I10632026

Brighton and Hove

PEVSNER ARCHITECTURAL GUIDES

Founding Editor: Nikolaus Pevsner

PEVSNER ARCHITECTURAL GUIDES

The *Buildings of England* series was created and largely written by Sir Nikolaus Pevsner (1902–83). First editions of the county volumes were published by Penguin Books between 1951 and 1974. The continuing programme of revisions and new volumes has been supported by research financed through the Buildings Books Trust since 1994.

The Buildings Books Trust gratefully acknowledges
Grants towards the cost of research, writing and illustrations
for this volume from:

ENGLISH HERITAGE

Assistance with photographs from:

ENGLISH HERITAGE
(photographer: James O. Davies)

Brighton and Hove

NICHOLAS ANTRAM

RICHARD MORRICE

PEVSNER ARCHITECTURAL GUIDES

YALE UNIVERSITY PRESS

NEW HAVEN & LONDON

For Sally and Charlotte, and for Liz

The publishers gratefully acknowledge help in
bringing the books to a wider readership from
ENGLISH HERITAGE

YALE UNIVERSITY PRESS
NEW HAVEN AND LONDON
302 Temple Street, New Haven CT06511
47 Bedford Square, London WC1B 3DP

www.pevsner.co.uk
www.yalebooks.co.uk
www.yalebooks.com

Published 2008
10 9 8 7 6 5 4 3 2 1

Designed by Ian Hunt
Set in Adobe Minion by SNP Best-set Typesetter Ltd., Hong Kong
Printed in Singapore by CS Graphics

Library of Congress Cataloging-in-Publication Data

Antram, Nicholas.
  Brighton and Hove / Nicholas Antram and Richard Morrice.
     p. cm. -- (Pevsner architectural guides)
  Includes bibliographical references and index.
  ISBN 978-0-300-12661-7 (alk. paper)
  1. Architecture--England--Brighton--Guidebooks. 2. Brighton (England)--
Buildings, structures, etc.--Guidebooks. 3. Brighton (England)--Guidebooks.
4. Architecture--England--Hove--Guidebooks. 5. Hove (England)--Buildings,
structures, etc.--Guidebooks. 6. Hove (England)--Guidebooks. I. Morrice,
Richard. II. Title.
  NA971.B76A58 2008
  720.9422'56--dc22
                        2008013122

Contents

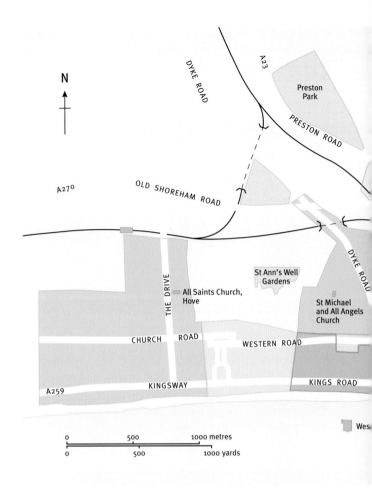

N

DYKE ROAD

A23

Preston Park

PRESTON ROAD

A270

OLD SHOREHAM ROAD

DYKE ROAD

St Ann's Well Gardens

THE DRIVE

All Saints Church, Hove

St Michael and All Angels Church

CHURCH ROAD

WESTERN ROAD

KINGSWAY

A259

KINGS ROAD

Wes

| 0 | 500 | 1000 metres |
| 0 | 500 | 1000 yards |

1. Brighton and Hove, showing areas covered by walks and major buildings

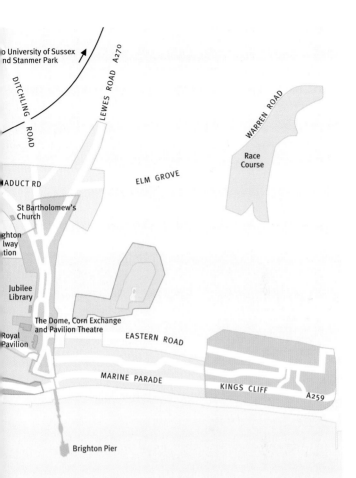

to University of Sussex
and Stanmer Park

DITCHLING ROAD

LEWES ROAD A270

WARREN ROAD

Race Course

ELM GROVE

VIADUCT RD

St Bartholomew's Church

Brighton Railway Station

Jubilee Library

The Dome, Corn Exchange and Pavilion Theatre

Royal Pavilion

EASTERN ROAD

MARINE PARADE

KINGS CLIFF

A259

Brighton Pier

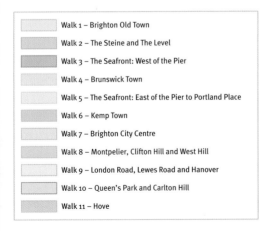

Walk 1 – Brighton Old Town

Walk 2 – The Steine and The Level

Walk 3 – The Seafront: West of the Pier

Walk 4 – Brunswick Town

Walk 5 – The Seafront: East of the Pier to Portland Place

Walk 6 – Kemp Town

Walk 7 – Brighton City Centre

Walk 8 – Montpelier, Clifton Hill and West Hill

Walk 9 – London Road, Lewes Road and Hanover

Walk 10 – Queen's Park and Carlton Hill

Walk 11 – Hove

Acknowledgements

Our first debt is to Sir Nikolaus Pevsner whose text on Brighton and Hove for *Sussex* (1965) forms the foundation on which this City Guide is based. His perception and impressive economy of word set a standard we have sought to emulate. Secondly we owe a debt to the pioneer of research into Brighton and Hove architecture, Antony Dale, whose numerous books published from the 1950s to the 1980s are still unsurpassed. His widow, Yvonne, has been generous with her time, hospitality and access to her husband's library of books and prints. Current scholars of Brighton and Hove have also been generous with their time and knowledge, in particular Sue Berry, editor of the Victoria County History *City of Brighton & Hove*, and supporting volunteers, Chris Christian, Jan Lank, Janet Sate and Ninka Willcock, who tested out the walks. Equally, David Beevers, Keeper of Fine Art at the Royal Pavilion, Libraries and Museums, read much of the text, shared his knowledge, particularly of the Victorian period and of the Pavilion, The Dome and Preston Manor, and was an enthusiastic supporter of the project. Andrew Barlow, Keeper of the Royal Pavilion, answered questions concerning the Pavilion's complex history.

We would like to thank the staff of Brighton & Hove City Council, in particular Rob Fraser and Roger Dowty (formerly Conservation Officers for Brighton and Hove respectively) who must be thanked for their kindness and help over the years. Roger's team of conservation officers, Geoff Bennett, Catherine Jeater, Tim Jefferies and Lesley Johnson have also answered questions and read text in draft. Also at the council assistance was given by Shane Maxwell and Philip Randall, whilst Kevin Bacon, Curator of Photographs at Brighton Museum, helped with advice on the council's photographic archive and Nigel Imi, Professional & Collections Manager at Brighton Library, was our guide to the new Jubilee Library. A general thank you must go to the staff at the Brighton History Centre and to staff at the East Sussex Record Office, especially Andrew Bennett, Brighton & Hove Archivist.

At the University of Sussex, Geoffrey Mead read through drafts and shared his local knowledge. Other archivists and librarians to thank are Reg Barrow (Masonic Centre), Lucy Dean (Brighton & Hove High School), Joyce Heater (Brighton College), Judy Middleton (former

2. The Royal Pavilion, Music Room ceiling

Hove librarian), Charles Noble (Keeper of the Devonshire Collection), Karen Sampson (Lloyds TSB archivist), Alison Scott (NatWest archivist) and the staff at the RIBA library and Drawings Collection and at the V&A library in London. Staff at English Heritage, Elain Harwood, Ian Leith, Kathryn Morrison and Simon Wartnaby have all answered questions and the enthusiastic English Heritage photographer, James O. Davies, took the excellent photographs, going to great lengths to ensure the best images.

Many other scholars shared their unpublished research, in particular we would like to thank John Allen (churches), Nick Barratt (Fife House), Geoffrey Brandwood (pubs), Peter Cormack (early c20 stained glass), Fred Gray (West Pier), Virginia Hinze (parks and gardens), Sharman Kadish (Jewish Heritage), Michael Kerney (Victorian stained glass), David Martin (vernacular), Robert Minton (St Nicholas's Church), Michael Hall (Bodley), Chris Morley (c20 buildings), Selma Montford (Brighton Society), Steve Myall (Montpelier & Clifton Hill Association), Michael Ray (former Hove Chief Planning Officer), Andrew Saint (Willetts), John Sakey (c19 sculpture), Teresa Sladen (churches), Nick Tyson (Regency Town House Curator). Many architects assisted, among them Mark Hills, Nick Lomax, Neil McWalter, Alan Phillips, David Pursey, John Small and John Wells-Thorpe.

For more general help we must thank Malcolm Airs; Roger Amerena; Anne and Michael Antram; Sidonie Bond; Leila Brosnan and colleagues at DCMS; Andrew Brown; Jefferson Collard and Sue Craig; Robert Gregory; Fred Gray; Richard Hawkes; Prof. Maurice Howard; Pamela James; Peter Kendall; Martin Knott, who kindly read through the text of the walks; Jill and Jeremy Lever; Scott Ralph; Dorothy Scruton who uncomplainingly delved into the archives in pursuit of repeated requests for information; the late Brian Spielman; Elizabeth Wardle; Henry Smith, who generously shared his knowledge of Brighton and Hove, the work of Clayton & Black and of historical engravings of the city. It was he who established that Wilds's Western Pavilion is but a portion of what was originally built. Closer to home we must thank our respective wives for encouragement and understanding. And we must thank each other; we have enjoyed working together and sharing our enthusiasm for the city.

The authors and photographer are indebted to church custodians and clergy, staff at town halls and other public buildings and to all those owners and occupiers of private buildings who kindly answered questions and allowed access, usually with enthusiasm and sometimes with hospitality too! They are too numerous to name individually but without their contribution the book would be the poorer.

Special thanks go to staff at Yale University Press. Charles O'Brien, always enthusiastic and encouraging, enriched the text through his careful editing, with interest and support from Simon Bradley. The Commissioning Editor, Sally Salvesen, oversaw the design and production, assisted by Sophie Kullmann. Ian Hunt designed the volume. Louise Glasson coordinated the illustrations. Bernard Dod was the copy editor, Judith Wardman compiled the index and Gavin Watson provided administrative support. Thanks are due to Colum Giles and staff of the Historic Environment Enabling Programme of English Heritage, which funded the volume.

Lastly, readers' responses dating back to 1965 informed this City Guide, including contributions from Rodney Hubbuck and Geoffrey Brandwood. We hope this will encourage a new generation of readers to respond to the traditional appeal for corrections and omissions, especially as this City Guide precedes a revision of the *Sussex* county volume. Comments can be sent by e-mail to pevsner@yaleup.co.uk or to the publisher's office.

3. North Street, former National Provincial Bank on the corner of Bond Street, by F.C.R. Palmer, 1921–3, details of bronze entrance doors

How to use this book

This book is designed as a practical architectural guide to the inner area of the City of Brighton and Hove. The first section of the gazetteer, following the Introduction, covers eight major buildings. All of these can be found within the area described in the rest of the gazetteer and their location is shown on the map on pp. vi–vii. The map also shows the areas of the city covered in the guide. With two exceptions, these have been arranged and described as walks. Each walk is preceded by a short history of the area and is accompanied by a street map for ease of navigation. It should be noted that although interiors of several buildings are described this does not indicate that they are open to the public. The final section is a suggested excursion to Stanmer and the University of Sussex, both of which can be reached by rail and are accessible to the public.

While this guide surveys the buildings of principal architectural and historical significance in central Brighton and Hove, a full account of the suburbs and villages within the city's boundaries will be undertaken in the forthcoming volume on *East Sussex* in the *Buildings of England* hardback series.

Throughout the book, certain topics are singled out for special attention and presented in separate boxes:

Laines, Furlongs, Paul Pieces and Leak Ways p. 5
Building Materials p. 6
Bows and Bays p. 12
West Pier p. 21
Orientalism: Chinese Styles p. 32
The Fall and Rise of the Royal Pavilion p. 43
Orientalism: Indian Styles p. 45
Sea Bathing and Bath Houses p. 70
Arthur Wagner and Ritualism p. 101
Houses in Brunswick Town: Planning, Function and Decoration p. 115
Henry Phillips and the Anthaeum p. 121
Magnus Volk p. 131
Thomas Read Kemp p. 145
Constable in Brighton p. 174

Introduction

Introduction

Brighton – 'The Queen of Watering Places' – is the pre-eminent English seaside resort, unrivalled architecturally, socially and artistically. No other resort has been so closely associated with the capital in the minds of its visitors, nor achieved the unique mixture of the regal, the metropolitan and the profane: 'London with prawns and the seaside air' was Thackeray's opinion. It was here in the C18 that the style of English seaside architecture was invented, the reputation of Brighton's light promoting the streets and squares of houses with bowed and bay-windowed elevations in pristine stucco, and in the enchanting oriental humour of the Royal Pavilion lay the inspiration for a century or more of eclectic, playful and spectacular buildings around England's coasts. The exuberance of the street scene set off the grander set pieces and gave Brighton a fantasy façade: the front, stretching some four miles from end to end and spreading into Hove (known for many years as West Brighton, until rivalry caused Hove to assert its independence). In the course of the C19 and C20 the select Brighton became the people's Brighton, boosted by the railways, cheaper travel, rising living standards, bank holidays and finally annual holidays but somehow it has stayed the same, a familiar brew of raffishness, emotional excitement, love of experimentation, fondness for the arts and sexual tolerance. Modern Brighton is not that different from Regency Brighton, while Hove (actually) has its own distinctiveness deriving from its spacious Victorian character. That there has been a convergence in mood since the joint city was created in 1997 may have more to do with the rest of England becoming more like Brighton than the other way round.

Early History

Brighton derives from the small fishing village of Brighthelmstone which was established by Late Saxon times. There was a small house of possibly Cluniac monks established at St Bartholomew as early as the C12, and the parish church of St Nicholas [5] has a Norman font, although the building's fabric appears no older than the C14 (substantially renewed in the C19). A market charter was granted in 1313 by King Edward II and by the early C16 the settlement was emerging as a town. Medieval Brighton is still represented by the grid plan of the 'old town'

4. Brighton beach, view looking E

5. St Nicholas, view from the SE, before the Victorian restoration

enclosed by three outer streets (North, East and West) with the principal internal thoroughfares running N–S with alleyways or 'twittens' between. Within the town was the large space of the Hempshares, set aside either for the growing of hemp or for rope-making. A street also ran along the cliff edge and there were buildings and net-huts at the head of the beach below, though these succumbed to constant erosion by the sea. To the E was a bourn or periodic winter stream which ran down by what is now the London Road, with a second smaller one along the later Lewes Road, going into the sea through the open space of the Steine. Surrounding the town were the open fields of the **laines** (*see* Topic Box) and to the w was the single-street village of Hove, with its church. Despite destructive C19 restoration this must have been a substantial early C13 building.

The earliest known view of Brighton, showing houses on West, North and East Streets, allegedly depicts a French raid by the Gascon Admiral Pregent de Bidoux in 1514. The drawing has been dated to *c.* 1520 and the date 1545, which also appears on the drawing, was probably added later by someone who knew of another French raid in that year. Much has been made of the damage done to the town by French raids but there is little evidence to support the claim that Brighton was razed to the ground. As far as we know there is no C16 or earlier fabric surviving (apart from the two churches), although Nos. 1–3 Black Lion Lane and No. 43 Meeting House Lane have jetties and could pre-date the C17. As part of the Tudor **defences** of the s coast a small circular fort or blockhouse was built (erected on land, close to the southern end of Ship Street, given for the purpose in 1559), to seaward of which was the so-called gun garden – intended to keep the cannons' firing line clear. Small gates were placed at the heads of paths down to the beach: East Gate, Portall Gate, Middle Gate and West Gate. These do not appear to have been defensive, being little more than barriers to stop livestock straying to the beach. A town house was built close to the blockhouse but both fell victim to the constant coastal erosion, the last remains of

Laines, Furlongs, Paul Pieces and Leak Ways

The old town of Brighthelmstone [7] was surrounded by farmland divided into five large open fields called **laines** (derived from the Anglo-Saxon word for 'loan' or 'lease'): Little, Hilly, North, West and East; beyond was sheep pasture. Each laine was divided into smaller fields called **furlongs**, in turn subdivided into narrow strips, called **paul pieces**, all of which might have different owners. This land division and ownership dictated the layout of streets as Brighton developed. The wide paths, known as **leak ways**, that separated one furlong from another usually became important roads, (e.g. Western Road and St James's Street), while small groups of paul pieces were developed in long rectangular blocks. The effect on Brighton's street plan is most obvious in the areas E of the Steine and in the North Laine, in marked contrast to the streets of the old town.

the fort falling in 1761. In 1759 a new battery was built at the s end of East Street (but this too succumbed to erosion and collapsed in 1786). The meagre defences were augmented in 1793 by two new batteries, the West (demolished 1859, on the site of the Grand Hotel) and the East (at the southern end of New Steine); the latter only lasted a dozen years, once more owing to erosion from the sea. Both were designed by *Colonel Twiss*, architect of the Martello towers further E along the coast.

The Georgian Town and Resort

Although Brighton was the largest town in Sussex by 1640, the Yarmouth fisheries, to which Brighton had sent an increasing fleet, had begun to decline and the town turned to coastal trade. But Brighton had no harbour (Shoreham to the w became more important because of its natural harbour at the mouth of the River Adur), and the fishing fleet, like that at Hastings today, was beach-launched. As the foreshore was eroding quickly the future for Brighton didn't seem bright. So the fashion from the mid C17 for **spas and sea bathing** was a boon (*see* Topic Box, p. 70) and proved so popular that by the 1750s we read of Brighton having lodging houses, assembly rooms, coffee houses, a subscription library and walks, all essential to the leisure of visitors. By the time that Dr Russell of Lewes published his famous *Dissertation on the Use of Sea Water in Diseases of the Glands* (1750, in Latin), he was cashing in on an already established market. Another physician, Dr Relhan, provided the town with its first guidebook in 1761: *A Short History of Brighthelmston, with Remarks on its Air and Analysis of its Waters.*

What visitors found in these early years is known from views of the town published for their purchase; these were supplemented by satirical prints, particularly after the Prince of Wales took up residence in the 1780s. The town was still defined by its medieval street pattern [7] and the

Building Materials

The character of pre-Regency Brighton was much like that of other Sussex and Kent coastal towns and defined by local **building materials**. Brick was used (the grand brick house at No. 15 Prince Albert Street appears to be mid Georgian but may be later) but mostly the buildings were of **cobble** and **flint** with brick dressings (e.g. No. 57 Ship Street, with a weathering coat of pitch), or weatherboard, painted or tarred. No. 37a Duke Street [43] of *c.* 1780 is a rare Brighton example of another Kent and Sussex speciality, the façade of wooden blocks imitating rustication.

Mathematical tiles, a cladding material of interlocking tiles imitating brick, became common in the town only after about 1760, although their use was widespread in the southern counties by that date. Brighton has a distinctive black-glazed version, seen at the former Cowley's Bun Shop (Nos. 9–10 Pool Valley), one of the most striking of the earlier buildings of Brighton, but it was used to best effect at Royal Crescent [72] and Patcham Place. They were a cheaper alternative to brick, mostly being used over timber framing (thus their use on early bow windows). Brighton, however, is also the chief location for '**bungaroosh**' ('bunga-rooge', 'bunglarooge'), a composite mass-walling material consisting

of a variety of materials, including perhaps cobble, flint, broken brick, even rubble stone, whatever was available, shuttered and usually set in hydraulic lime. It isn't known when it was first used but it was common for the century after 1750 for party walls and even for façades. It is most noticeable in boundary walls, obvious from the use of bricks laid diagonally, but it can suffer badly if water gets in; it has been said that half Brighton could be demolished with a well-aimed hose.

The history of **stucco** is complicated, moving from traditional lime plaster via experiments by Adam and others in the 1770s to Parker's Roman Cement of 1796, but its use in Brighton and Hove only became common in the 1820s. Plain facing, lining out and pseudo-rustication as well as ornament were usually carried out in varieties of lime plaster until past the mid-century mark. Early on stucco seems to have been used in conjunction with brick, as in the part brick, part stucco façades of Regency Square [10] and Kemp Town, but by 1830 it was largely an overall coating.

6. Building materials (left to right): flint and cobble, mathematical tiles, bungaroosh, No. 1 Arundel Terrace, detail of mid-c19 stucco decoration

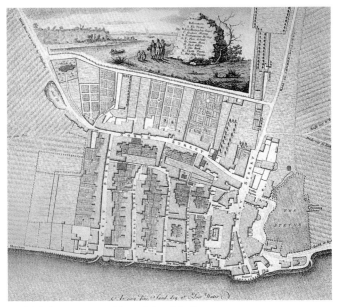

7. Brighthelmstone surveyed by Yeakell and Gardner, 1779

E side of the Steine remained undeveloped in the 1760s with only a library and a small bandstand. The established inns, principal among them the Castle, in business from the 1740s close to the Steine, and the Old Ship, began to compete for custom by providing impressive **assembly rooms** in the latest architectural styles. The first rooms were built at the Castle in 1754; the Old Ship followed in 1761 with an assembly room [54] and a ballroom to the design of *Robert Golden*. Only the ballroom retains something of its late Palladian character, both rooms having been redecorated in an Adamish style, presumably following the rebuilding of the Castle's rooms in 1776 by *John Crunden* (now preserved at the First Base Day Centre in Montpelier Place). At this time the lodgings used by visitors were largely indistinguishable from the houses of the locals; usually let furnished and sometimes serviced, complaints were frequent of the standard of accommodation at resorts throughout the C18.

Attendance at social events at the assembly rooms was a main activity during **the season**, which started in late summer and lasted into the late autumn, though occasionally extended when the Prince of Wales stayed until January. Visitors would bathe in the sea or in Dr Awsiter's Baths (on Pool Valley, opened 1769 following his publication of a book about the medicinal uses of seawater) or, after 1787, at Sake Deen Mahomed's Indian Shampooing Baths, a little to the w; promenade or watch cricket matches on the Steine; drink the waters at St Ann's Well; visit the libraries and coffee houses; go to the races (after 1783); visit local beauty spots; attend the theatre; and, if of the right rank, hope for an invitation to dinner at the Royal Pavilion.

Private houses for visitors first appear during the 1760s: Henry Thrale bought or inherited in 1760 a house on West Street where Dr Johnson stayed, and in 1771 the Duke of Marlborough bought Marlborough House on the Steine which the proprietor of the Castle Inn had originally built *c.* 1765 to let to visitors. The Prince of Wales first visited in 1783, returned in 1784 and 1785 and acquired a house on the Steine in 1786. This was rebuilt as the Royal Marine Pavilion by *Henry Holland* (1786–7 and 1801–4), first in a rather stilted classical style, though it showed an Ionic rotunda and dome to the Steine [18]. It is hard not to feel that there was competition from *Robert Adam* when he, in turn, rebuilt and extended Marlborough House for William Hamilton M.P. in 1786–7, as a miniature Neo-Palladian great house [47, 8] with spatially arresting interior. It is a pity that his designs for Mrs Fitzherbert's house, next door, were not built; *William Porden*'s house for her of 1804, with a fine staircase (now gone), has been grievously altered both inside and out. The Duke of Marlborough, meanwhile, had taken Grove House, immediately N of the Pavilion, which was demolished during Nash's rebuilding (1815–22).

The adherence to old or vernacular fashions even for new buildings continued. Pattern-book detailing, particularly of doorcases, can be found on a number of houses around the old town, including Nos. 7 and 63 Ship Street; Nos. 3–4 Pavilion Parade [52] have segment heads, definitely old-fashioned by the 1780s. The Steine was by now established as the promenade for the town's visitors and a magnet, because of the presence of the Pavilion, for the most expensive lodgings. But even here the first attempt at **planned development** – the terraces of North and South Parade – were of cobble and brick. As development spread further E into Hilly and Little Laines, regularity grew, as can be seen in the little houses in Camelford Street and the larger ones in Charles Street, but the palette is still basically vernacular, with little symmetrical arrangement of houses or central emphasis. These are not the artificial palaces familiar from Bath of the Woods. The New Steine, the first square open to the sea, was laid out 1790–5 with two terraces facing each other across a garden, black mathematical-tiled façades (refronted 1825–30) but again without attempt at palace fronts. To the w Bedford Square (begun in

8. Marlborough House, altered 1786–7 by Robert Adam, detail of an alcove in the study

1801 but not finished for many years) was likewise irregular and it was followed by Clarence Square (before 1810) and Russell Square (from 1809), both set back from the sea. Even Royal Crescent [72] (1799–1802), Brighton's first crescent and the first development actually facing the sea, was less than palatial and stood far from the centre on the East Cliff.

Regency and Early Victorian Brighton

The post-Napoleonic period, the time of the Prince's Regency and then his succession to the Crown, was the high summer of exclusive Brighton. The Prince's improvised villa now became a much grander affair at the hands of *Nash*, *Crace* and *Jones*. It was the Prince's stables (now The Dome) by *William Porden* in 1804–8 which gave the first hint of something altogether more monumental. If the Pavilion, undoubtedly more sumptuous than its predecessor, lacks something of the Dome's stylistic rigour, it more than makes up for it in its vitality and dynamism, and it remains a fascinating insight into the complex artistic mind of the Prince Regent.

With the building booms of the second and third decades of the C19 the resources for monumental domestic architecture in the town became available, snowballing as confidence built and producing one of the great sequences of Regency and Early Victorian town planning in England. Brighton's population tripled from *c.* 7,000 in 1801 to 24,000 in 1821, and in the decade up to 1821 it grew faster than that of any other English town. For the first time too, development spread across the boundary into Hove, known as West Brighton until the later C19, thus eroding the distinction between the two places. Building was at a new scale, indicated from 1817 by Regency Square [10] with its larger houses around a broad open space facing the sea.

Amon Wilds, his son *Amon Henry Wilds* and *Charles Augustin Busby* are the **architects** associated with the grand new developments of Regency Brighton. The Wilds came from Lewes and were active in Brighton from about 1814 when Hanover Crescent was laid out N of the Steine. Wilds senior, builder as well as architect, died in 1833, but A.H. Wilds continued working into the 1850s. Charles Busby arrived in Brighton in 1823 and was for a short time (June 1823–May 1825) in partnership with the younger Wilds. His career at Brighton lasted just eleven years and saw his financial ruin before his early death in 1834.

Wilds and Busby were no doubt brought together by Thomas Read Kemp, for whom the Wilds had previously worked, to realize his ambitious plans for Kemp Town at the eastern edge of Brighton's seafront [79]. Initially projected as a much wider development with houses of various different classes, at its centre it famously combines the three important forms of town planning: the flanking Arundel and Chichester terraces; Lewes Crescent, which curves in towards the centre; and, set back in the middle and above, Sussex Square. The scale is massive and monumental with the ranges of terraces, crescent and square each treated as palace fronts with pilastered pavilions. The height of grandeur is reached in Arundel Terrace where the use of the giant

9. Montpelier Crescent, 1843–7

Corinthian order, detached in the centre, attached elsewhere, reaches the monumentality of the grandest of Nash's Regent's Park terraces.

By 1825, when Brunswick Town was under construction, Busby was working alone. What Brunswick Square lacks in novelty of layout is more than made up for by the force of the Neo-Greek architecture, particularly in the emphatic bowed façades along the sides of the square [62] (here following earlier Brighton precedent in using bows to allow views down to the sea, as in Marine Square of 1823–5 where again the top elevation, facing the sea, is flat). It has been well said that the bows of Brunswick Square 'make one forget that Neo-Classical design was ever meant to be flat' (Stefan Muthesius). On the seafront Busby built two immense palace-fronted terraces, as grand as anything in St Petersburg, and an enjoyable and much more varied group, Nos. 1–6 Brunswick Terrace, with a tall centre, bowed links and pavilions, almost Vanbrughian in its movement and monumentality.

Outside their brief partnership both Wilds and Busby were prolific, yet the absence of documents and drawings makes it often difficult to be sure what they designed. Attributions to A.H. Wilds rely on his characteristic handling, in particular using ammonite capitals for the Ionic order, a motif which was first used by George Dance the younger and which Wilds's father had appropriated for the house in Lewes which was reconstructed for Dr Gideon Mantell, the palaeontologist, in 1819. A second motif is the scallop shell, used commonly in arches over first-floor windows. On this basis a large number of buildings have been attributed to the Wilds, no doubt hopefully at times. For Busby (for whose work some two hundred drawings survive) it is a matter of a certain urbanity and expansiveness of handling. The stylistic variety of the Wilds' buildings is wider than Busby's, from primitive Neo-Greek at Nos. 4–6, Richmond Terrace (from 1818) and the relatively pure Grecian of the Unitarian Chapel in New Road (1820), to The Gothic House, Western Road (1822–5), a rare instance of that style in Brighton although Wilds may also have designed the similar Wykeham Terrace, Dyke Road, in 1827–30. For his own house, the Western Pavilion [59] (1831), Wilds opted for a pretty straight crib from Nash's Pavilion.

A.H. Wilds was a capable town planner and he occasionally worked as an engineer, including the laying out of King's Road between 1818–34, part of the Regency improvements to form seafront walks in succession to the Steine and to which *Thomas Cooper*'s seawall along the East Cliff (1830–3) also belongs. Wilds's layouts (from Hanover Crescent begun 1814 to Park Crescent in 1849) recall Bath and Nash, particularly in the sweep of the developments and the realization that extended façades need to be varied if used as streetscape. Hanover Crescent was designed as a crescent of Palladian villas; Regency Square as a rectangular square open to the sea; and Oriental Place (1825–7) as a street open to the sea at one end and with an oriental garden and conservatory at the other. Montpelier Villas [94] (*c.* 1845) may also be by Wilds and has a rectilinear group of semi-detached Italianate villas in individual gardens. Montpelier Crescent [9] (1843–7) is another, larger crescent of linked individual villas; and Park Crescent sets a continuous line of terraced Italianate villas in an irregular curve around a large garden [102].

Busby built less. He designed a pair of schemes for shortish streets leading up from the seafront to focal-point villas: Portland Place (1824–8)

Bows and Bays

The **bow window** is wholly characteristic of the domestic buildings of Brighton and Hove from the end of the c18. The earliest bows are tall and very narrow, as shown in views of Marlborough Place (now largely altered) or in smaller and more hidden-away terraces such as Charles Street on the East Cliff. Whether half or full height the bow allowed both movement in façades and wider views out from houses; particularly, in terraces at right angles to the seafront, they granted all-important views of the sea. The bows began to fill out, as at Royal Crescent [72] or Bloomsbury Place (after 1810), but it was only after the Napoleonic war that the bow reached maturity in Brighton, in the very stately form of Regency Square (attributed to *A. & A.H. Wilds*, 1817–30), with their very generous and architectural canopies [10]. In that way they could become the dominant element of the wider architecture of the terrace. *Busby* of course made bows the main feature of the façades of the sides of Brunswick Square [62] (1825–30), but Powis Square, as late as 1856–7, uses deeper full-width bows to give an extraordinarily pneumatic character to the architecture. Canted **bay windows** are almost exclusively a Victorian development and have often replaced earlier bows. They were easier to build using the larger window panes then beginning to be favoured (no curved glass). At Vernon Terrace, Montpelier, one can find bows and canted bays in combination as late as 1856–7.

10. Regency Square, 1817–30

is similar in its staccato provision of pilastered pavilions to Lewes Crescent, leading up to a monumental villa, Portland House, which until destroyed by fire had a hexastyle portico to a cubic central block; Cavendish Place, from 1826, a rather French scheme with massive sixteen-bay pilaster-fronted blocks leading up to a villa with hexastyle portico and a Pavilionesque dome (not built). Among the most attractive, and most distinctive, of his designs are the semi-detached villas of Lansdowne Place (broadly complete 1833) in Brunswick Town, with their combination of low hipped roofs, paired bows and roofed balconies.

Many of the early to mid-c19 schemes in Brighton and Hove took many years to complete, of which Adelaide Crescent [64] and Palmeira Square are the most notorious examples. Work began in 1830 at the sea end on a crescent to the design of *Decimus Burton* [63]. This rather Neo-Renaissance, if not Neo-Neo-Palladian scheme, was soon abandoned, but was then picked up again *c.* 1849–50 in similar style on the E side and in a plainer way on the W, and then, in Palmeira Square, it was continued in a more full-bloodedly Victorian Italianate with canted bays and tri-partite windows. It was topped by Palmeira Mansions of 1883–4 by *H.J. Lanchester* across the head of the square, which continued the theme but breaks into little Netherlandish gables over the centre of each block.

Associated with these suburban developments was a modest degree of **church building**, principally for the Nonconformists. New or rebuilt **chapels** included the Trinity Chapel, Ship Street (by *A.H. Wilds*, 1817, originally for Thomas Read Kemp's sect but consecrated as an Anglican church in 1826); the Unitarian Chapel in New Road (A.H. Wilds, 1820); the Countess of Huntingdon's Chapel, North Street (although founded in 1766 and later rebuilt, it was enlarged with a new front 1822–3; rebuilt 1870–1, later demolished); the Hanover Chapel, Queen's Road, by the local architect *Thomas Cooper* (1824); and the Union Chapel in Union Street (1689, extended 1810, but rebuilt by Wilds, 1825). But four new Anglican chapels of ease were also built during this decade: *Busby*'s St Margaret, Cannon Place (1824, dem.) and St George, St George's Road at Kemp Town (1824–6); A.H. Wilds's St Mary, Egremont Place (1826–7, later rebuilt by *Emerson* [75], 1877–9); and most prominently *Charles Barry*'s St Peter, Valley Gardens [49] (1824–8). To that can be added his St Andrew, Waterloo Street (1827–8) in Brunswick Town. This introduced the Quattrocento style to Brighton, seen also in Barry's very Tuscan Attree Villa, Queen's Park [108], of 1829–30 (dem. 1972). Wilds and others responded to the lessons. Cornices became more heavily bracketed, round-arched windows appeared and both asymmetry and a varied roof-line became popular. Most important, perhaps, was that this remained an architecture which could accommodate stucco.

11. Former St John the Evangelist Church (now Greek Orthodox), Carlton Hill, by George Cheesman Jun., 1839–40

Victorian and Edwardian Brighton and Hove

Although the Regency had a long tail in Brighton, change came with the advent of the railway in 1841 as the town began its transition from Georgian exclusivity into a more popular resort (it has been estimated that more people visited Brighton that first railway weekend than during the whole of the previous year, and the resident population increased by half in the following decade, from 46,000 to 65,000). The royal presence at the Pavilion ceased after Victoria built Osborne in the 1840s but 'the season' continued, with that of 1848–9 being reported in the press as the most brilliant the town had seen. Perhaps this was in fact already a sign that 'the season' was in decline, and its significance gradually waned as the century progressed. In spite of this the wealthy and aristocratic were still drawn to the town, albeit increasingly as a place for retirement. The effect of this had a consequence for the **churches** of the mid and later C19 where, in common with other resorts such as Bournemouth, the combination of wealth with a revived Anglicanism produced one of the finest groups of churches outside London.

In spite of the activity in building new chapels of ease in the 1820s, there were still considerable gaps, particularly in the E and N of the town. This prompted the new vicar of Brighton, the Rev. Henry Michell Wagner, into a major campaign of church building. To his initiative were due All Souls, Eastern Road (*Henry Mew*, 1833–8; dem. 1968); Christ Church, Montpelier Road (1837–8, by *George Cheesman Jun.*; dem. 1982); and his St John the Evangelist, Carlton Hill (1839–40, now Greek Orthodox [11]). Like the Nonconformist chapels these were almost all in a classical style, but Barry's St Peter had introduced the flamboyance of Gothic to Brighton in a very conspicuous location and it was Gothic which was to see its most extraordinary flowering in the Anglican churches built during the mid-Victorian years under the Rev. Wagner's son, Father Arthur Wagner. For him the elder Wagner built St Paul, West Street [55] (1846–8, by *R.C. Carpenter*). Here for the first time a more archaeologically correct Gothic was adopted, in this case 'middle pointed', the Gothic of the late C14.

In Father Wagner Brighton gained not just a very rich clergyman of advanced religious beliefs (*see* Topic Box, p. 101) but a very knowledgeable patron of art and architecture. He was the reason for the change of tone in the last of Henry Wagner's church plantings: at All Saints, Compton Avenue (also by *Carpenter*; first projected 1847 but not opened until 1852; dem. 1957) and St Anne, Burlington Street (*Benjamin Ferrey*; 1862–3, dem. 1986). Wholly at Arthur Wagner's initiative were built two smaller churches of distinction: St Mary and St Mary Magdalene, Bread Street, by *G.F. Bodley* (1862; dem. 1950) and the appealing Annunciation, Washington Street [105], by *William Dancy* (1864), extended by *Edmund Scott* (1881) and *F.T. Cawthorn* (1892). But it is the big churches, lavishly fitted for High Anglican worship in poor areas, for which Father Wagner is best known: the tall, plain St Bartholomew, Ann Street [98, 30] (1872–4) and St Martin, Lewes Road (1872–5, by *Somers Clarke Jun.*), more Northern European in its Gothic and the vessel for an assemblage of fittings unsurpassed at its date in England [103]. Sadly lost is the little-known 'Underground Church' of the Resurrection, Russell Street by *R. H. Carpenter*, (1876–7, dem. 1968). These were joined by two related churches which were the venture of others: the spatially dynamic St Mary, Upper Rock Gardens [75] (1877–9, the only major English work by *William Emerson*), and St Michael and All Angels, Victoria Road [28] (1858–61 and 1893–5), with its contrasting approaches to muscular Gothic by *Bodley* and *W. Burges. Pearson*'s All Saints [31], just as high and luxurious, was built as the new parish church for fast-expanding Hove.

The **stained glass and furnishings** of these buildings are accordingly outstanding. At St Paul, West Street, is *Pugin*'s most complete set of glass for an Anglican church (1849–53); the w window at the Annunciation, Washington Street, of 1853, is the earliest known window by *J. R. Clayton* (formerly at St Nicholas), and the *Morris, Marshall, Faulkner & Co.* glass in St Michael, Victoria Road, is a first-class ensemble from the earliest years of that company (1862–3) with designs by *Morris, Ford Madox Brown, Peter Paul Marshall, Philip Webb* and *Edward Burne-Jones* [29]. Also of significance is the glass by *James Powell & Sons* at St Martin, Lewes Road (1874 onwards); *Kempe*'s at St Nicholas (1878–87); *Clayton & Bell*'s at All Saints, Hove (1891–1920); the more mixed glass at St Mary, Upper Rock Gardens; and for the C20 there is the *Christopher Webb* glass in the s chapel at St Andrew, Waterloo Street (1927 and 1938). Other **furnishings** of note include the C16 reredos in the Bodley chancel at St Michael and All Angels, decorated by *Kempe* to *Bodley*'s design (currently dismantled); the Aesthetic Movement touches to the superlative fittings in St Martin's; the wonderful lectern of 1888 by *Hardman, Powell & Co.* at St Paul's [12]; *Pearson*'s chancel furnishings at All Saints'; *Romaine-Walker*'s sanctuary at St Michael's (1899–1909); *Henry Wilson*'s superb Arts and Crafts fittings at St Bartholomew, Ann Street [30]; and *Randoll Blacking*'s Italianate baldacchino and font (1925) at St Andrew's, Waterloo Street.

Worth a special mention is the Middle Street Synagogue [42] (*Thomas Lainson*, 1874–5). Not Gothic at all but in a spirited and free Italianate style, it is a strong reminder of the continuing history of synagogues in the town. Late C19 Brighton continued to be a major centre of Nonconformity too, *John Wills*'s Baptist Church in Holland Road, Hove (1883) being a fine surviving example. Brighton and Hove have several Roman Catholic churches of note, including St John the Baptist, St George's Road, Brighton (*William Hallett*, 1832–5), which harks back to the early classical Anglican churches, and the Sacred Heart church in Norton Road, Hove (*John Crawley*, 1880–1) with its distinguished interior. The most impressive is St Joseph, Elm Grove [104], originally begun in 1879 by *W. Kedo Broder* in a fully vaulted C13 Gothic but finished by others.

The largest group of Victorian Gothic buildings is Brighton College, Eastern Road, with original buildings of 1848–9 by *George Gilbert Scott*,

12. St Paul's Church, brass lectern by Hardman, Powell & Co., 1888

'joyless' according to Pevsner, with chapel of 1859 and grander work by *T.G. Jackson* of 1884–8 [77] and chapel extension of 1922–3. Scott's most extraordinary Brighton building was demolished in 1929, the new Gentlemen's Swimming Bath at Brill's Baths, an astonishing 65-ft circle in Venetian Gothic polychromatic brick.

Brighton and Hove's **suburbs** were continuing to develop in the mean-time. The architectural evolution is telling. The streets of Montpelier, largely Regency or post-Regency in style, i.e. stuccoed with tented balcony roofs and bows but also some Italianate detailing, date largely from the 1840s and 1850s, with infilling continuing later. Smaller-scale Hanover, again largely post-Regency in spirit though unarticulated, was developed from the 1850s. Round Hill, from the 1860s, is similar and Roundhill Crescent of as late as *c.* 1865 is still post-Regency in character.

Cliftonville in Hove, however, developed in the 1850s and extended towards the railway in the 1860s, though still largely stuccoed, shows how distance from Brighton, and from the Regency in date, allowed more variation, in this case towards both the Italianate and the Tudorbethan. It was only in outer Brighton and particularly on the Stanford estate in Hove, developed from 1872, that the Regency tone was finally lost.

Because development had been restricted on Stanford land, Hove village was still in 1850 detached from Brighton and Brunswick Town (although the latter was actually in Hove parish). Cliftonville followed that date but the land between was only released for development in 1871 with *Sir James Knowles* drawing up the masterplan. Although there are touches of the Regency in the resulting development, particularly in the more palatial terraces with their tent-roofed balconies, the *Willett*-developed northern section of the estate was laid out with large gault brick villas, both detached and semi-detached, with a very distinct and wholly Victorian character. Later development on the estate, by *Harry Measures* and *Amos Faulkner*, even went over to a red brick Queen Anne Revival style, spacious and suave. The Vallance estate to the w of Sackville Road was developed first by *Lainson & Sons* from 1890, then by *Clayton & Black* in a more suburban Olde English style, yet there is very little vernacular revival architecture of the Arts and Crafts variety in Brighton and Hove. Nos. 8–11 Grand Avenue, Hove [113], 1900–3, by *Amos Faulkner*, are prominent examples of a rather Ernest Newtonian Arts and Crafts domestic with tile-hanging and multi-columned porches. Wilbury Lawn in Wilbury Road, Hove, is in a free Neo-Georgian style slightly reminiscent of Philip Webb by *J.H. Ball*, 1905. *Clayton & Black* built a small block of early Brighton council housing in the High Street, off St James's Street in East Cliff (1910) and the John Nixon Memorial Hall [73] in St George's Road, Brighton (1912) is a surprising example of the Arts and Crafts free style (architect unknown).

At this time, too, one should note the redecoration of the large **houses** of the great Regency estates. Preserved, if heavily restored, is the scheme for the drawing room of No. 1 Lewes Crescent, by *J.G. Crace* in an Italian style (1848), but the most extraordinary survival is the Late Victorian interior of No. 33, Palmeira Mansions [13, 66]. It appears to have been carried out for A.W. Mason of Mason's Inks and is in the most eclectic and opulent taste, including both a first-floor conservatory and a Moorish room. The fashion for the revived styles of the late c17 and c18 is in evidence in the last decades of the c19, e.g. the dining room of No. 2 Eastern Terrace with early c18-style mahogany panelling supplied by Messrs *Lenygon*, c. 1905. No. 34 Adelaide Crescent, Hove, similarly has an interior with an English Baroque ceiling [65], though here apparently dating from the 1880s, and No. 37 First Avenue, Hove, has an early c18-style interior by *A.N. Prentice* dating from 1895. *Raymond Erith* redecorated the interior of No. 11 Adelaide Crescent, Hove, in 1933.

Now for new buildings along the seafront and in particular the **piers**, the first of which belonged to the Regency. This was the celebrated

13. No. 33 Palmeira Mansions, Hove, Moorish style ceiling, *c.* 1899

Chain Pier, opposite New Steine, erected at the base of the East Cliff in 1822–3 by *Captain Samuel Brown* RN, engineer and pioneer of suspension structures (e.g. Union Chain Bridge across the Tweed, 1819–20). 350 yds long with A-shaped cast-iron towers decorated in Egyptian style and with its roadway suspended from iron chains, the pier began as a landing stage but was soon adopted as a platform for promenading over the sea. It was the Victorians who introduced the concept of the 'pleasure pier' with buildings for entertainment, although Brighton's West Pier of 1863–6 by *Eugenius Birch* (*see* Topic Box p. 21) was deliberately aimed at attracting a more select clientele than was the case with the Palace Pier [32], proposed in 1891. Now the only pier to survive, the Palace Pier was built on condition that the storm-damaged remains of the Chain Pier should be cleared away. It was erected closer to the heart of the seafront where other attractions for trippers and holidaymakers were also concentrated, including The Aquarium (opened 1872, again by Birch, with a striking Gothic interior [70] providing a strangely sepulchral setting for the fish) and the peculiar Volk's Railway taking visitors along the shore E of the pier. The **seafront** itself also largely dates from the later C19, King's Road reaching its current width in 1883–7 as part of improvements with the Upper Esplanade, by the Borough Surveyor, *Philip Lockwood*, and Madeira Drive of 1872 being given its signature decorative cast-iron terrace in *c.* 1889–97. The design of Brighton's seafront railings dates from 1880 and was generally followed thereafter; the ornate lamp standards date from 1893.

As diversions for visitors grew, so purpose-built **hotels** emerged, as the practice of taking houses for a season fell out of fashion. Brighton is one of the few places in Britain where Victorian grand hotels on the European model can be seen. Larger free-standing and architecturally distinct establishments had first developed in the 1820s, including the Royal Albion Hotel [38] (unmistakably by *A.H. Wilds*, 1826) and the Royal York Hotel (enlarged from two houses in 1819) on the Steine. In their position and names these hotels clung to the regal era of Brighton's popularity, but the most fashionable hotel for the next generation was the Bedford (by *Thomas Cooper*, 1829, dem. 1964), a grand Grecian palace on the seafront. The age of the monster hotel was heralded with the development of the passenger lift, and from 1864 the nine-storey bulk of the Grand Hotel by *J.H. Whichcord* dominated the seafront. To emphasize its sumptuousness it was wholly Italianate. It was followed by the smaller Norfolk Hotel in 1865, by *H. Goulty* in a stuccoed French Renaissance manner. That the wealthier class of visitor was still attracted to Brighton at the end of the C19 is shown by the opening of the Hotel Metropole in 1890. Larger even than the Grand and with the full panoply of ballrooms, dining rooms, smoking rooms, winter gardens, Italian gardens etc., the Metropole also broke the orthodoxy of stucco along the seafront, with red brick and terracotta wholly typical of its architect, *Alfred Waterhouse*. But then hotels need or like to stand out.

West Pier

The pathetic remains of the West Pier standing in the sea opposite Regency Square belie its significance as one of the most important piers ever built. Erected in 1863–6 it was intended as an exclusive attraction at the smarter w end of the esplanade, where the major hotels were emerging and the best residential addresses were to be found. The designer was the engineer *Eugenius Birch* (1818–84), who was also responsible for thirteen other piers – from Margate Jetty in 1853–5 to Plymouth Pier in 1884 – and two seawater aquaria of which only Brighton's survives, although altered. In his construction of the West Pier, Birch perfected his use of *Alexander Mitchell*'s innovative patent screw pile, which could be screwed directly into the seabed. It was also important as a transition between promenade piers, typified by Brighton's Chain Pier of 1822–3, to the grander type with buildings devoted to sideshows and entertainments. The West Pier had kiosks of a distinctively oriental character that soon became synonymous with seaside architecture. But the prototype for the Late Victorian pleasure pier was Birch's Hastings Pier (1869–72) with its large domed pavilion for entertainments. Such a pavilion was added to the West Pier in 1893, by which time the Palace Pier had been projected as a direct competitor. A second concert hall was added to the West Pier in 1916 but from this date the attractions of piers were in decline and the West Pier's distance from the heart of tourist Brighton around the Palace Pier was to be its downfall. Although well maintained until after the Second World War, and listed in 1974, it was closed in 1975 and spiralled into decay, twice ravaged by fire in 2003–4. Efforts continue to campaign for its restoration.

14. The West Pier, as originally designed, photographed *c.* 1870s

The proliferation of styles in the architecture of Victorian Brighton followed national trends but with some of the local peculiarities that one associates with the seaside. The legacy of the Pavilion's exoticism lasted in the town for years to come, even being adopted for the extraordinary private mausoleum built for Sir Albert Sassoon in Paston Place in 1892 [80]. This was at a time when the Pavilion itself was generally regarded with contempt (*see* Topic Box p. 43), but the associated sense of fun recommended its Oriental motifs for **buildings for entertainment** ranging from the determinedly lighthearted styling of the piers, the seafront walks at Madeira Terrace and the Esplanade's kiosks and bandstand, to the remodelling in 1901 of the former Hippodrome in Middle Street by *Frank Matcham*, who gave the boxes onion domes. This had originated as an ice rink and in Matcham's conversion doubled as a circus, an indication of the variety of pleasures on offer to Victorian visitors. The town's principal theatre was the Theatre Royal, remodelled in 1866 by *C.J. Phipps*, the theatre specialist, and refronted by *Clayton & Black* in 1894 in a red brick Jacobean style [15]; the interior was enlarged and overlaid in a Louis Seize style by *Sprague & Barton*, 1927.

From the second half of the C19 Brighton also began to see itself as a regional centre and thus accrued **commercial, institutional and public buildings** of the kinds familiar from other large British towns. Although many of these buildings tend to have been redeveloped, particularly in the heart of the town where the key commercial streets of North Street (from the 1870s), Queen's Road (1878), West Street (1928–38) and Western Road (1926–36) have all been widened, the survivors show the emergence of **local architects** to fulfil the demand for new types of buildings, to such an extent that there are few important commercial and institutional buildings by outsiders. *George Somers Clarke* (1825–82), though not himself local, was responsible for the full-blown Venetian Gothic of the Blind Asylum on Eastern Road (1861, dem. 1958) and the German Gothic Swan Downer School on Dyke Road [86] (1867); but his nephew George (1841–1926), whose father was a Brighton solicitor and for sixty years Vestry Clerk, designed St Martin's, Lewes Road [103] (1872–5). From 1876–92 he was in partnership with *J.T. Micklethwaite*, the architect of the fine Neo-Perp chancel at St Peter, Valley Gardens (1889–1906). *Thomas Lainson* (c. 1825–98), the architect of the Middle Street Synagogue, began in practice in 1862 and was joined by his sons (Thomas James and Arthur H.) in 1881. Surveyors to various estates, they were also architects to the Brighton and Hove Co-Operative Supply Association, for whom they designed Palmeira House (1887) in an Italianate style appropriate to its setting at the head of Palmeira Square, yet at the Repository in Holland Road they adopted a French Second Empire style (1893), for the Royal Alexandra Hospital for Children, Norman Shaw's Queen Anne style (1880–1) and for several blocks of flats, including St Aubyn's Mansions in Hove (1899), a Free Renaissance style. Equally prolific was the solidly

15. Theatre Royal, façade altered in 1894 by Clayton & Black

commercial firm of *Clayton & Black* (i.e *Charles E. Clayton* (1853–1923) and *Ernest Black*), in practice from the 1870s through to the 1930s with their sons *Charles L. Clayton* and *Kenneth E. Black* and other successor partners. Their commercial architecture is spread across the city from the Flemish Renaissance of Gwydyr Mansions in Hove (1890) and the rather limp François Premier Revival of the French Convalescent Home in Kemp Town (1895–8) to the more assured Lloyds Bank (*c.* 1901) and their *chef d'oeuvre*, the Edwardian Baroque of the Royal Assurance Society offices [89] (1904), both in North Street. Only the stately NatWest Bank of 1905 nearby, is claimed by an outsider: *Godfrey Pinkerton* of London.

From the 1860s to 1889, civic architecture was mostly in the hands of the Corporation's engineer and surveyor, *Philip Lockwood* who converted the Pavilion stables into the Dome concert hall (1867–73) and undertook the 1880s seafront improvements. His successor, *Francis May*, is the epitome of the versatile late C19 civic architect, showing in his monumental classical reconstruction of the Town Hall interior (1898–9) and the 'Hindoo' style remodelling of the Art Gallery and Museum in the Dome (1901–3) an outstanding facility with historic styles. His original works are equally eclectic: from garden structures for the Corporation at Preston Park and Queen's Park, to free Jacobean at the Municipal Technical College in Richmond Terrace (1895–6) and Free Baroque for the Market Buildings (1900–1; dem. 1940 and 1987). The distinguished group of late C19 schools for Brighton School Board were in the hands of their architects, *Thomas Simpson* and his son *Gilbert*. Gilbert's better-known brother *(Sir) John Simpson* is also credited with some schools but is represented in central Brighton by his Boer War Memorial (1904) on the seafront and the First World War memorial in Valley Gardens. Hove's public buildings were designed by outside architects: *Alfred Waterhouse*'s Town Hall (1882) was lost to fire in 1967 (his son's Prudential Buildings, North Street, of 1904, went in the same year) but still preserved is the excellent Neo-Baroque Hove Public Library [16] by *Percy Robinson & W. Alban Jones* of Leeds (1907–8).

Brighton and Hove in the Twentieth Century

Brighton first began to lose exclusivity after 1900; it was at this time, for instance, that the larger terraced houses began to be divided into flats. Both Brighton and Hove continued to attract retirees and their commercial life was maintained, especially as the resort grew ever more popular at a less exclusive level. Indeed the heyday of Brighton as a genuinely popular resort were the three decades around the Second World War when visitors peaked at around ten million every year.

Something of the fun spirit is best represented by the interwar **pubs** with two fine examples in the 'Brewer's Tudor' of that era; the Hotel du Vin, formerly Henekeys, in Ship Street by *Ernest F. Barrow*, 1934, and the King and Queen in Valley Gardens by *Clayton & Black*, 1931–2, fitted out by *Ashley Tabb*. That they both have portcullises gives something of their flavour. Other fine pubs of this date include the Neo-Georgian Good Companions in Dyke Road and The Brunswick in Holland Road, both 1939 and (probably) by *Arthur Packham* for Tamplins, and the very jazzy Freemasons, Western Road [68], by *J.L. Denman* of 1928.

It is the varieties of early C20 classicism, from stripped classicism through the various revivals to less generic Neo-Georgian, which predominate among **commercial buildings**. Associated with the redevelopment of Western Road as the town's main shopping street are large stores for the national chains, e.g. *Bromley, Cartwright & Waumsley's* former Boots store (1927–8) in a rather Beaux-Arts style, the blocky jazz-American British Home Stores (now Primark), probably by *Garrett &*

16. Hove Public Library, by Percy Robinson and W. Alban Jones, 1907–8

Son of 1931. Of interwar **banks** there are several of which the best is the former National Provincial in North Street (1920–1, by *F.C.R. Palmer*; now a bar) in a Louis XVI style. Just up the hill is the much larger Barclays Bank of 1957–9 by *Denman & Son*, combining an entrance block and top-floor loggia with a long flank in a sort of brick and Portland stone chequer. *J.L. Denman* (1882–1975) was the master of this sort of mid-century Neo-Georgian, seen in the former offices of the Citizen's Permanent Building Society in Marlborough Place (1932), the former offices of the *Brighton & Hove Herald*, Pavilion Buildings (1933) and in the former Richmond Hotel, Richmond Place (1934), one of a series of pubs he designed along the s coast for the Kemp Town Brewery. He also designed in a more jazzy style, as can be seen in Regent House (1934), off North Street behind the Chapel Royal, with its canted walls at high level (now slightly altered) and its almost *pointilliste* brickwork, and in the Sussex Eye Hospital on Eastern Road (1935). Denman's too are the free classical stone pylons, on the A23 N of Brighton, built as a gateway to the town on its newly extended boundary in 1928. His son, *John B. Denman* (1914–2001), was responsible for the well-mannered extension to the Old Ship Hotel (1963–4).

True **Art Deco** architecture in Brighton is represented by the former Savoy Cinema by the cinema specialist *William Glen* but its greatest monument, the Regent Cinema by *Robert Atkinson* (1921), was demolished in 1974. His auditorium of 1934 for the Dome survives as some compensation (though slightly reworked by *RHWL/Arts Team*, *c.* 2000). The best interior in that style belongs to Barford Court, an idio-syncratic former private house off the Hove seafront also by a cinema architect, *Robert Cromie* (1934–7). The interwar seaside attracted modern architecture of its various kinds and Brighton is no different, from the *moderne* of the Saltdean Lido and the Ocean Hotel (*R.W.H. Jones*, both 1938) to the gigantic Marine Gate of 1937–9 by *Wimperis, Simpson & Guthrie*, given something of the nautical by the use of port-hole windows. Rather more typical of multi-storey mansion flats, of which Hove has many mid-century examples, are No. 4 Grand Avenue by *Murrell & Piggott* (1935–8) with its curved balconies and Crittall windows, Mitre House, Western Road (*J. Stanley Beard & Bennett*, 1935) in brick and stone, and Furze Croft, by *Toms & Partners* (1936).

Again in a nautical vein is *Wells Coates*'s Embassy Court of 1934–5 [58], on the seafront, right on the border with Hove. This is Brighton's most prominent example of early **Modernism** at its most polished even if it is, as Pevsner wrote, far too tall for its site and therefore, in its horizontality and disregard of context, an unfriendly neighbour to the Regency hous-es next door. In a less sensitive setting but a much more idiosyncratic and edgier version of Modernism is Prince's House in Prince's Place by *H.S. Goodhart-Rendel* (1935–6), steel-framed and brick clad with expres-sive use of coloured decoration. (A sometime resident of Brighton, Goodhart-Rendel also designed its greatest interwar church, St Wilfrid, Elm Grove, 1932–4, sadly closed in 1980 and converted to flats).

Sir Herbert Carden (1867–1941), long time Alderman of Brighton, proposed the redevelopment of the entire seafront in the Embassy Court vein. This kind of pre-war indifference to the historic fabric of the town inspired the formation of the Brighton & Hove Regency Society in 1945 (as a result of a scheme to redevelop Brunswick Town) and coincided with a revival of serious interest in the architecture and decoration of the Pavilion, for whose site Carden had advocated the building of a conference centre. Instead from 1951 it was transformed from its use since the mid c19 as a glorified community centre to become a museum and centre of scholarship.

Nevertheless much damage was done in the period up to the early 1970s in the cause of **postwar redevelopment**. Particularly offensive was the Churchill Square shopping centre, one part of a major mixed-use development by *Russell Diplock Associates*, 1964–5, extending between Western Road and the seafront where its public face was (and remains) the Kingswest Centre. Nothing can compensate for the full ghastliness of this building, or that of the brutal Brighton Centre next door (1974–7), neither of which shows any concern for setting but which were considered essential in providing further facilities for daytrippers and particularly for the lucrative conference trade. Even *Hugh Casson*, advising the council, could only comment that the Diplock scheme had 'architectural potential'. Three residential **tower blocks** were also threatened for this site. Although only one was com-pleted, high flats for private and public housing were scattered without thought throughout the town at this time. The majority followed the programme of slum clearance initiated before the war in the area between Edward Street and Albion Hill and continued by the council through the 1960s. The first tower (1961) at the newly laid out Grove Road/Ashton Rise was followed by six eleven-storey blocks that now dominate views on the eastern side of the city. Most damaging, however, is *R. Seifert & Partners'* Sussex Heights of 1966 behind the Hotel Metropole on the seafront. The tallest building in Brighton, it is destructive both in long views and to its immediate environs.

Not all new buildings of the 1960s and 1970s should be dismissed. A significant number fit in well, particularly the concave front of the University of Brighton (Grand Parade Annex) [51] of 1967 by *Percy Billington*, the then Brighton Borough Architect (with *Sir Robert Matthew & S.A.W. Johnson-Marshall*) which chimes well with Grand Parade. Brighton Square (*Fitzroy Robinson & Partners*, 1966) blends in with the architecture and layout of The Lanes [44] in the old town, which were becoming a tourist attraction at this time. Hove Town Hall (*John Wells-Thorpe & Partners*, 1970–3), with its pendant multi-storey car park, is an interesting exercise in a well-mannered Brutalism (as one might expect in Hove). And, of course, *(Sir) Basil Spence's* University of Sussex shows what an outstanding architect with an eye for history, layout, materials and setting could do in a beautiful landscape. Eaton Manor Flats, The Drive (1963 by *Hubbard Ford & Partners*) is a rare example of Spence's influence. There is even a certain pleasure to be had from the Thunderbirds whooshiness of the white and blue Amex House in Edward Street [17] (*Gollins, Melvin, Ward & Partners* 1977, as part of the redevelopment of that area).

In 1973 Brighton rejected the 'Wilson Report' (by *Sir Hugh Wilson* and *Lewis Womersley*) that proposed large-scale road-building and the

17. Amex House, Edward Street, by Gollins, Melvin, Ward & Partners, 1977

demolition of North Laine. Five town-centre conservation areas were designated instead (five more followed in 1977). But the next decade was, architecturally, a low point for Brighton and Hove reflecting the nation-wide decline of the seaside resort. It was beginning to be understood that context was important for new buildings but first attempts to engage with it were half-hearted. Neither Castle Square House (*Fitzroy Robinson Miller Bourne*, 1985) nor Trustcard House, Gloucester Place (*Christopher Beaver Associates*, 1985) really manage to update the character of Regency Brighton, and the Thistle Hotel, and its adjoining blocks as part of the redevelopment of Bartholomew Square (*Michael Lyell & Associates*, 1984–7), mistakes Brighton for a bloodless version of Las Vegas. Full-blooded Postmodern is rare in Brighton but is best seen in the Nile Street redevelopment in The Lanes (*Robin Clayton Partnership*, 1987–9), which benefits from the use of inflated features in closed-up surroundings.

And then, for some reason, the fun returned. Perhaps it was the Van Alen Building, with its 1930s *moderne* streamlining (*PRC Fewster*, 1999) which revived the spirit of interwar Brighton. Perhaps it was the Education Pavilion for the Museum and Art Gallery in the Pavilion Gardens (*RHWL/Arts Team*, 1998–2001), with its hint of the Indian. Or perhaps it was the Japanese-inspired pavilion for Moshi Moshi Restaurant in the middle of Bartholomew Square by *Alex de Rjike* of *drmm* (2001) which changed the tone. Now there are plenty of little drop-in site redevelopments across the city and many are conscious of context. *Mark Hills*'s mixed-use development adjoining Pelham Square (1998) is typical, in massing and materials responding both to the post-Regency stucco of the square and to the late C19 brick in Pelham Street. Avalon, a residential development by *Acanthus LW Architects* (2004–6), filling a large hole between West Street and Middle Street, is a smaller but much more thoughtful counterpoint to the anonymous residential development by *Chetwood Associates* of the New England Quarter (phase one completed 2007), as are the town houses of 2004 by *Alan Phillips Associates* in Brunswick Street West. More crisply Modernist is the Glass Pavilion by *3W Architecture* (2006) filling another gap site, this time opposite the Pavilion. And the Jubilee Library [35] in Jubilee Street (*Bennetts Associates* with *Lomax Cassidy & Edwards*, 2003–5) is a triumph, a carefully wrought but nonetheless striking glass box.

The future development of Brighton and Hove is clearly a problem – like all seaside towns they can only expand inland but that is constrained by the South Downs (currently proposed as a new National Park). So the pressure is to go up, with tall buildings proposed or granted consent at both ends of the seafront. As it stands the city has largely balanced the need for development with the conservation of a collection of buildings richer than for most towns its size. There are threats, particularly in the closure of Anglican churches, tall buildings and the management of traffic which damages both the open spaces of Valley Gardens and the linkages between the seafront and the beach, but the city is at least aware of the problems.

Major Buildings

The Royal Pavilion

Introduction

The Prince of Wales first came to Brighton shortly after coming of age in 1783, staying with his uncle, the Duke of Cumberland, at Grove House on the Steine. He had not been allowed to visit earlier but he enjoyed the relaxed ways of the town and took Grove House himself for the season in 1784. In 1785 the Prince was busy in Brighton with his pursuit of Mrs Fitzherbert but in 1786 Louis Weltje, his Clerk of the Kitchen and the Cellars, arranged the lease of a house, generally referred to as a farmhouse, between Grove House and the Castle Inn, for three years from Thomas Kemp Sen. The Prince's Pavilion was then begun and extended in three main stages: the conversion and extension of the farmhouse in 1786–7 by *Henry Holland*, the architect of the Prince's Carlton House in London; its extension to Holland's design, but perhaps by his pupil, *P.F. Robinson*, in 1801–4, with complete internal redecoration by *John Crace* and his son, *Frederick Crace*; and finally the almost total rebuilding and aggrandizement by *John Nash*, largely but not wholly in an Indian style, apparently begun in 1815 and largely complete externally in 1822. Decoration, by *Frederick Crace* and *Robert Jones*, continued until 1823. The result is a Pavilion fit first for a Prince and then, in Nash's incarnation, for a King.

The Pavilion as we have it is only part of the building as Nash left it. After inheriting the Crown, George concentrated on Windsor Castle and Buckingham Palace, visiting his Pavilion for the last time in January 1827. Although King William IV enjoyed the Pavilion, Queen Victoria was only an occasional visitor before she purchased Osborne on the Isle of Wight in 1845, and much of the interior was stripped out before the town's purchase of the Pavilion from the Crown in 1850. Soon after the extensive office ranges at the s end were demolished (*see* Pavilion Buildings, p. 167), but redecoration of the interior was undertaken almost immediately by *Christopher Wren Vick*, who had worked for both William IV and Victoria. Paintings and fixtures were returned after 1864 and some time later *John Diblee Crace* undertook to restore his grandfather's work where it survived (the Music Room and the Saloon, for instance), while redecorating anew those rooms where nothing remained.

More scholarship informed the works after 1920, under the supervision of Henry Roberts, the Director, particularly as Queen Mary was interested in the building and returned much furniture that was unused in other royal palaces and in further loans following the Second World War. Under Clifford Musgrave the first artist-restorer, *Roy Bradley*, was appointed, but the Pavilion continued in community use into the 1970s when it was finally devoted wholly to its own exhibition. A fire in 1975, which almost destroyed the Music Room, led to a major programme of repairs which set in motion increased scholarship, an innovative approach to the conservation of a major building and the now almost complete renovation of those remaining unrestored 1822-period rooms, under the direction of John Morley and later Jessica Rutherford. What survives is more than enough to give a vivid impression of the leisured life and patronage of the most artistically aware royal builder and collector since King Charles I.

The Marine Pavilion 1786–1815

The original farmhouse faced E onto the Steine. Holland repeated it to the N and connected the two buildings by a rotunda with two apsidal extensions. To the outside the rotunda came forward and had a detached Ionic colonnade, and each wing had (as in the original farmhouse) a pair of shallow bows – parents to many at Brighton. A shallow dome on the rotunda showed to the outside too. The rotunda had one tall storey, the wings two. This was not great architecture and it is hard to liken it to such suave Continental prototypes as Schloß Sanssouci at Potsdam (Georg Wenzeslaus von Knobbelsdorf, 1745–7) for Frederick the Great, Lustschloß Solitude at Stuttgart by Philippe de la Guêpière and J.W. Weyhing (1763–7) or the Hôtel de Salm in Paris by Pierre Rousseau (early 1780s). It had, however, a gawky vernacular charm, particularly on the entrance (W) front with its long plain wings enfolding a rather overlarge tetrastyle portico. Little of this building can now be seen, but hidden away here and there are stretches of its original facing of gault clay mathematical tiles, a favourite building material of Holland's.

In **Holland's Pavilion** there is much that is comparable to the Prince's London home, Carlton House. Both were enthusiasms of the Prince's from the time of his majority; both were intended for private living initially, for relaxation and comfort but also for display and entertainment. Both were too small and were inconveniently planned. And both were subject to changes in the Prince's taste.

18. Engraved view of Holland's Royal Pavilion, as built 1786–7

Internally Holland's Pavilion remained a classical house until at least 1802. It was fitted up in a largely French style, as Rowlandson's attractive drawing of the interior of the Saloon shows, until the wars with France demanded a change of taste. Plans of 1787 show the central domed Saloon or Drawing Room with the Breakfast Room and the Ante Room to the s, divided by a staircase which led up to the Prince's apartment above, and the Dining Room and Library to the N. Kitchens and the kitchen yard stood to the N of the house with other offices while sizeable stables were to the s, divided from the sw wing by 'Mr Weltje's House'. Although Holland planned rearrangements and extensions in 1795 at the time of the marriage to Princess Caroline, it was instead the *rapprochement* of 1801 with Mrs Fitzherbert which led the Prince to consider the first major rebuilding.

Orientalism: Chinese Styles

Trade with Asia encouraged the unscholarly appreciation of Chinese art and architecture in European decorative arts from an early date. *Chinoiserie* found its greatest popularity from the earlier c18 in the light-hearted Rococo styles of that period and the enthusiasm for picturesque modes of landscaping. These imported styles were used in Europe, however, not only for garden pavilions but also for major houses such as Schloß Pillnitz designed by Mattaeus Daniel Pöppelmann for Elector Augustus the Strong of Saxony (*c.* 1720). In royal circles the Prince of Wales's mother, Queen Charlotte, had a fondness for Chinese ornaments and his sisters were taught japanning. Sir William Chambers published his *Designs of Chinese Buildings, Furniture etc.* in 1757 and had put up a Chinese pagoda (as well as a mosque and an Alhambra) at Kew as early as 1762. The Prince's architect, *Henry Holland*, designed the Chinese Dairy at Woburn in 1787 and the first of several Chinese rooms at Carlton House, *c.* 1790. Those were the years of the most ingenuous playing with the architectural forms of other cultures, and by the 1790s they were on the whole over. No one knows why the style was adopted for the Pavilion as late as 1801–2. That the Prince was given eight sheets of Chinese wallpaper in 1802 may only have been the result of a decision already made, rather than inspiration, since Holland had already supplied a very pretty scheme (dated July 1801) for dressing up the house externally in this style. *Chinoiserie* was maintained as the principal decorative influence through the many changes to the interior up to 1822, a unique loyalty in the age of Neoclassicism and typical of the Prince, whose taste was often both forward-looking and conservative. Though Chinese styles were often associated with women and women's rooms, David Beevers considers that the Prince's use was a reaction against an architecturally conservative father, a stylistic innovation encouraged by picturesque eclecticism, and by boredom with the ambiguity of the Greek revival.

As part of these discussions Holland produced the first design for an exterior in Chinese guise. The choice of style was not a surprise. Holland had designed a Chinese Room at Carlton House *c.* 1790 but there it was one style among many – what he intended for the Pavilion was quite different. But the Prince decided only to extend the house and rearrange the accommodation. The major additions erected under the supervision of *P. F. Robinson*, Holland's assistant, were two wings on the E front angled at 60 degrees to the main range for a conservatory (s) and a new eating room (N). These were in a style to match the rest of the early Pavilion but the Prince must have been tickled by the Chinese style, for the chaste and elegant interiors were reconfigured and converted to a thoroughgoing *chinoiserie* at the hands of *John Crace* and *Frederick Crace*, his son. New staircases were added in projecting lumps between the portico and the wings on the w front: the main stair appears to have been symmetrical, a reduced version of Holland's stair at Carlton House.

Unfortunately, there are now only tantalizing glimpses of this phase of interior decoration, and its overall character is only alluded to by the Craces' many sketches. With the exception of the Saloon, the appearance of several rooms had been changed (in some cases frequently) before the penultimate programme of redecoration began in 1815. Of the lost interiors the most extraordinary, and certainly the most mourned, was the Glass Corridor set between the new conservatory and library at the s end of the Pavilion. It was formed of glazed screens of stained and painted glass within a framework of Chinese lattice, all back-lit, with a ceiling painted in imitation of tea wood and pagoda roofs projecting at both ends.

Nash's Pavilion 1815–22

The land on which to extend the Pavilion was severely constricted by East Street along the w front, the Steine to the E, Marlborough House (formerly Grove House) to the N, which the Prince used for guest accommodation, and the Castle Inn to the s. This had proved fatal to Holland's earlier plans for extension, and from 1802 efforts were made to acquire East Street and the land to its w for gardens and the erection of

19. The w front from Nash's *Views of the Royal Pavilion*

William Porden's stables (1804–8, *see* The Dome, p. 44). This building raised a further question: how should the Pavilion compete with a structure so unexpectedly monumental and archaeological in style? *Humphry Repton*, who had been engaged in 1805–6 for the laying out of the new gardens with buildings in an Indian style, also proposed, it seems at his own suggestion, rebuilding the Pavilion in a manner to match the stables but this was not acted upon. The Prince's desire for ambitious redesigning revived in 1812 when acquisition of Marlborough House offered limited opportunity for extension to the N (although the surrounding ground was granted on condition that it remain undeveloped) and the site of the old stables presented room for expansion to the S for new kitchens and offices. The commission in that year to *James Wyatt* to rebuild was aborted by his death late in 1813 and, owing to the inevitable need to economize, Nash inherited an unenviable situation in 1815 in which he had to remodel, rather than start afresh, while at the same time monumentalizing with the requisite flair to satisfy the Prince's need for comfort and pomp. This is where Nash's genius shone. He was always good at varied and extended façades, as the Regent's Park terraces show. His performance at Brighton was even better, being in three dimensions.

Exterior

Nash kept Holland's building but added as outer pavilions on the E **front**, in place of the 1802 wings, larger rooms than any so far: the Banqueting Room (S) and the Music Room (N). Basically of course the classical scheme was not given up: central motif, angle motifs, unstressed links between them. But the Prince and Nash could not tolerate anything unstressed, and so in addition to the capital onion dome and naughty (as Pevsner described them) pagoda roofs of the new pavilions, each of the four shallow bows of the links, two left and two right, received another dome and the parapets were fairly sprinkled with little finials. In doing so, as John Morley points out, it is as though he put all of Repton's unexecuted garden buildings on the roof. From Porden Nash took the scalloped arches ending in an ogee tip which, though Islamic in feel, are also at once reminiscent of the Gothick. Indeed the most curious of features is that in places Nash has frankly Gothic friezes of cusped lozenges, a Perp motif. The domes of course are Indian, the pinnacles are Indian and columns starting bulbously and ending in lotus shapes are Indian too. But there is something more bulgy and Baroque here than the two-dimensional merits of Porden's stables; unlike Indian architecture, here the roof furniture is strongly related to the architecture below, not floating about somewhere behind the façade as at the stables. Fretwork screens tie the main pavilions of the E façade together and minarets pin the building to the ground while raising the eye in a building largely without a base.

On the W **front** the entrance is not symmetrical, owing to the interference of houses on its S side. Its centre here is a deep porte cochère, neither an Indian nor an Islamic motif. The projecting wings allowed

20. The Royal Pavilion, detail of the domes, view from the NE

Nash to increase the depth of the Pavilion for additional suites of rooms by bringing ground-floor accommodation forward and then extending the building on both sides more or less level with the wings, with the King's Apartment on the left and services on the right (although the southern block was not completed to follow the northern scheme with its seven-bay loggia and veranda). The ends of the C18 wings were given clerestory strip windows, domes and minarets, and these are replicated at the corners of the N front, where there is a five-bay loggia and veranda, possibly intended as a secondary entrance to the Pavilion (as Repton had suggested). Extending beyond the s pavilion Nash created the Great Kitchen and mighty service ranges. Work began with the kitchen and was complete in 1822.

Planning, Function and Decoration after 1815

The major loss since the Prince's time has been the majority of the office ranges, including most of the areas subsidiary to the Great Kitchen. That about a quarter of the **ground plan** of the Pavilion [21] was devoted to the preparation or eating of food, may be taken as indication not only of the Prince's prodigality but also the great care taken to ensure the comfort of his guests. From the start few visitors stayed overnight owing to the lack of bedrooms, and dinner companions would be invited from the town. Dinner was served at 6 o'clock, followed by music, conversation and cards lasting beyond midnight. All of the rooms along the E front would be in use for these entertainments as a single suite, including the Gallery, which divides the plan E–W and allowed access to all the public rooms. On the W front, by contrast, the rooms to either side of the Entrance Hall functioned effectively as waiting rooms; to the N was the Yellow Ante Room for those waiting on the King, to the S the Red Drawing Room, apparently mostly used as part of a suite of rooms for ladies to prepare themselves for, or to withdraw from, the evening's entertainment. Servants were cleverly provided, furthermore, with a tiled passage running alongside the Gallery for the full length of the house (and indeed the office range) with stairs leading up and over the Entrance Hall (parts are still in use for visitors).

Although the **decoration** of the Pavilion was never subject to quite the same capriciousness as Carlton House, the schemes for each room were (sometimes frequently) altered. The Prince's apparent irresolution was often the result of a fastidious taste that called for decorative effects, whether trivial or an entire scheme, to be tried for his approval. Thus, for example, the colour of the bamboo ceilings in the alcoves in the Music Room was changed following painting, and a drawing by Frederick Crace shows a kind of chart for the Prince to select the colour. Although his taste was sure, and once selected tended to be firm, there was no attempt at purity of decoration. The interiors have a mainly Chinese flavour but use motifs which may also appear to be Indian, Gothic or classical; the final effect is undeniably Empire in manner but resolutely eclectic. The same was true of the furniture, with objects selected for their impact rather than the latest *goût du jour*. Older pieces were used too but all, old and new, were of the highest quality.

Similarly the Prince was fascinated by the latest **technology**, whether in kitchen equipment, the organ in the Music Room (the largest in England when it was installed) or the use of underfloor heating systems. Visitors to the Pavilion all remarked on the warmth, not to say suffocating heat, of the rooms, and all would have been impressed by the **lighting**. This came from two sources, natural and artificial, though much of the apparently natural light was also artificial. Thus the clerestory eyebrow windows in both the Banqueting and Music rooms were lit from outside after dark (by gas, in 1821 a very early use) and back lighting was also employed for the stained glass in the Gallery; the precedent was the lighting of the Craces' Glass Corridor of 1802–4

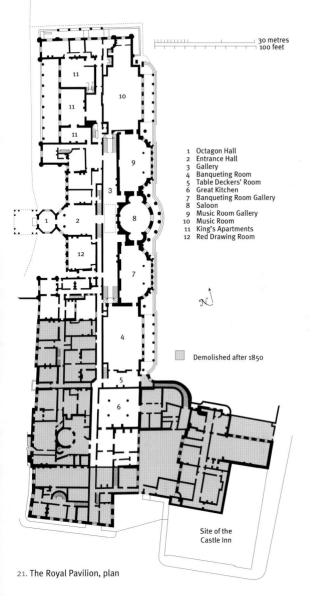

1   Octagon Hall
2   Entrance Hall
3   Gallery
4   Banqueting Room
5   Table Deckers' Room
6   Great Kitchen
7   Banqueting Room Gallery
8   Saloon
9   Music Room Gallery
10 Music Room
11 King's Apartments
12 Red Drawing Room

Demolished after 1850

Site of the
Castle Inn

21. The Royal Pavilion, plan

(*see* above), and something of the original effect may be gauged from the
painted glass windows in the staircases. Painted glass lay-lights provided
light to the Gallery as well as to the South Galleries on the first floor.
Structurally the Pavilion was also innovative with an iron frame to
the central dome and iron cores to the minarets. The pagoda roofs to
the Music and Banqueting rooms were iron-framed too, following the
design that Nash, with the assistance of the carpenter *William Nixon*,
had used for the Rotunda for the Victory Fête at Carlton House in 1814
(now at Woolwich Common).

22. The Royal Pavilion, Banqueting Room

Interior

Decoration of the **interior** has largely been restored to the appearance depicted in Nash's *Views of the Royal Pavilion* (1826). The initial phase of redecoration after 1815 was once more in the hands of *Frederick Crace*, but with the addition of Music Room and Banqueting Room after 1818 this work was revised and new schemes developed by *Crace* (the Music Room, the Gallery and the North and South Gallery rooms) and the otherwise unknown *Robert Jones* (the Banqueting Room, the King's Apartment, the Red Drawing Room and the Saloon). The contrast in the decoration of this time with the Rococo spirit of previous years clearly reflects the Prince's changing role: earlier more fun, later more regal. The work was carried out largely by assistants, mostly unknown. Many of the fittings were executed to Crace and Jones's designs by *Bailey & Saunders*, who provided doors, the dragon in the dome of the Banqueting Room, draperies and curtains, the sideboards, chairs, carpets and rugs, and the carved ornament, which was gilded by *Fricker & Henderson*. *Vulliamy* made the chimneypieces, to the design of *Sir Richard Westmacott* in the Banqueting Room and Jones in the Music Room, as well as clocks; *Ashlin & Collins* provided all the mirrors; *Perry & Co.* the lustres; and *Robson & Hale* all the wallpapers. The Banqueting Room is thought to have cost £41,886 4s. 0d.; the Music Room, £45,125 15s. 10d.;

in total the Prince is thought to have spent at least £502,000 on the Pavilion during his lifetime.

The visitor entered the Pavilion by the **porte cochère** in the centre of the w front topped by one of the smaller Indian onion domes, this one lit by windows and carried on doubled columns, tapering from the top, with lotus-leaf bases and tops with Indian finials. Two halls follow, the outer of which (**Octagon Hall**) has the form of a tent, complete with billowing, almost Baroque, ceiling and ropes down the walls. Beyond is the **Entrance Hall**, square but with a half-octagonal end behind a screen which has windows and a clerestory of painted glass above, the panels of which cleverly repeat the arched, rather Gothic form of the cornice to the room. Here is the first introduction to the Chinese world of the interior. Designed by *Frederick Crace*, the decoration is relatively subdued, doubtless to contrast with the Gallery beyond, with panels of serpents and dragons on banners on a pale green ground and the woodwork painted to imitate pollarded oak.

The **Gallery** beyond is the first of the truly sumptuous rooms and, in its predominantly pink with blue, red and gold colouring, is both the most obviously Chinese room and the closest in spirit to the lighter decoration of the Pavilion in 1802–4. The central section is taller with a painted glass lay-light and below a sort of false roof with bells running as a cornice, a motif to be found throughout the Pavilion. The space is compartmented down its length by bamboo fretwork. On the E wall are niches, the central pair a survival from the original Pavilion when they were exterior features at the back of the portico. The central lustre was designed for the Saloon in 1802–4. At each end are the **staircases**, of cast iron masquerading as bamboo, with paired lower flights framing doors which when open give views to the great rooms beyond but also have mirrored fronts to give the impression of compound stairs when closed.

The two rooms at the ends of the Gallery are a mirrored pair, although their ceilings differ in detail: the Music Room dome resting on an octagon and the Banqueting Room on pendentives, both with shallow recesses to N and S. The effect of both is as of tents, exotically decorated but entirely of their time in their Empire richness. First, the **Banqueting Room** [22], of which Princess Lieven wrote, 'I do not believe that, since the days of Heliogabalus, there has been such magnificence and such luxury'; the central lustre weighs a ton. Murals of scenes from Chinese life by *Robert Jones*, more than life-size, on a figured silver ground, stand against a background of blue and silver diaper; below is a red and gold Chinese trellis dado. The canopied ceilings of the ends are treated as if gold leather with stars, mythical birds and trees. The richness of the blue, silver and gold decoration continues above to an apparent opening in the centre of the dome, a clouded sky (a favourite motif of the Prince's) and a giant plantain tree spreading above. From this suspends the lustre, with mirrored star, lotus bowls and dragons, all topped by the biggest dragon in the Pavilion. In the pendentives flying birds, the F'eng of Chinese mythology, carry more lights.

Beyond the Banqueting Room survive the only kitchen offices, including the **Table Deckers' Room**, a lofty space which served as the main servery for the footmen, and then the **Great Kitchen**, tall like kitchens since the medieval period and top-lit by a clerestory. The ceiling is famously supported by cast-iron columns topped by palm leaves. Beyond are a small cluster of household rooms; the meat and game larders, the plate stores and stewards' rooms, the coffee, pastry, confectionery and ice-cream rooms and the bakery have all gone.

The **Banqueting Room Gallery** begins the suite of rooms laid out in enfilade along the E front and is deliberately calmer than the Banqueting Room. This room is the core of the old farmhouse (as its low ceiling reminds us) and in 1787 was the Breakfast Room and Ante-Room (with staircase between, leading to the Prince's Apartment above). In 1802–4, with the loss of the stair, it became the Ante Room and Library (with the Glass Corridor and Conservatory beyond). By 1815 it was one room, redecorated as the Blue Drawing Room in sumptuous Chinese style by *Crace* but altered by him after 1818 when Nash rebuilt the E wall (and that of its matching room to the N) to form a square window bay. The earlier building line is marked by a pair of palm-tree columns. Walls of 'flake white' with gilt embellishments and a 'rich green ground satin brocade' to windows and the recess. Similar decoration for the corresponding room to the N of the Saloon, the **Music Room Gallery**, which has a more distinctively Chinese character with supporting columns entwined by serpents and finished with umbrellas. Here the walls have shadowed gilt edging set off by yellow upholstery and draperies, a reminder of its redecoration in 1815 as the Yellow Drawing Room. This was in a livelier Chinese style and here was displayed much of the furniture from the original Chinese Room of 1790 at Carlton

House. In Holland's Pavilion this was the Eating Room and Library in 1787 but was thrown together in 1802–4 as the 'Chinese Gallery' and by 1809 is described as the 'Egyptian Gallery'.

The **Saloon** is the only room to retain its form from 1787. Its decoration was first classical, by *Biagio Rebecca*, then 'à la Chinois' in 1802–4 but in its final form, as redecorated by *Robert Jones*, has pleated crimson silk and mirrors in panels with lavish, rather Indian-style crestings. Fire surround, 1860s by *John Thomas*, replacing one

23. Cross-section of the Saloon from Nash's *Views of the Royal Pavilion*

24. The Royal Pavilion, Music Room

taken to Buckingham Palace. The colour tones are gold on a ground of blue and silver diaper (like the Banqueting Room) but with crimson upholstery and draperies; the ceiling is clouded with a painted central coiling dragon supporting the lustre. This room was one of three, with the Banqueting and Music rooms, with hand-knotted Axminster carpets rather than the flat-weave Brussels carpets used elsewhere.

The **Music Room** was *Frederick Crace*'s major interior and climax to the tour of the public rooms [24]. Starting as a Rococo Chinese interior in blue and pink, the designs moved towards a much more startling and sumptuous red and gold and blue scheme. With painted blue and gold dado, the walls are decorated with paintings of Chinese scenes in gold on a very rich red, derived from William Alexander's *The Costume of China* (1805) and executed by *M. Lambelet*. The dome is supported on an octagon and eight pendentives (framing coloured glass panels) and has a convex ring with red and gold decoration on a blue and gold diaper under a gold dome of diminishing shellwork [2]. The huge central lustre hangs from a particularly spiky gilded centre via a sort of pagoda construction with bells to a huge painted glass dish with pearl edging and lotus-leaf base. This painted glass dish is repeated eight times around the room, dropping from giant floral brackets in the corners of the octagon. The extraordinary fire surround is a copy of the original, designed by Jones, now at Buckingham Palace.

The **King's Apartments** were added on the w front of the N wing after 1815, when the Prince moved downstairs from rooms over the Banqueting Room Gallery. These are sober rooms entered via the Yellow Ante Room

N of the Entrance Hall or by a door at the base of the Music Room staircase. Designed by *Robert Jones* as a suite of **Ante Room**, **Library** and **Bedroom** (with bathroom, page's room and dressing room), they are decorated with a green-ground dragon paper, a version of which had been used in the Red Drawing Room (s of the Entrance Hall), with a clouded ceiling, yellow upholstery and draperies. A loggia on the w side opens out into the Pavilion gardens.

The **first floor** was never very spacious. It comprised galleries to N and s, at the head of the two main stairs, serving the **Bow Rooms,** that to the s formerly the King's Apartment and the one to the N, recently restored to Jones's design, the bedrooms of the Prince's brothers, the Duke of York and the Duke of Clarence. Over the Entrance Hall, **Queen Victoria's Apartment** has also been re-created, a Chinese room in a more traditional country house taste. The **South Galleries**, which have also been restored, are odder, top-lit by painted lay-lights with painted bamboo trelliswork on an azure ground.

In 1821 the Castle Inn was acquired by the King and subsequently demolished, although its assembly room, designed by *John Crunden* in 1776, was converted for use as the **Royal Chapel**. After the sale of the Pavilion estate in 1850 it was dismantled and re-erected at St Stephen, Montpelier Place (*see* p. 171).

Pavilion Gardens

The grounds are a story of steady increase in size as the Prince moved to gain extra land around the Pavilion, first with part of the Steine to the E of the Pavilion in 1793, then in 1802 with land to the w including Promenade Grove, the town's first pleasure garden, at which time that part of East Street in front of the Pavilion between Castle Square and Church Street was closed to the public. Further ground was obtained in 1813, 1815 and 1827. The gardens were redesigned to encompass the increase in size by *Samuel Lapidge* in 1805 but then relandscaped by Nash with the royal gardener, *W. T. Aiton*, as shown in Nash's *Views of the Royal Pavilion*. The **North Gate** dates from 1832 and was designed by *Joseph Good* for William IV entirely in the spirit of the Pavilion; central arch with corner columns and minarets and onion dome. Lower side wings with tall finials. To its w, **North Gate House** is the remaining house (No. 8) of nine which comprised Marlborough Row and dates from *c.* 1784–1802. The houses were acquired for the Prince, occupied by him during the redevelopment of the Pavilion and mostly demolished in 1820–1. It was tricked out in oriental style by Good when the North Gate was built. A South Gate House, also by Good (1831), was demolished with the majority of the offices in the 1850s. The present **South Gate** dates from 1921. It was designed by *Thomas Tyrwhitt* in an archaeologically accurate Gujerati style to commemorate the Indian soldiers tended in the Pavilion during the First World War. Bath stone with square piers and attached octagonal columns, wide overhanging eaves and stone dome.

The gardens were restored in the 1990s to something like their original appearance of serpentine pathways and informal plantings, with the closure of what had become a public road between the North and South Gates. The fanciful wall with railings to the E of the Pavilion dates from 1922, a remnant of an earlier effort at landscaping by the then Superintendent of Parks and Gardens, *Capt. B.H. MacLaren*.

The Fall and Rise of the Royal Pavilion

The British have always been of two minds when it comes to marvels, and the reaction to the Pavilion was also coloured by the political complexion of the onlooker and their view of the King. George IV was not a monarch about whom one could be indifferent. Neither could one be of his Pavilion. William Cobbett, Tory radical and reformer: 'Take a square box . . . take a large Norfolk turnip . . . and put the turnip on the middle of the top of the box. Then take four turnips of half the size . . . and put them on the corners of the box. Then take a considerable number of the bulbs of the crown imperial . . . let the leaves of each have sprouted to about an inch; put all these, pretty promiscuously, but pretty thickly, on the top of the box. Then stand off and look at your architecture. There!' Even Sir Walter Scott thought that fire would be a suitable fate for 'a great eyesore'. Although the Pavilion's indirect influence was strong, especially on seaside architecture where it unleashed a spate of pagoda roofs and Indian domes around the coastal resorts, its eclecticism was abhorrent to later generations of architects. The sobriety of interwar Modernism, preferring a restrained garb for its 'fun' architecture and encapsulated by Mendelsohn's De la Warr Pavilion at Bexhill (1935), is reflected in the attitudes of mid-c20 architectural historians to the Prince's Pavilion. John Summerson, writing early in his career, considered it 'simply a minor historical monument . . . today the Pavilion is a curiosity which rouses only a vague, transient wonder in the visitor'. But it was also in the 1930s that a serious revival of interest in the art and architecture of the Regency began and led to greater appreciation of the Pavilion after the war. Work began on its restoration *c.* 1951, perhaps significantly coinciding with the Festival of Britain and renewed interest in British traditions of the Picturesque. By the 1960s Pevsner could respond to it more warmly, almost against his better judgement: ' . . . those of us who have grown up with the emotional appreciation of the International Style of the 1930s and the more intellectual appreciation of the finesses of Georgian proportion, details and craftsmanship, may well laugh at first, but then a feeling of intoxication will follow. There is in the end a great release in looking at and walking about in this folly, and so we stop asking questions.' Summerson too revised his opinion, noting the Pavilion as a 'felicitous materialisation of the careless, humorous, audacious genius of the architect'. But still not of his patron.

The Dome

(Museum, Corn Exchange and Pavilion Theatre)

Church Street

The Dome was built in 1804–8 as the Prince of Wales's **stables and riding house** by *William Porden*, who had replaced Holland as the Prince's architect. He had already built a house on the Steine for Mrs Fitzherbert in 1804, while also working on the incorporation of the site of the Promenade Grove into the Pavilion Gardens and in laying out what would become New Road (p. 81). Following the sale of the Pavilion estate in the 1850s, the buildings were converted from 1867 to 1873 for a concert hall, corn exchange and picture gallery (the first purpose-built municipal picture gallery in the country), museum and library, all by *Philip Lockwood*, Corporation Surveyor. It was further remodelled in 1901–2 by *Francis J. May* and again in 1934 by *Robert Atkinson*. Although the Dome was not the first addition to the Pavilion estate, it was the first to turn to Indian and Islamic styles for its influences and this has been maintained, with greater or lesser confidence, in the numerous additions and remodellings since. A cool Modernism has been added to the stylistic mix only in 1998–2001 during major refurbishment by *Renton Howard Wood Levin/Arts Team.*

Despite many changes Porden's building still dominates the s front overlooking the gardens and gives the main key to the N elevation on Church Street. Though Indian in its details and form, it has little of the verve of the handling of the Pavilion, its success lying in an undeniable monumentality. It is a big block of yellow brick, and one never gets over noticing that. As designed, it consisted of a central domed stables with further stabling in the N court, flanked by the riding house in the W wing and matching screens to the E behind which a Real Tennis court was to have been built, eventually completed as stables for Queen Adelaide in 1832 by *Joseph Good*. These elements are expressed in the tripartite composition of the N and S façades, and each has its own tripartite features. The centre has two rows of windows and the façades have much of the flatness of Islamic architecture (as shown, for example, in Thomas Daniell's illustration of the Jami' Masjid at Delhi (1644–58), published following 1795), with the character of screens behind which domes rise up without any hint of their relationship to the buildings below. The centre of the **s elevation** cants forward without really affecting the two-dimensionality of the architecture. Set back behind is the dome, large but relatively wide and shallow in its curves and almost wholly Roman in its forms and not obviously related to the building beneath.

It was something of a constructional feat for its time, its cast iron construction pre-dating the famous glass and iron dome with which François-Joseph Bélanger re-roofed the Halle au Blé between 1809 and 1813; the glazing appears to have been modelled on that of its predecessor, the timber roof of 1782–3 by Jacques-Guillaume Legrand and Jacques Molinos.

The N façade to Church Street has been altered, principally by *Francis May* who in 1901–2 introduced a more vigorous Eastern character by replacing Porden's rather underplayed centre with a much richer, not to say more congested, two-storey block of seven bays (for the library), divided into three by full-height buttress-columns carrying minarets,

Orientalism: Indian Styles

Although establishment of the Dutch and English East India Companies in the C17 established opportunities for greater exposure to Indian culture, it was only at the end of the C18 that accurate information on its architecture was available through William Hodges's *Views of India* (1786) and Thomas & William Daniell's *Views of Oriental Scenery* (from 1795). Among other buildings, these depicted the Jami' Masjid, Delhi, which clearly influenced *William Porden*'s design of 1804 for the Prince's riding stables (although he still proposed Chinese re-cladding for the Pavilion at about this time). Porden had already exhibited at the Royal Academy 'a design for a place of amusement in the style of the Mahometan architecture of Hindustan' in 1797 and was also connected with Samuel Pepys Cockerell, who with advice from the Daniells designed Sezincote (Gloucestershire) *c.* 1805 (i.e. after the Dome) in an Indian Islamic style for his brother, who had made a good deal of money in India. Repton also worked at Sezincote and drew on its style for his unexecuted designs for ornamental structures in the Pavilion's gardens and his proposals for transforming the Pavilion into a Moghul's palace, aspects of which reappeared in Nash's great reconstruction after 1815, perhaps symbolic of the almost total control which Britain held over India by that time.

25. Perspective view of the Dome stables, s elevation

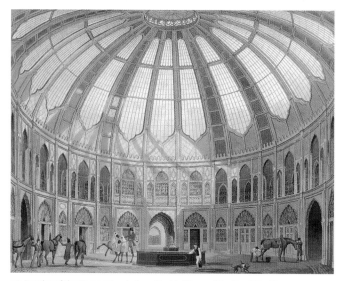

26. Interior of the Dome rotunda from Nash's *Views of the Royal Pavilion*

and with two Pavilion-style domes at the outer bays. In the bays to left and right entrances with cusped arches. At the w end of this front is a modest four-bay addition of 1934 by *Robert Atkinson* for an entrance to the **Corn Exchange**, remodelled at this date for exhibitions and banquets. Central tall arch and a relief figure of Ceres in a vesica flanked by angels, by *James Woodford*. This block, and Atkinson's **Pavilion Theatre**, at the sw corner of the complex with its front to New Road, use Indian or Islamic embellishment but almost with embarrassment. Yellow brick, windows with round-arched heads and spiral-fluted columnar mullions and battlements of lunette form, all rather dull.

Internally, the Victorian and c20 work is much more interesting. The only surviving interior of the Prince's stables is the 178-ft long former Riding House (converted as the Corn Exchange in 1868), which in spite of the alterations in 1934 remains very close to its appearance in Nash's *Views of the Royal Pavilion*. Like the Dome the construction of the timber roof is interesting and innovative in its adoption of an arched form to span the width of the building without the use of tie-beams, producing a high and uninterrupted space. Five trios of elliptical arched principals are stiffened longitudinally by what amount to staggered butt purlins, a technique that appears to take timber engineering as far as it can go. Atkinson's painted scheme remains.

The **Concert Hall**, formerly the circular stables, was reconstructed in 1998–2001 but largely preserves the spirit of Atkinson's Art Deco interior of 1934. As depicted in Nash's *Views* this was originally two-storeyed with grooms' and stable-boys' quarters above the stables. The decoration was essentially flat with architraves around the ground-floor openings and rather Indian-looking pilaster strips rising to the similar ribs to the Dome, though the main structure was hidden in pairs of thicker ribs on the diagonals of the space. The most impressive feature was the glazed roof with openings of an immensely satisfying form, scalloped at top and bottom and therefore in their form rather petal-like, like water-lily flowers. The structure survives, at least in part, but concealed by Atkinson's ceiling (above, the roof has an extravagant paint scheme in an Indian/Islamic style, apparently dating from Lockwood's reworking in 1867), and his single horseshoe balcony carries widely spaced trefoiled arches to a ceiling with a very shallow dome and two tiers of sixteen and eight lobes. Walnut-veneered walls, the whole effect very plain and cinematic.

Of Lockwood's work, the main survival is his large two-storey Picture Gallery in the **Museum**. It would appear to survive virtually intact but the rooms all around, though Lockwood in their bones, were altered by May and show his preference for a decorative treatment of an eclectic Neo-Jacobean kind, though that might underplay just how well thought out they actually are. The exceptions are May's very fine twin **entrance halls** to the Dome and the library, both lined in polychrome tiles and modelled terracotta in a Victorian version of an Indian/Islamic style. The tiles were designed by *George Elphick* and manufactured by *Craven Dunhill & Co*. The E entrance to the Museum with its porte cochère by May, originally of 1901–2, is now in a plain modern style by *RHWL/Arts Team*, contemporary with the rather flat redecoration of the Museum and Art Gallery, including the former public library on the ground floor in the centre of the Church Street façade. RHWL/Arts Team's interventions were mostly technical, but adjacent to North Gate House their small timber **Education Pavilion** is the most felicitous intervention. Though contemporary in much of its handling, it is kiosk-like and, with wide eaves and shutters, rather Indian in feeling.

27. The Dome, staircase in the Art Gallery

St Michael and All Angels

Victoria Road

1858–61 by *G.F. Bodley;* one of his earliest commissions. Enlarged 1893–5 to designs of 1865 by *William Burges.* Of all the great Victorian churches of Brighton, St Michael and All Angels in Montpelier combines grandeur and artistry in the most satisfying way. More stately than St Bartholomew, Brighton, its fittings are more rewarding than All Saints, Hove. Only St Mary, Upper Rock Gardens, approaches its inventiveness as a theatre for Anglo-Catholic worship.

The history of the church is surprisingly complex. The church was one of a number of plantations in expanding suburbs of Brighton which emanated from the Anglo-Catholic centre at St Paul's, West Street (p. 98), and the ministry of the Rev. Arthur Wagner (*see* Topic Box, p. 101). The Rev. Charles Beanlands had been one of a number of curates at St Paul's, coincidentally the young *Bodley*'s local church. It is possible that, on being presented with the new living of St Michael, Beanlands asked his acquaintance for designs. Bodley remained in contact with Beanlands, or at least the church, into the 1870s but Beanlands had turned to *Burges* for work as early as 1862 (he designed a house near Bingley, Yorkshire, for Beanland's cousin). Thus a new and splendid, soaring nave and N aisle were designed in 1865 but only built after Burges's death with his friend and office manager, *John Starling Chapple,* as executant architect. The original plans, like those of many of the greater Victorian churches in Brighton, were more extensive than as built, including a cloister and a campanile; his scheme of decoration for the chancel was later entirely changed.

Although the church is the outcome of two campaigns, the newer and higher nave hides that from outside by following, a bit more lushly, the red brick with stone dressings and plate tracery of Bodley's church, which now serves as the s aisle. This church originally comprised a nave with N and s aisles and s chapel, the latter entered under an internal flying buttress. Four-bay nave with s clerestory and plain s arcade on low paired marble piers with foliate capitals, all different and perhaps carved by *Thomas Earp.* Walls and arches are articulated by use of stone and black brick banding with moulded stone and black brick voussoirs to the chancel arch. E window with shafting and rose window. Rose window also at the w end of the nave.

The older part opens out into the 1890s additions through a taller four-bay arcade, broadly C13 in its details, which is much grander owing

28. Interior view of St Michael's and All Angels Church, Burges's nave, 1893–5

in part to internal facing wholly in stone, with double attached piers with foliate capitals carved by *Thomas Nicholls* as private memorials. c13 in style and cathedral-like, it has a triforium and a clerestory tied to the arcades below by shafting running up beside the piers, clustered shafting to the upper parts and detached inner arcading to the triforium which repeats the tracery. The effect would have been richer had the stone vault been executed, but the timber vault is not inadequate. The nave here is of three bays, with the chancel occupying the bay corresponding to *Bodley*'s fourth nave bay and the sanctuary beyond of a marbled splendour often aspired to but rarely achieved in the later c19.

Furnishings

Sanctuary. Burges's scheme of decoration was largely changed, indeed somewhat subverted, by *W.H. Romaine-Walker* during the incumbency of Canon Sanderson, vicar from 1899 to 1909. Romaine-Walker, formerly a pupil of Sanderson at Lancing College, is an architect normally associated with lush country house interiors though he did some church work, including the sumptuous chapels at the church of the Immaculate Conception, Farm Street, Mayfair. His work here has low **screens** to both chancel and sanctuary of Derbyshire alabaster and Mexican onyx, the **walls** of the sanctuary panelled in the same material with brass studs, wrought-iron **screens** in a Renaissance style to the sides of the chancel and **rood** very high because of the height of the church. The **reredos** represents the Universal Church of Christ with central panel of Christ in Majesty flanked by the Doctors of the Church, and with seven saints in niches. Broadly Perp in style with lavish gilding. **High altar** by *Temple Moore* of 1914 in red Sussex marble. **Pulpit** of marble and alabaster by *Bodley* originally for the old church. **Lectern** by *C.E. Kempe* in N aisle, *c.* 1862, modelled on one in the Hôtel de Cluny, Paris. **Choir stalls** designed by *Burges*, in walnut with misericords by *Nicholls*. **s aisle**. **Gates** of wrought iron in low marble screen. **Rood** also wrought iron with foliate cross. Plain pedimented alabaster **reredos**, presumably by *Bodley*. From 1871 it was hidden by a large early c16 winged **altarpiece** (now in store). Made in Antwerp, it appears to have been found on the Continent by Beanlands who told Bodley. The latter, however, bought it without Beanlands' knowledge for his St John's, Tue Brook, in Liverpool. When the Bishop of Chester refused to consecrate the church with such an overtly Catholic furnishing, the altarpiece came to St Michael's, where it was restored and painted by *Kempe* to *Bodley*'s design and installed in 1871. It depicts the Passion with various groups of figures.

On the E wall above the reredos is a **painting** of twelve angels carrying golden reeds, similar to the group of angels painted in the tympanum of the W door, variously ascribed to 'a lady' and to Frank Holford, churchwarden. They were in place by 1867. The **roof** of the chancel was painted with diaper ornament by *William Morris*, *Philip Webb* and *Charles Faulkner*, part of a larger scheme which was not executed. **Reredos** in the s chapel by *Cecil Hare* (*c.* 1919).

Stained glass. No church in Sussex has better Victorian glass than St Michael's. That in the old part of the church is by *Morris, Marshall, Faulkner & Co.*, and was the company's second commission (1862–3), following Bodley's All Saints', Selsey, Gloucestershire. *Morris, Ford Madox Brown, Peter Paul Marshall, Philip Webb* and *Edward Burne-Jones* (i.e. all the founding partners of the firm) were responsible for designs. Sewter describes it as 'the earliest of the firm's windows to show real distinction in colour', particularly in the way that the typical Morris greens highlight 'the small areas of brilliant gold, blue, and the luminous pale quarries above and below the subject panels'. Although not carried out to a unified scheme, the glass appears largely to have been conceived by Morris and Webb. Some windows, however, in the old church were designed by *Clayton & Bell*, and *William Worrall* designed one in *c.*1889 (second from the w in the s aisle). Worrall was also responsible for making the e window in the main, new, chancel, to a design by *H. W. Lonsdale*, and *Clayton & Bell, Jones & Willis* and *C.E. Kempe* also designed windows for that part of the church. St Michael's also has rich holdings of plate and vestments, as might be expected of what was a wealthy Anglo-Catholic parish.

29. Detail of the Flight into Egypt, St Michael and All Angels, s window, s chancel aisle, by Edward Burne-Jones, 1862

St Bartholomew

Ann Street

If St Michael (*see* p. 48) is Brighton's most celebrated combination of church architecture and art, then St Bartholomew, built in 1872–4, is the most unforgettable experience. Yet it is by a local architect, *Edmund Scott*, who never achieved anything remotely comparable. It owes its existence to the munificence and devotion of the Rev. Arthur Wagner (*see* p. 15) and succeeded the mission chapel built by him in 1868. Two designs appear to have been made. The first was for a very different church, only 41 ft 9 in. to the roof plate (i.e. less than half the present height) but it was also to be very long, incorporating the school that Wagner had built in 1868. The second scheme more than doubled the height but reduced its length to eleven and a half bays long, leaving a gap between church and school.

St Bartholomew is Gothic in style but of no historical or local class. Plain brick throughout. The view from Ann Street prepares for the impact to come [98]. An immensely high wall with nothing to relieve it, until the eye reaches high up four lancets in a row, some bold stone banding and a gloriously large rose window. The side to the w (liturgical n; interestingly, Wagner was never very concerned about liturgical orientation in his churches) is plain and relies unhesitatingly on lancets only. Indeed, this side is treated in two parts, a plain lower elevation because the church was masked by two-storey houses, now cleared, on this side. The effect can be seen very well from higher up as one reaches the station by train. The e wall's unfinished appearance outside suggests that Scott and Wagner had intended a chancel.

One enters, and there is this **nave**, 135 ft high, i.e. a good deal higher than Westminster Abbey and nearly as high as, say, Palma Cathedral, and 58 ft wide. The wagon roof, timber with tie-beams and kingposts, Italian rather than English, disappears in darkness. There are no aisles. Indeed, as at Albi Cathedral (of which one may be reminded a little), internal buttresses, forming very high and very narrow arched side chapels. Only above that level is a kind of triforium of three slit lancets per bay, and then at last follow the wide and tall clerestory windows. There is hardly any enrichment, only mouldings to the sides of the internal buttresses, various kinds of diaper patterning, both to the vaults of the side chapels and to the e wall of the church and, on the upper side walls, plain brick shafts with stone caps and corbels to demarcate the bays at high level and to carry the wall-posts and braces to the tie-beams of the roof. The e wall

30. St Bartholomew's Church, interior looking E, by Edmund Scott, 1872–4, with enrichments of 1895–1910 by Henry Wilson

is bare except for ornamental brickwork, in various kinds of chequer below the string course and diaper above. The blankness above the string course is relieved by the giant rood, with Christ outlined on the Cross, partly painted and partly incised on encaustic tiles. This is one of the few original **furnishings**, designed either by *S. Bell* or *Daniel Bell*, who was also responsible for the **altar.** The **Stations of the Cross** are of 1881, carved wood from Bruges. The confessionals, 1880, have onion domes.

Within thirty years, however, the whole church had received a decoration not in the initial spirit of Scott, but of so high a quality as to stand up to it. It was gradually installed between 1895 and 1910 and was designed by *Henry Wilson*, Sedding's most brilliant pupil, who also drew up plans to extend the church in 1906. What there is of metalwork is purest Arts and Crafts of the very top quality; what there is of variegated marbles is Byzantine, in the Westminster Cathedral spirit and distinguished by surfaces and forms as plain and direct as Scott's. Thus the **baldacchino**, the first major introduction by Wilson (1899–1900), has square pillars with capitals and arches to a groin-vaulted ceiling under a square top. It is faced in marble and alabaster, green and then black to the bases of the columns, pink to the columns themselves, white alabaster capitals with interlaced vine patterns and green to the upper sections, again with a pink and white border. The ceiling is in gold mosaic and mother-of-pearl with a dove in the centre. Predating this are Wilson's six large brass **candlesticks** on the earlier altar. **Tabernacle** door of beaten silver. **Mosaics** by *F. Hamilton Jackson*, 1911, jarring with the abstraction and simplicity of the baldacchino. Christ in Glory flanked by four angels carrying symbols of the Evangelists. **Crucifix** by *McCulloch* of Kennington, 1912. Sanctuary **lamps** by *Barkentin & Krall*, 1915. In front of the baldacchino two enormous **candlesticks** delimiting the sanctuary, plain round pillars of grey and white marble, but on them candle-holders of convoluted metal forms, apparently a combination of flaming urn and pineapple. The **altar rails**, of brass with enamel inserts, are seemingly a later addition of 1905. The sanctuary stands up five grey marble steps from the nave with a marble **pavement**. Flanking the baldacchino more **mosaics** by *Hamilton Jackson*.

In the same Byzantive taste is Wilson's **pulpit**. It dates from 1905, six red African marble columns with white marble caps and bases on a Tournai marble base, carrying green Irish marble panels canted out from the sides and again in the centre to the central pulpit. Pink alabaster background to both ground and first floor; the staircase rises in a spiral behind. The final marble introduction by Wilson was the **baptistery**, dating from 1908, towards the w end of the church's e side (liturgical s). Recess lined in pale green marble, framed in darker green and black. Central **statue** of St John the Baptist by *Giles Gilbert Scott*, made by *W.D. Gough* in 1925. Giant green marble **font** with beaten copper mounts and huge timber cover, standing on three Tournai marble steps.

In all this astonishing richness, perhaps the most extraordinary is the **Lady Altar** (e side, third bay from the n), which, although small in comparison with Wilson's other work here, is sumptuous in the extreme. Repoussé **altar frontal** of silver plate on copper, showing the Adoration of the Magi within a central wreath of vine leaves. Assyrian symbols of the planets on either side. Single silver **gradine** with symbols of the Evangelists carrying two silver candlesticks. **Crucifix** originally designed by Wilson for the high altar, again repoussé silver with broad arms. The **ceilure** of timber, painted silver and green, slightly Eastern in design. Finally **stained glass**, 1910, largely by *W.E. Tower*. Only four windows of the sixteen proposed for the nave were ever installed. One window has glass by *J.C.N Bewsey*, Kempe's pupil, who was also responsible for the glass in the four windows over the gallery.

All Saints, Hove

Eaton Road

Brighton has several great Victorian Gothic churches; Hove has only one but in some ways it is the most splendid of all. This superb building, begun in 1889, is *J. L. Pearson*'s largest parish church, and here in Goodhart Rendel's opinion 'Pearson gave of his best', while Summerson called it 'a work of extraordinary subtlety'.

Hove parish had an ancient church, St Andrew's (p. 195), held in plurality with Preston, where the vicarage was located. The two were split in 1879 and the Rev. Thomas Peacey, the new vicar of Hove, began to build new churches away from the seafront. He started with St Barnabas, Sackville Road (1882–3, also by Pearson), to serve the area developing to the w of the railway station, and contemporary with this the new vicarage for All Saints at the eastern end of a sizeable plot running E from The Drive (*see* below).

Peacey had already obtained designs from Pearson in 1880 for a new parish church for the rapidly expanding resort, but these were rejected in 1886 and various alternatives considered before the design as built was accepted in 1887. The foundation stone was laid in 1889, nave and aisles were consecrated in 1891, the E end was built between 1891 and 1901 but the narthex and stump of the sw tower were only completed in 1924. Although Pearson designed the church and many of its fittings, he died in 1897 and much of the execution was in the hands of his son, *Frank L. Pearson*. The cost was about £40,000. It became the parish church of Hove in 1892.

The church is built of ashlar, with the sw tower left alas as a stump. Side view with buttresses and the five-light s transept window against Eaton Road. The N transept has three two-light windows and a large rose window above, the chancel three windows of two lights. Fine E end flanked by two turrets, but apsed s chapel. Lean-to entrance narthex at the w end.

Pearson used here a Gothic both more English and later than one might expect, particularly in the nave with its piers of many clustered shafts and great transverse stone arches. The sanctuary is vaulted and thus more typical of Pearson, the effect one of great richness, flowing and supremely elegant, the scale reminiscent of cathedrals. Five-bay **nave** [31] with wide s aisle and narrower N aisle. Piers of clustered shafts carry vaulting shafts, and transverse stone arches carrying the posts and purlins of the timber roof. This is interesting as an example of historicism in action and is a type of roof first used by Pearson at Chute

Forest, Wiltshire, in 1870–5 and several times thereafter. It also has a local precedent in the small number of high status mid-c14 great halls around the High Weald of Kent and East Sussex, which have big timber roofs carried on stone arches, e.g. Ightham Mote. The transverse arches appear as a series of frames leading the eye to the chancel because of the lightness of the stone against the dark of the roof. Crossing with single-bay transepts, the chancel arch is narrower than the nave with internal buttressing, i.e. the shafting projecting forward of the wall line. The **sanctuary** is groin-vaulted, as are the two-bay s chapel with apse, the interior of the tower, the narthex and the w end of the N aisle.

Furnishings

Reredos, sedilia, bishop's throne and **pulpit**. Designed by *Pearson* (though erected posthumously, 1902–9). Sumptuously carved by *Nathaniel Hitch* who was responsible for woodwork in Pearson's Truro Cathedral. **Pulpit**, stone, with panels showing the spreading of the Gospels and niched figures of the four Evangelists. The **reredos** is cathedral-like in its sweep, bigger than Truro's. Stone, in two main tiers (i.e. figures under tall canopies) and broadly late Gothic, with life-sized figure of Christ crucified in the centre, being crowned by angels. At his foot, figures of Mary, Mother of Jesus, the Apostle John, Mary Magdalene, Mary, the sister of Martha and Lazarus, the Centurion and Nicodemus. To left and right, one on top of the other, figures of Isaac, Moses and David, and Isaiah, Jeremiah and Daniel, respectively. The side wings have figures under canopies, St George, St Stephen and St Andrew to the left, St Patrick, St Alban and St David to the right. **Bishop's throne**, with carvings of early Sussex Bishops, and **sedilia** with carvings of more recent bishops, a dean and Queen Victoria. **Altar rails**, brass, 1901. **Choir stalls**, **canopies** and **screens**, designed by *F.L. Pearson* and installed in 1915, as a memorial to the Rev. Peacey (d. 1909). Flamboyant Gothic style, very lavish and featuring many biblical and post-biblical figures. **Screens** in finely carved timber to the Holy Trinity chapel (s chancel aisle) are a First World War memorial; wrought-iron **screen** of the 1940s to N chancel chapel. **Organ case**, N side of the chancel, again by *F.L. Pearson* and installed 1915. It closely resembles his father's organ cases at Westminster Abbey. (The organ, by *William Hill & Son*, was originally installed in 1894; rebuilt and considerably extended in 1905.) **Font cover**, very tall and spire-like, made by *Evelyn Ormerod*, 1928, whose carving is also to be found in the Holy Trinity Chapel (lectern and two folding chairs.) **Stained glass** by *Clayton & Bell*, 1891–1920, (some by *John Clement Bell*), one of their largest commissions and best seen as a whole. Clayton & Bell were especially favoured by Pearson for their close adherence to the forms of medieval stained glass design. The Jesse window at the w end of the s aisle is the last of these, *c.* 1926 by *Reginald Bell*, son of Clement. Four windows in the Holy Trinity Chapel and two windows in the narthex by *Martin Travers*, 1932, in memory of Canon Peacey and his wife Ellen by their children.

31. Interior view of All Saints, Hove, by J.L. Pearson, *c.* 1889–1901

The **vicarage**, E of the church, is of 1882–3 by *Pearson*, red brick with Bath stone dressings, a rambling Tudor-Gothic house with bays and oriels and mullioned and transomed windows. Large staircase window with Gothic tracery.

Brighton Pier

Madeira Drive

Built for £137,000 in 1891–1901 as the Palace Pier for the Brighton Marine Palace & Pier Company. They had bought the remains of the Chain Pier (*see* p. 18) on the removal of which the building of the new pier was conditional. The designer was *R. St George Moore*, engineer (also responsible for the earlier St Leonards Pier; dem. 1951), the builder *Arthur Mayoh* of Manchester. The main pier was complete by 1899,

32. **Brighton Pier**

the seaward end with its pavilion theatre in 1901. Building was protracted because of disputes with the owners of the West Pier (*see* Topic Box, p. 21), damage caused by storms during its construction and the folding of the company itself. The pier quickly accrued further buildings, including a Winter Garden in 1910–11 by *Clayton & Black*, but was altered in 1930 and restored *c*. 1945. Damage to the pierhead in 1973 was followed by repairs, but these did not restore its former richness and the pavilion was dismantled in 1986.

The pier is 1,760 ft long with a wider than normal deck. Originally the main promenade down to the pavilion was flanked by a series of kiosks, smoking and grill rooms. Balustrading remains as does the central windscreen, with pairs of cast-iron columns, added in the early C20, and the remains of original filigree arches, which carried decorative electric lights. Semicircular **entrance area** with central rectangular **entrance pavilion** and **clock tower** added postwar in place of the clock tower taken from the Aquarium (p. 127) in 1930. Flanking are the two original entrance kiosks. The wings were added in the early 1990s. The next **kiosks**, just in front of the Palace of Fun, are a surprising survival of two octagonal former toll booths from the earlier Chain Pier; they date from 1872 when that pier's original toll house was lost to the building of the Aquarium. The iron-framed Winter Garden of 1910–11 is now the **Palace of Fun**. Low rotunda with N and S projections, i.e. on axis with the pier, the N entrance façade with flanking towers distantly reminiscent of the Art Nouveau façade of the pavilion of the Wellington Pier, Great Yarmouth. Internally a ring of twelve doubled columns, vestigially Baroque in some of its internal detailing. Further S is the early C20 restaurant building, now altered. Squarish central pavilion with N and S wings. Beyond are a pair of original hipped-roofed **kiosks**, cast iron with BMP & P on their panels. In place of the original **pavilion** is a low-domed building, too low to act as a proper focal point for the pier. The seaward end (widened in the 1990s) is now largely taken up by the **fun-fair**; rides were first introduced in 1938 (the helter-skelter may date from then). The best that can be said for its popularity is that it provides a usefully remote location for such a typical seaside entertainment, discouraging others on the seafront.

The main **structure** of the pier survives intact, though in places replaced and enhanced with more secure members. Understanding of iron pier structures was well known by the 1890s and there is little that is particularly innovative in its straightforward arrangement of columns running in braced triple pairs down the length of the pier (except where the pier has been widened, i.e. around the Palace of Fun and the restaurant as well as around the pierhead). The columns, standing on screw piles, carry the braced longitudinal and cross-trusses which support the deck. Its structural clarity is only marred by the extension of the seaward end with columns on a different grid pattern, supporting the widened deck.

Brighton Railway Station

Queen's Road

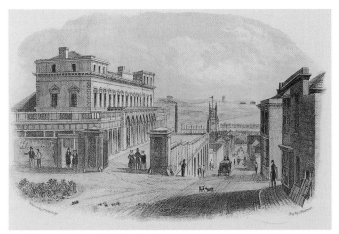

33. Mid-c19 engraving of Brighton Station

1841 by *David Mocatta*, extended 1882–3 by *H.E. Wallis* (and with alterations by *F.D. Bannister*). Refurbished in 2000.

Railway stations are always important for resorts and the opening of the line from London to Brighton had a more striking impact perhaps than most. It has been estimated that more visitors came to Brighton during the first weekend that the line was open than had visited in the past year. Similarly the population increase in the town in the decade prior to the opening of the line was 15 per cent; the following decade saw an increase of 41 per cent. The railway was one of the principal reasons for the change in the market for resorts, from exclusivity towards something more popular, and that was especially true for Brighton.

Although a railway between London and Brighton had first been proposed as early as 1823, the line as built, with branches to Shoreham and Newhaven, is the result of the London and Brighton Railway Act of 1837. The railway, with its London terminus at London Bridge Station, was engineered by *Sir John Rennie* and *John Rastrick*, and ran s to Selhurst, then Coulsdon and Redhill, Haywards Heath and Burgess Hill. The most notable feature of the line is the viaduct [100] over the Ouse near Balcombe designed by John Rastrick, the most impressive railway viaduct in southern England. The line opened in stages, with the full length down to Brighton opening on 21 September 1841. In 1858 it was extended at the London end to Victoria, which became the terminus of the London, Brighton & South Coast Railway. Famous for luxury Pullman cars, which were first run on the line in 1875, it never really had any expresses, only trains euphemistically called 'fast'. It was only in November 1908 that 'the most luxurious train in the world', the Brighton Belle, first ran down to Brighton. The train, which had its own platform with arch at Victoria, was discontinued in 1972, to considerable protest.

The original Brighton terminus was designed by *David Mocatta* and replaced a plain building for the branch line to Shoreham. The site was not an easy one and necessitated the creation of an enormous raised and levelled area running along the side of West Hill. It also had inadequate connection to the town: Queen's Road was laid out to give easier access to the station only in 1845, and a bridge was therefore needed over Trafalgar Street which dives down the hill to the E just in front of the station. Below the bridge one can see best how the station sits on its massive platform with great vaults beneath. Its E side is like a cliff, with two- and three-storey buildings at the foot and the timber-clad side of the train shed curving round above. The tall arch at the bottom of the building on Trafalgar Street leads to the former hackney carriage road, a quarter-mile of surviving late Victorian street which runs in semi-darkness, lit by occasional arches in the side of the station, up to the end of platform six. The vaults are now occupied by wine storage and the Brighton Toy Museum.

Mocatta's **station** is a two-storey stuccoed building in an Italianate style with pedimented first-floor windows and a prominent cornice to low-pitched roofs. The central nine-bay range is flanked by pavilions of three bays which rise to low pyramidally roofed attics. The ground floor is obscured by the decorative iron forecourt **canopy**, added during the major extensions of 1882, which projects out further still over the Trafalgar Street bridge. Mocatta's building has lost its ground floor colonnade-cum-arcade (though it survives at the rear), along with window and door-surround articulation.

The marvel, however, is the **train shed** added in 1882–3 by *H. E. Wallis*. It consists of three spans running roughly N–S in an easy curve. Two of the spans are very broad and extend wider and higher than the Mocatta block. The narrower E span is shorter and is itself narrowed towards its N end to take account of the short lengths of platform which run along outside the main shed. These have nicely detailed cantilevered roofs of the type more familiar from London suburban stations but here cleverly engineered with braced trusses and decorative use of fret valances. The main shed is 597 ft long of twenty-one bays of tall columns; with abbreviated bays at both ends. The columns have octagonal bases with fluted capitals which carry the iron braces longitudinally and laterally across the spans. Iron-braced purlins and remarkably slender trusses, all members of which have the expressed rivet heads (here of

34. Brighton Station, detail of train shed roof, 1882–3

some size) which are so typical of late Victorian engineering of this kind. The result is a great space, very light and airy, and entirely characteristic of the greater Victorian railway station. Unlike many such roofs, it is as impressive outside as in; because it is built against the side of West Hill, one gets a very good view from Terminus Road as it runs along beside the train shed and up above it, following its curve.

Various other alterations were made around 1882–3 to the designs of *F.D. Bannister*. Ancillary buildings to either side of the concourse, including two-storey **offices** to the w and single-storey offices to the e in a utilitarian style of yellow and red brick. A free-standing blank-panelled two-storey block was built on the e side of the concourse in 1987, at the same time as the indicator board was added in an over-engineered High-Tech style.

Jubilee Library

Jubilee Street

2003–5 by *Bennetts Associates* with *Lomax Cassidy & Edwards* of Brighton; a rare example of first-class design emanating from the controversial Private Finance Initiative (PFI).

Plans for a central library on the present site, a long-derelict quarter of the once artisan district between Church Street and North Road, were first laid in 1991. From the outset the library was considered integral to the wider regeneration of this area and under the masterplan agreed in 2000 rows of commercial and residential buildings have been created along the w side of Jubilee Street, facing a major public square in which the library forms the centrepiece.

The building appears as a crisp, slightly austere, translucent glass box (containing the library) with an over-sailing brise-soleil, sandwiched between lower elements (for offices, conference rooms etc.) that are given solidity by facings of dark blue glazed tiles, a reference to the traditional fashion in Brighton for glazed mathematical tiles. Projecting forward to the E, and similarly treated, is a low wing containing a café. Tiles are continued along the Jubilee Street elevation, which is highly glazed at ground floor but otherwise contrastingly solid, with an irregular pattern of rectilinear window openings. The other elevations are largely concealed by buildings. Above the entrance, recessed to the left of the main façade, is a large window, filled with an art installation by *Georgia Russell*, a filigree of suspended cut-paper letters. The roof was to have been dramatized by a trio of revolving funnels – apparently a casualty of the design and build contract in which they were superseded by insignificant vents.

In the square, two **benches** by *Caroline Barton*, their primeval forms sharply contrasting with the slickness of the building. Laminated sections of timber and glass, the latter illuminated after dark.

35. Jubilee Library, entrance front, by Bennetts Associates with Lomax Cassidy & Edwards, 2003–5

36. Jubilee Library, view of the interior looking across the front, by Bennetts Associates with Lomax Cassidy & Edwards, 2003–5

The low-key entrance leads into a foyer and shop before emerging into the lofty double-height forum at the heart of the **interior**. Walls are lined with beech boarding, visually warm and attractive. The whole space is illuminated through the louvred screen behind the sheer glass façade. Top lighting penetrates to the ground floor by setting back from the outer walls the two-storey internal structure whose roof and floor plates are carried at each level on eight soaring white concrete columns branching out at the top – an allusion to the C19 tradition of tall, well-lit, columned libraries such as Labrouste's Bibliothèque Nationale and Bibliothèque Sainte Geneviève in Paris. At the upper level steel and glass bridges connect to plain openings in the outer walls, providing controlled vistas through to rooms in the outer ranges including the Children's Library with its colourful 'Wall of a Thousand Stories' by *Kate Malone*. Further visual permeability is achieved vertically by square openings in the floors below the roof vents. This design has environmental purpose: air is drawn down through the long side ranges, through voids in the concrete floor plates, and into the library where it exhausts through the roof vents. Heating and cooling are supplemented with mechanical systems only when the temperature rises or falls beyond set limits. After the thrill of the architecture, several details seem rather meagre – a single cantilevered staircase links the two main floors and leads into corridors that feel claustrophobic after the openness of the library. The shelving in particular falls well below the quality of design established for the building and, such is the scale of the main spaces, there seem remarkably few books.

Brighton and Hove

Brighton Old Town

This walk covers the area of medieval Brighthelmstone, which is defined by East, West and North streets, with Middle Street running N–S. From the late C16 this grid was infilled by a complex network of narrow alleys (in Sussex called twittens), which are partly preserved, most memorably in the area known as The Lanes [44]. Very few of its buildings, however, are older than the mid C18 when the town began its transformation into a resort. The old town continued to maintain a separate character as a working centre, with its market, town hall and

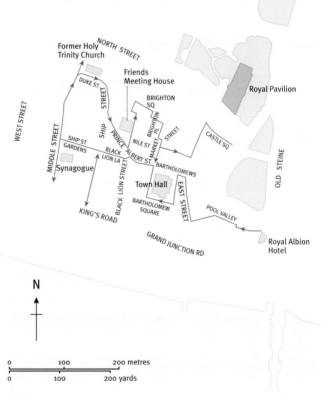

37. Walk 1

38. Late C19 photograph of the N front of the Royal Albion Hotel

commercial life and in the C20 The Lanes became a tourist attraction. Today, although parts are scruffy and neglected, the Old Town is still a vibrant mix of domestic and commercial activity.

A walk can start in **Old Steine** at the **Royal Albion Hotel** of 1826 by *Amon Henry Wilds* (built on the site of the house erected in 1752–3 for Dr Richard Russell of Lewes, an early advocate of sea bathing, *see* p. 70). At this date the important aspect was still towards the Steine rather than the sea. The original stuccoed frontage is four storeys with five giant Composite columns in the middle and three plus three giant pilasters. The pilasters are taken round to the E side as well. In the attic storey shells set in blank arches above the windows, one of the hallmarks of Wilds. To its right, continuing the theme of giant orders, is an extension – perhaps *c*. 1847 when the hotel was granted the epithet Royal: three bays treated as a distyle *in antis* with fluted Ionic columns. Top-heavy C20 additions to the upper parts and, at the rear, ungainly Edwardian embellishments, by *Clayton & Black*, for a lounge overlooking the sea. The hotel has incorporated its neighbour, formerly the Lion Mansion Hotel built in 1856, also with fluted Composite pilasters and stacks of canted bays. Set forward to the road at this point is the **Royal York Hotel** (on the site of the old manor house of Brighthelmstone), converted in 1819 from two houses, the name was adopted with the permission of the Duke of York, a frequent visitor to the town. Enlargements of 1827 and later leave a somewhat incoherent façade but the centre (dated 1819) has three-storey bows, highly glazed and divided by Roman fasces prettily reeded, a motif used in French Empire design and seen elsewhere in Brighton's early C19 domestic buildings. C20 cast-iron porte cochère. Nos. 44–6 to the right, despite being drastically rebuilt as an office block in the 1990s, is a striking late C18 group with bold canted bays and nice doorcases. For the rest of the Steine, *see* Walk 2.

Sea Bathing and Bath Houses

39. Brill's Baths, *c.* 1869

Sea bathing as a pastime, first for the wealthy, has its origins in the popularity of spa towns where mineral waters were drunk and bathed in for their health-giving properties. Popular first in Continental Europe, by the late C17 spas were already well established in England (Bath, Epsom and Tunbridge Wells) and the chalybeate spring at St Ann's Well, Hove, was an attraction to visitors long before Brighton became a resort. The first reference to bathing in the sea at Brighton dates from 1641 when the burial is recorded of Mary Askall who came for 'the cure'. Dr Richard Russell's *A Dissertation on the Use of Sea Water in Diseases of the Glands* (1750) promoting the health-giving properties of bathing and drinking seawater, was crucial to the future of Brighton as a resort. Russell, a doctor in Lewes, first sent patients to drink the water at St Ann's Well but in 1752–3 built his house by the sea on the Steine for their benefit. Horse-drawn bathing machines (for discreet changing) quickly became a familiar site on the shore, as were the 'dippers' – men and women who submerged bathers in the sea. The career of the best-known dipper, Martha Gunn, spanned well over half a century.

Several purpose-built bathing establishments followed. The first seawater baths were opened in 1769 by Dr Awsiter at Pool Valley, providing six cold baths, a hot bath, a showering bath and a sweating bath. Awsiter also advocated the drinking of seawater mixed with milk and cream of tartar. In 1787 Sake (Sheikh) Deen Mahomed opened Turkish baths on the seafront (the Queen's Hotel now stands on the site), the first in the country, with the novelty of a 'shampooing' (massaging) service. George IV appointed Mahomed his 'Shampooing Surgeon'. Nearby in East Street were Lamprell's (later Brill's) baths, opened in 1823, which contained the first communal swimming pool in the town. Bruce's 1834 Brighton guide lists five baths in the town but their popularity waned from the mid C19 – William's Royal Hot and Cold Baths, on Old Steine, were demolished in 1856 but Brill's was not demolished until 1929 (to make way for the Savoy Cinema).

A passage between the two hotels leads to **Pool Valley**, today an unprepossessing backwater, serving since 1929 as Brighton's coach station. Originally an inlet or small pool, it was paved over following the culverting of the Wellesbourne stream in 1792–3. Several bathing establishments were clustered here, including Brighton's first baths, in 1769 (*see* Topic Box). Older buildings survive only on the NW corner of Pool Valley, notably Nos. 9–10 built in 1794, although the big hipped roof perhaps suggests earlier origins, with a façade of black mathematical tiles – the Brighton speciality. For many years it was Cowley's Bun Shop and to Goodhart-Rendel it was 'as charming a relic of the Brighton that was called Brighthelmstone as anyone could wish to see'. The view to the sea was obscured after the embanked Grand Junction Road was created in 1829. Before then, the main access between the Steine and western town was along the narrow paved passage which cuts through to East Street and was 'occupied by gay shops of fancy dealers of every description' in 1833 (Parry's Guide). **King's Road** led w onto the cliff-top road before it was bypassed by Grand Junction Road. No. 6 (s side) is of *c.* 1825 by *A.H. Wilds*, with giant fluted pilasters and Wilds's usual motif of ammonite shell capitals.

By the early C19 (Great) **East Street**, running N–S, was a densely populated commercial street, servicing the large houses on the Steine and in Castle Square. Today little tells outwardly of a pre-C19 date. Nos. 5–6, Scoop & Crumb, has a painted cobbled front of a kind seen on several early buildings within the Old Town and visible tiled roof, suggesting an C18 date. Big Victorian first-floor shop window. No. 10 (Long Tall Sally) has a pair of early C19 bows, with tall first-floor windows and bold entablature. From here the scale of the buildings steps up to four storeys, several with bows above the shopfronts, often replaced in the mid C19 by canted bays. A few later C19 façades dominate on the E side, e.g. No. 67 (Reiss), dated 1883, red brick Queen Anne, typical for its date, and No. 63 (Cargo Home Shop), also brick, but overpainted and with a cheerful timber loggia beneath the gable, dated 1888. At the point where East Street becomes pedestrianized there are views through to the onion domes of the Pavilion (for the N end of East Street *see* below).

Nos. 20–1 East Street (Jones the Bootmaker) has an early C19 stucco front with an upper floor divided by Doric pilasters. It turns the corner into **Bartholomews**, a street which takes its name from the medieval priory of St Bartholomew. Of this nothing remains and the street is now entirely dominated by the Town Hall, but before considering it we can turn left into **Little East Street** which runs along the Town Hall's E flank. Here a few early relics, including **The Cottage**, of tarred cobbles with brick quoins and gambrel roof; a small group beyond, including No. 6 (Strand Restaurant) with two original bowed Regency shopfronts; and closing the street, No. 8, a rather grim cement-rendered front but evidently a once fashionable Early Georgian town house. Little East Street was opened up by the demolition of buildings along its w side for an extension to the Town Hall, a dire set of offices (**Priory House**) with curtain-walled flanks of 1984–7 by *Michael Lyell & Associates*. It spans steps leading into the contemporary **Bartholomew Square**, a feeble attempt to create a civic space for the town centre, with the Town Hall eating into its NE corner. The creation of the square destroyed the s end of Market Street, which previously continued down to the seafront. Enclosing the square's s side, and thus obscuring the long views to the sea that are so characteristic of the old town grid, is the rear of the Thistle Hotel (*see* p. 96). On the w side, further council offices on the site of the pre-C19 town hall. The architecture is dull and the landscaping sterile, only partly countered by a Japanese-style pavilion (**Moshi Moshi** restaurant) in the centre, 2001 by *Alex de Rijke* of *drmm*. This crisp 'lightbox' is raised over a deck with prefabricated lightweight walls of translucent fibreglass panels which, on the E side, can slide across to open up the interior.

So to the **Town Hall** itself, won in competition in 1827 by *Thomas Cooper*, a Brighton town commissioner, built in 1830–2, and enlarged and altered in 1898–9 by *Francis May*, Borough Surveyor. It has two fronts to the N and w, both with a portico in two orders, Greek Doric below, Ionic above. A s wing to make the building cruciform was never built. The main upper windows have pilaster aedicules. Much of the interior is taken up by the remarkably intricate and airy staircase hall, of 1898–9, with Ionic and Composite columns creating aisled colonnades at each floor, emulating the superimposed orders of Cooper's exterior. The stair rises in two stages straight through and then turns left and right to the top-lit galleried landing. Cast-iron balustrades to the stair and landing continuing around an open well beyond the staircase.

Returning to Bartholomews, we continue w into the elegant curve of **Prince Albert Street**, cut through the Old Town in 1842. The houses on the left (Nos. 2–8) are of this date (though substantially rebuilt *c.* 1990) and still in Regency style, with a regular rhythm of two-storey bows with tripartite windows, stopping short of the continuous cornice that oversails them. The effect is greatly enhanced by the regularity and discipline of the shopfronts. At the bend of the street where it meets **Black Lion Street** is the **Cricketers Arms**, with two full-height bows, probably of 1824 when it acquired its present name. The building itself may date from the late C17, and there are references to alterations in 1790, but the earliest internal feature is an attractive early C19 curved stair in a compartment behind the bar. The rest is of 1886, a lavish display of Victoriana, many fittings original but exaggerated to satisfying effect [41]. The lower block to the right incorporated the town pound.

Its neighbour to the left, the **Black Lion**, is a deceptive vernacular pastiche faced in cobbles and with a slate-hung, tall gabled centre. It is largely a facsimile rebuilding of part of the Black Lion Brewery, whose site was redeveloped with banal and overbearing offices to the s by *Wells-Thorpe & Suppel*, in 1974. The façade opposite, dated 1889, with

40. Brighton Town Hall, staircase of 1898–9 by Francis May, Borough Surveyor

41. Cricketers Arms, Black Lion Street, interior of 1886

a moulded brick frieze and a lion beneath the pedimented gable, may have been built as stabling for the Black Lion Inn.

Squeezed between the pubs is **Black Lion Lane**, one of the claustrophobically narrow medieval twittens for which the Old Town is famous. Midway along, Nos. 1–3 is timber-framed with a jettied upper floor and the ground floor faced in flush timber boards, but it has otherwise been much renewed. From Black Lion Lane we emerge into **Ship Street**, by the mid C18 colonized by the professions and higher-quality lodgings, a status reflected in its buildings. On the w side opposite, No. 15, despite the later shopfront, is evidently an early C19 double-fronted town house with a Doric doorcase and full-height bows with tripartite windows. To its right, Nos. 16–17 are probably later C18, set back, with ramped side walls to the front area enclosed by railings and with steps up to the front doors, both with good doorcases. An Edwardian bay window addition to No. 17. Opposite, further N, a doorcase with broken pediment indicates that No. 59 began life as a three-bay symmetrical town house. Returning down the E side: Nos. 60–1 do not have a parapet and may be a late C18 refronting of an older house (the remodelled rear has a re-set datestone of 1713) when the s end (No. 61) was given stucco quoins, pedimented doorcase and first-floor bowed oriel window. No. 63 has a narrow frontage but still with a good Doric doorcase, and a second doorcase adjoining the altogether grander No. 64. This has first- and second-floor bands, suggesting that it is essentially early C18.

After a C20 intrusion, No. 68 is dated 1738, again with brick bands; polychrome effect of red and grey bricks. Inside, an altered staircase and two panelled rooms on the ground and first floors at the southern end of the building all accord with its date. No. 69 is lower and has a façade of dressed flint with brick quoins: its date (1685) may be accurate but the staircase is of Late Georgian character. Most of the remainder of the street on this side has been absorbed into The Old Ship Hotel (*see* p. 97). Facing, at the bottom of the street, is the eyecatching **Hotel du Vin** (on the site of the C17 New Ship Inn), built for Henekeys in 1934 in their customary Tudor style, and done with panache by their usual architect, *Ernest F. Barrow*. Wonderfully phoney, with carved gables and oriels and even a portcullis, a piece of Olde England dropped into Brighton. The main internal space is treated as an aisled barn. Returning up the street, No. 7 is another Late Georgian town house, believed to date from *c.* 1787. Pretty fluted Doric doorcase and bows, all with the motif of a dentil frieze. Generous open-well stick-baluster staircase towards the back of the house lit by an arched landing window. Later ballroom to the rear with octagonal lantern. **Smugglers** has a busy late C19 pub front, arranged as a tripartite composition with a broad canted bay and extensive glazing to the first floor.

On the left **Ship Street Gardens** continues the E–W twitten, paved with red bricks in the manner traditional to Sussex. On the left the twitten opens to the gardens of a mid-C19 stucco terrace at right angles (Nos. 1–3). Nos. 13–16 opposite have Victorian shopfronts (though the shops themselves are unfortunately not used as such), which seem over-scaled in this intimate space.

The twitten debouches into **Middle Street**, the principal street at the heart of the old town grid and with buildings of commensurate significance. No. 20, ahead, was refronted in the early C19, asymmetrical with a broad bow on the left. A commemorative plaque, recording that William Friese-Greene carried out early cinematographic experiments in this house, is of a standard design by *Eric Gill* commissioned by Brighton Corporation in the 1920s. **Avalon**, to the right, a recent infill development, has its main frontage in West Street (*see* p. 98), whilst No. 19, to the left, is set back, its diminutive proportions indicative of earlier origins than the C19 exterior.

Turning around, No. 60, on the corner of Ship Street Gardens, is a double-fronted C18 house with a chequerwork façade of flint, knapped flint and red brick dressings. Towards the sea is a much larger Victorian building squeezed into the dense urban fabric: the **Brighton Synagogue** of 1874–5 by *Thomas Lainson*. Emanuel Hyam Cohen is credited as founding the Jewish community in Brighton in 1782. The first synagogue was in Jew Street (near Bond Street), moving first to West Street and then to Devonshire Place (*see* p. 139). By the 1870s a much larger synagogue was needed and the site in Middle Street was acquired. Iron-framed, clad in brown brick to the sides, the street façade Italian Romanesque of yellow brick with diverse stone and blue and red tile dressings. Two tiers of paired round-arched windows with sandstone columns and foliage capitals, set in four-square projecting bays, with narrower recessed bays, all with a heavy corbelled cornice and a broad gable above with a central wheel window and paired pilasters at the angles. The basilican-plan galleried **interior** [42] is a delight: round-arched arcade on two tiers of columns, the galleries (for women) with

42. Middle Street Synagogue, interior, by Thomas Lainson, 1874–5

filigree fronts, repeated in front of the seating area below (for men). Continuous arcaded clerestory, interrupted only by the transverse arches supporting the pitched roof. Curved roofs to the aisles. Canted apse framed by two tiers of columns with Byzantine-style columns and with a completely glazed half-dome. The whole interior is sumptuously decorated with mosaic, marble, brass, stencilling, gilding and stained glass. The iron columns are covered in scagliola and have capitals of flora from the Holy Land, of hammered iron and copper. Much was paid for by the Sassoon family, the synagogue's chief patrons. The Ark is set in the apse behind elaborate wrought-iron gates of 1905. The central area is taken up by the **almemmar** or bima with a wooden base and elaborate cast iron and brasswork (added in 1892). Non-figurative **stained glass** throughout, added between 1887 and 1912, some of it signed by *Campbell Smith & Co*. Brass **electroliers** dating from 1892.

Next, No. 69 has a reset Doric doorcase, Nos. 74–6 full-height bows, and **The Globe** pub, mid C19 with twisted colonnettes to the bays. No. 1, opposite, 2007 by *Turner Associates*, has a faceted glazed corner, the floors at upper levels brought forward to form enclosed balconies looking towards the sea.

Middle Street's other major building is at the street's N end: the former **Hippodrome**. It was opened in 1897 as an ice rink – of this date the long and low unassuming stucco exterior with towered ends. The glazed awnings were renewed c. 1990. Converted and enlarged in 1901 as a circus and theatre (later variety theatre) to designs by *Frank Matcham*, whose hallmark decorative richness is found inside. Narrow crush bar and foyer leading into the horseshoe-plan auditorium. The seats were arranged around a circular ring set in front of the stage with proscenium arch with intertwined dolphins flanked by female figures. Ornate plasterwork, making liberal use of Rococo forms. A touch of the Royal Pavilion in the squat onion domes above the stage boxes. All this can still be appreciated, though a level floor was put through c. 1967. Former bars and a conservatory to the N, with more exotic Middle Eastern decoration.

Further N on the right is the entrance to **Duke's Lane**, a shopping street created in 1979 by *Stone, Toms & Partners*, in a tactful, if self-consciously 'old Brighton' style. Beyond, Nos. 44–5 Middle Street look c. 1800 and of the modest scale of Brighton's houses before the Regency expansion. The last cottage has been taken in to **The Victory** pub, early C19 with a gambrel roof, but distinguished by its c. 1910 remodelling for Tamplin's Brighton Brewery. Glazed tiles in bands of pale and dark green and glazing with elliptical-arched lights and the upper parts multi-paned. The interior retains the bar back and other features of the period.

Duke Street, crossing the N end of Middle Street, was widened on its N side in 1867; the w end is now pedestrianized. The only earlier survivor is the remarkable No. 37a, which stands well back from the street at right angles. Built c. 1780, it has a façade of wooden blocks imitating stone. Further w, on the s side, Nos. 12–13 have the early C19 bows and mathematical tiles by now familiar to us in the Old Town.

At the E end of Duke Street on the junction with Ship Street the former **Holy Trinity** (Fabrica art gallery). Built in 1817 as a chapel for his own sect by Thomas Kemp, developer of Kemp Town (*see* Topic Box, p. 145); his architect was *A.H. Wilds*. In 1826 it became an Anglican chapel of ease and was altered by *Charles Barry*. The widening of Duke Street in 1867 exposed the s side, which was remodelled as a blind

43. No. 37a Duke Street, façade of wooden blocks, c. 1780

frontage, stuccoed and Italianate with round-headed arcading. The surprise is the front to Ship Street, all of a radical Gothic remodelling by *Somers Clarke & Micklethwaite* in 1885–7. Thin tower growing out of the façade, with two projecting buttresses and an open stone lantern. Chequerwork parapets. Inside, the preaching house remains obvious in the galleries on columns, but the timber roof and clerestory are by *Somers Clarke*, of 1882. Chancel added 1869 by *G. Lynn & Son*; it has a triplet of round-headed lancets with **stained glass** by *James Powell & Sons* to designs by *Henry Holiday*. Marble **font**. 1887, a neat design, the bowl on a cruciform shaft rising from a square base.

Opposite the chapel on **Ship Street**, the former **Post Office**, with a crisp Portland stone façade of *c.* 1925 by *D.N. Dyke* of *H.M. Office of Works*, to a building of 1892 (partly visible in the brick and terracotta gable-end). To its s, a stucco frontage, with first-floor pedimented windows, follows the curve of the street; it dates from 1849. The next stretch forms an engaging streetscape with full-height bows on the inner, right curve and a stepped arrangement on the outer curve. Here No. 53 has a first-floor bow with a semi-domical roof and Nos. 54–5 turn the corner into Union Street. O'Neill's, on the other side of the street, built in 1897 as **The Seven Stars** by *Clayton Botham*, has a florid façade with columns, pilasters and recessed balconies, looking more like a theatre than a pub. To its left the other entrance to Duke's Lane (*see* above). Back to the E side and No. 57 is vernacular in character, with a gambrel roof and an unusual façade treatment of alternating cobbles and knapped flints, all with a weathering coat of pitch. No. 58 (Ask), has a rather plain early C19 double-fronted façade. Then, well set back on the left behind a garden, and until the 1840s concealed by buildings on Ship Street, is the **Friends Meeting House**, erected by the Quaker community in 1805. It was altered in 1850 and in 1876–7 when the N wing was built by *Clayton & Black*. The centre of three bays with pediment, but the details unmistakably Victorian. No. 22, opposite, is a cobble-fronted three-bay house with shops on the ground floor but retaining its central entrance.

In **Prince Albert Street**, on a slither of land on the left, a row of single-storey lock-up shops with original fronts and terracotta balustrade, *c.* 1907 by *Thomas Garrett*. Nos. 10–13 opposite date from the 1840s but the ground floor of the curved front of No. 10 is by *Clayton & Black* (whose offices were here from 1904) falsely implying an C18 date. Genuinely C18 is the grand mid-Georgian town house opposite (No. 15), set back in its own grounds and facing down Black Lion Street towards the sea. It belonged in the C19 to the Bass family, members of the Meeting House congregation. Five bays and three storeys over a basement. Keystones to all windows, stone quoins and cornice. Stuccoed Doric porch. Inside, the detailing of the entrance hall and stair suggests an early C19 date; elliptical arches and the staircase set in a semicircular projection.

Meeting House Lane is the start of the dense jumble of pedestrian streets comprising **The Lanes** with its rows of tiny shops. It runs through to North Street with a dog-leg in the middle, but also has a spur running E. The first stretch has older properties on the right and a late C19 shopfront of two tiers, on the corner, no doubt originally the lower half opening onto display slabs. The buildings in The Lanes are generally modest and have layer upon layer of alterations such that real antiquity could only be ascertained through archaeological study. On the right Nos. 29–30 (weatherboarded and with a gambrel roof) and Nos. 27–8, with overscaled late C20 shopfronts but the upper parts rendered and lined as ashlar, are probably C18 or earlier. Then an abrupt left turn and the lane narrows right down, passing Nos. 1–3: probably of C18 origin, very low, the upper windows have 12 by 12-pane horizontal sliding sashes, indicative of the need to maximize light for craft workshops. Ahead, the **Bath Arms** was rebuilt in 1864 and looks somewhat gargantuan in this Lilliputian grid. Its N side faces the former **Presbyterian Meeting House** (also known as Union Chapel, now The Font pub), established in 1689, from which Meeting House Lane took its name. The chapel was enlarged in 1810. Consistent with this date is the cobble front to Meeting House Lane, with two tiers of windows. In 1825 the chapel itself was rebuilt by *Wilds & Busby*, though the design is credited to Wilds. Façade to **Union Street**, very Grecian, especially the door and window surrounds whose tapering form accentuates the scale, but with the middle three bays emphasized by Doric pilasters carrying a pediment. It is difficult to appreciate such a grand composition in the confined surroundings. The interior has a deep semicircular balcony on two tiers of cast-iron columns (leaf capitals below, Corinthian above), leaving only a small full-height area with half-domed ribbed ceiling. The pulpit was in an arched recessed balcony set at an intermediate level on the rear wall, later replaced by an arcade of blind arches and three large high-level windows.

44. View of The Lanes

Back in **Meeting House Lane**, No. 22 (Doyle's), E side, has early C19 detailing but is much restored. It occupies a corner plot opposite the former chapel and has a charming bow and decorative railings enclosing a roof terrace visible from the Lane to the side, created in the 1960s as an approach to **Brighton Square**. This is of 1966 by *Fitzroy Robinson & Partners*, sensitive infill, shops and flats of load-bearing brick placed over a reinforced concrete basement car park, the entrance to which is discreetly tucked away. Architecturally of its time, with projecting upper bays clad in tile-hanging and shiplap boarding, successfully keeping to the scale and variety of The Lanes. It was well received when built, earning a Civic Trust award, and is still a model for urban renewal. In the centre of the square a fountain and Dolphin **sculpture** by *James Osborne*.

From the square's SE corner a lane leads into **Brighton Place**, the first of a sequence of informal squares between The Lanes and East Street. On the N side the rear parts of the former **Hannington's** department store, its skyline with a hexagonal turret and a row of round-arched windows, part of mid-C20 alteration by *J.L. Denman*. The **Druid's Head** has a brick and flint Victorian façade, not at all urban looking. Before leaving The Lanes, a brief sally once more into **Meeting House Lane**, where No. 43, on the left, is one of the oldest buildings in the area, timber-framed with a weather-boarded jettied upper floor. No. 32, opposite, also has a jetty, side on to the lane. (These early buildings have been much altered and would repay detailed study. Back to Brighton Place, which flows into an irregular W–E square at the junction with Market Street. On the left corner is a quirky High Victorian Gothic intrusion (*c.* 1867) on the site of the House of Correction built in 1835. On the right **The Pump House** (its name first recorded in 1776), has an upper storey faced in glazed mathematical tiles, the much restored bowed shopfronts and the tripartite first-floor windows give an unusually strong horizontal emphasis. Its overscaled but characterful neighbour to the s is a Postmodern design by *Robin Clayton Partnership*, 1987–9, for shops and offices, filling a whole block from Market Street to Black Lion Street. Massive corner drum, the lower two storeys with banded channelled rustication; the upper two with smooth render. Big tripartite windows, Diocletian at the top, and a rounded front to the upper parts, all somewhat menacing when viewed against the intimate scale of The Lanes, but well handled and, with interest along **Nile Street** in the projecting semicircular oriels and shopfronts. This lane was renamed after Nelson's victory at the Battle of the Nile in 1798.

Back now to the E part of the 'square', where in the lower corner is a late C18 double-fronted house (No. 11) with mathematical tiles and a pedimented Tuscan doorcase and elliptical-arched entrance. No. 12, with gambrel roof, faces due s, almost against the rear of the **Sussex Tavern**, down the side of which runs another twitten, emerging into another small informal 'square' at the N end of **East Street**, where the entire front of the pub is bowed. Here all is irregular and attractive.

To the left and facing N, first No. 28, with a front which appears mid C19, with a large balconied window above the shopfront. The later C19 top floor above the cornice creates an ungainly appearance. To the right, No. 29 is more elegant, with a three-storey bow, with original glazing and louvred storm shutters at the top. Nos. 30 and 31 (**English's Restaurant**) are stepped and set back, with gambrel roof. Probably late C18, with a good later C19 shopfront. The shaped gables of the building facing E add some fun to this varied and wholly unplanned corner. To the right of the Sussex Tavern No. 35 has a C19 brick façade to an C18 building, see the upper wall barely masking the pitched roof and the cobbled side elevation. Nice C19 shopfront. No. 36 (Al Forno) is late C18, painted cobbles with a later canted bay window. This was the home of Martha Gunn, the famous bathing 'dipper'.

East Street continues N, taking on a more C19 commercial appearance. On the left, Nos. 39–42 (Monsoon) is High Victorian Gothic of 1866 by *Henry Jarvis*, with colonnettes with foliate capitals to the windows and probably polychromatic brickwork under the later paint. Then another entrance to **Market Street** which here has a bridge (1989) from when these buildings were all part of Hannington's department store. The **Market Tavern**, just beyond, has two early C19 first-floor bow windows but is otherwise much altered.

East Street finishes at **Castle Square**, a square in name only and now no more than the eastward continuation of North Street (*see* p. 163). Until 1805 East Street continued N past the Royal Pavilion to form the main road out of town, and it was here that the coaches from London arrived. In that year the Prince of Wales requested its closure and paid for the construction of New Road further w. Widenings and realignments have destroyed the visual and functional significance of this once important space. Here were several hotels, principal among them the Castle Inn (adapted from a residence in the 1740s, acquired by the King in 1821 and dem. *c.* 1823*), which stood at the corner with the Steine (*see* Walk 2). On the s side, a few minor Late Georgian survivals: Nos. 1–7, developed piecemeal and far from uniformly. For No. 1 *see* p. 85. Nos. 2–3 are conventional early C19, whilst the five storeys of No. 4 soar to almost twice the height. No. 5 is stout and short, with giant pilasters and a pediment, whilst No. 6 is skinny and tall, just one bay but with giant elongated pilasters with laurel-wreath capitals and a vertiginous mansard. The tall, bow-fronted **Royal Pavilion Tavern** was built as the Royal Pavilion Hotel, established *c.* 1816 and altered in 1820 by *A.H. Wilds*. Intertwined dolphins as finials to the first-floor balcony. Finally, on the corner of East Street, **Castle Square House**, 1985, by *Fitzroy Robinson Miller Bourne*, a lame attempt to update the Brighton style. For North Street and Pavilion Buildings, *see* pp. 163 and 167.

---

*The assembly room was preserved as the King's chapel and is now at the former St Stephen's Church, Montpelier Place (*see* p. 171).

Walk 2.

The Steine and The Level

45. View of the Steine at Brighthelmstone, by J. Donowel, 1778

The Steine (the name deriving from the Anglo-Saxon word for a stony place) had been an ill-drained area of manorial common land forming a flat-bottomed valley at the E edge of town, with the Wellesbourne (seasonal stream) flowing down its w side into Pool Valley (*see* p. 71). Its importance as a place of residence grew only with the beginnings of Brighton as a resort when its level ground, with its sheltered aspect to the sea, was adopted for promenades. So it was here rather than on the seafront that the rich and fashionable, including the Prince Regent, took lodgings. By 1778 the s end, generally known as Old Steine, was turfed and enclosed and the activities previously carried on here by the townsfolk banished. J. Donowel's print of 1778 [45] shows the enclosed ground with its w side colonized by several private houses including the Duke of Marlborough's, and diversions for visitors in the form of the 'Circulating Library' and 'The Orchestra' on the E. More sustained development with terraced houses around the w and E frontages of the Steine began in the 1780s. This was given impetus by the enclosure in five sections of the entire length from the seafront to The Level in 1787 and drainage and culverting of the Wellesbourne in 1793, eventually forming the sequence of landscaped green spaces that today comprise Valley Gardens. As before, the townspeople were ousted and

46. Walk 2

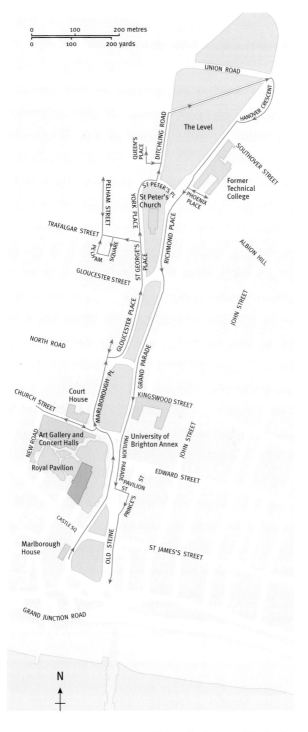

Scale

0   100   200 metres

0   100   200 yards

UNION ROAD

HANOVER CRESCENT

The Level

DITCHLING ROAD

QUEEN'S PLACE

SOUTHOVER STREET

PELHAM STREET

YORK PLACE

ST PETER'S PL

St Peter's Church

PHOENIX PLACE

Former Technical College

TRAFALGAR STREET

PELHAM SQUARE

ST GEORGE'S PLACE

RICHMOND PLACE

ALBION HILL

GLOUCESTER STREET

GLOUCESTER PLACE

JOHN STREET

NORTH ROAD

GRAND PARADE

MARLBOROUGH PL

CHURCH STREET

Court House

KINGSWOOD STREET

JOHN STREET

NEW ROAD

Art Gallery and Concert Halls

University of Brighton Annex

PAVILION PARADE

EDWARD STREET

Royal Pavilion

PAVILION ST

CASTLE SQ

PRINCE'S ST

Marlborough House

OLD STEINE

ST JAMES'S STREET

GRAND JUNCTION ROAD

N

the fairs and games which had been held on the Steine were gradually pushed N to The Level. By 1824 when the new church of St Peter was built at the N end of the Steine, development ran virtually unbroken on both sides of the central gardens, with the showpiece of the Pavilion on its w side.

The Steine's attractions as a smart address declined once the seafront promenade was improved. Since the arrival of the motorcar it has become increasingly dominated by traffic, much to the detriment of its buildings. From 1904 trams and buses terminated here and a one-way traffic system was introduced in 1926. As early as 1911, *George Ward*, the Corporation's head gardener, was asked to report on how the Steine could be improved for viewing from road vehicles. The 'Valley Vistas' scheme, which removed railings and shrub planting in favour of dwarf railings and colourful bedding plants, was implemented during the 1920s. In 1929 the *Brighton Herald* reported that 'M.P.s were urging the LCC to abolish the railings in Hyde Park because of Brighton's fine example', and that the removal of the railings 'now presented the visitors from London with the magnificent sight of three-quarters of a mile of boule-vard effect'. Few would endorse such praise today as this opening up, combined with increasing traffic, has so eroded the quality of one of the city's significant green spaces that they are now little used for recreation.

The land to E and w of the Steine was never smart; the area of North Laine (one of the five open fields around the Old Town) to the w was developed in the 1820s–40s with a grid of streets as an artisan and industrial area. The North Laine itself extended from Church Street to Preston Circus but today the name applies only to the smaller area between Church Street and Trafalgar Street. On the E side of the valley were two open fields, Little Laine, s of Edward Street, and Hilly Laine, N to present-day Elm Grove. The former, being closer to the town and the sea, developed first, from the 1790s, whilst the latter was developed for artisan housing from the early 1800s, but more extensively up the hill from the 1850s. Slum conditions in the area between Albion Hill and Edward Street led to extensive clearance and redevelopment from the 1930s.

The hotels at the s end of Old Steine are described in Walk 1. This walk starts on the w side at **Marlborough House**, the finest late C18 house, or rather villa, in Brighton. It was built *c.* 1765 for Samuel Shergold, proprietor of the Castle Inn, to let to rich visitors. The third Duke of Marlborough bought the house in 1771 but its present appearance follows its sale in 1786 to William Hamilton M.P., who commissioned its enlargement and remodelling in Neoclassical style by *Robert Adam* [47]. The building evidence indicates that Adam kept the external shell, extending the house to the s. The rear parts retain the floor levels of the 1760s building whilst at the front more generous storey heights were provided. Evidence of blocked dormer windows in the front of the roof also indicates that Adam worked largely within the confines of an exist-ing structure. The façade to Old Steine was made up-to-date as a nicely

47. Marlborough House, front elevation by Robert Adam, 1786

balanced front with a delicately detailed doorway with Tuscan columns. The façade is of five bays and two storeys, stuccoed. It has pediments left and right over advanced bays creating pavilions. Windows on the ground floor under them with the Adam variety of the Venetian type, i.e. like a Venetian window but with a blank band making the whole into a round-arched feature. Balustrades across the windows. Amply spaced windows between these two and the doorway. This is the Palladian great house in miniature. No less fine and sophisticated is Adam's suite of interiors, although their decoration typifies the restrained style of his later career. Modest **hall** with asymmetrical elevations, given a greater scale by the use of a concave ribbed ceiling. The **dining room** to the right has a groin-vault with wreaths playing round the ridges and segmental lunettes. Serving alcove to one side. To the left of the hall the **drawing room** with mouldings that have a maritime theme, Cupid astride a dolphin. Octagonal **study** behind the entrance hall; its lower ceiling tells that we are in the earlier house, though the finish is entirely Adam's. Compartmented ceiling with guilloche ornament, octagonal frame in the centre, fan decoration to the four cardinal points and Wedgwood-style plaques in the diagonal bays. **Staircase hall** awkwardly squeezed in to the E of the study. Open-well stair with Vitruvian scroll to the tread ends and newels in the form of columns. The interior plasterwork has been attributed to *Joseph Rose*.

To the left of Marlborough House are irregular groups of altered early C19 town houses, and to the right, the house built in 1804 by *William Porden* for Mrs Fitzherbert, wife of the Prince of Wales (now YMCA). Refronted in 1927, the house has been cruelly treated and nothing of Porden's work survives. Standing forward of this and taller, **Blenheim House**, largely reconstructed in 1875 by *Clayton & Black* and made more Regency in character with the addition of the first-floor balcony in the early C20.

Next comes No. 1 **Castle Square** with its segmental bowed front to Old Steine, faced in mathematical tiles, now painted. Later C19 cast-iron corner shopfront. On the N corner of Castle Square the former Brighton Corporation Electricity Department offices (now **Royal Bank** of Scotland); Art Deco classical of 1933 by *W.H. Overton*, built on the site of the Castle Inn (*see* p. 81).

Within the broad central gardens opposite this group is the 32-ft high **Victoria Fountain** of 1846 by *A.H. Wilds*, cast at the Eagle Foundry, Gloucester Road. Two shallow basins, the lower supported by entwined dolphins (modelled by *W. Pepper the elder*) over rockwork and set within a large pool. *The Builder* (1847) called it 'gawky and ungraceful'. It was partly financed by Sir Cordy Burrows, surgeon and first mayor of Brighton, whose own **statue** of 1878, by *E.B. Stephens*, stands at the gardens end. Granite plinth and a white marble standing figure in mayoral robes. In the northern part of the Old Steine gardens is the **Brighton War Memorial**, 1922, by *John Simpson*, an Italianate water garden with a plain rectilinear colonnade at one end of a rectangular basin. Bronzework by *H. Cashmore*. N again, the **Egyptian Campaign Memorial**, a plain obelisk erected in 1888. Along Old Steine are numerous **shelters** built for trolley bus stops, 1939 by Borough Surveyor *David Edwards* in streamlined International Modern style with curved glazing and deeply overhanging flat roofs. Displaced by the war memorial to the N end of the gardens of the Royal Pavilion (*see* p. 42) on the Steine's w side is a **statue** of George IV, 1828 by *Francis Chantrey*. Standing bronze, 9 ft high, on a granite base.

Now a brief detour w along the N side of **Church Street** (for the s side *see* The Dome, p. 44 and Pavilion Gardens, p. 42). First, the former **County Court House** (now council offices and lecture theatre) of 1869 by *Thomas Sorby*, County Court Surveyor. Tudor-Gothic dress but the shallow hipped roof and overall proportions still consistent with the Italianate style of court houses of the previous generation. Red brick with Bath stone dressings. Archway to the left, with Royal Arms carved by *Mansel Bayly*, the public entrance to the court room in the parallel rear range lit by high-level windows. To its w a funny juxtaposition of the ponderously classical former offices of the Brighton & Hove General Gas Co., built *c.* 1925, and a narrow, diminutive Italianate Victorian façade. Then a huggermugger group of earlier buildings including the cobble-fronted No. 111. No. 2, on the corner of New Road opposite, is an altogether grander cobble-fronted building of *c.* 1807 with a nice doorcase to Church Street. More vernacular buildings further w, e.g. Nos. 5–8 of the 1790s, with steep tiled roofs.

N of Church Street, the Steine is divided once more by green spaces, collectively known as **Victoria Gardens** since 1897 but previously called North Steine. **Statue** of Queen Victoria by *Carlo Nicoli* of Carrara, at the centre of the s garden. Along the w side of the southern garden is **Marlborough Place**. Development began in 1771, when it was called North Row and lay at the edge of town, but by the 1790s this was fast becoming attractive for lodging houses. Part of the terrace is no doubt of Georgian origin (Tuscan doorcase at No. 9) with a good run of decorative iron balconies, but with much Victorianizing including the curious protrusion of brick in the middle of the façade of No. 10.

Then the first of two striking interwar interlopers: the **King & Queen** pub. A theatrical rebuilding of 1931–2 by *Clayton & Black* with a wonderful assembly of features culled from English C16 domestic building and in every material. Lower wing to the right of 1935–6, timber-framed with brick nogging. It even has a portcullis and a gallery. The pantomime continues inside with Tudor-style fireplaces, staircases and minstrels' galleries. The interior was fitted out by *Ashley Tabb* of *Heaton, Tabb & Co*, but the original divisions were removed in 1967. **Stained glass** of knights and ladies, coats of arms and stylized trees. Upstairs **function room** (originally the Children's Room) with shallow barrel-vaulted ceiling.

Almost contemporary, but a strict contrast to the pub's display, are the offices of the **Allied Irish Bank** (formerly the Citizen's Permanent Building Society), 1933 by *J.L. Denman* in his well-mannered but individual Neo-Georgian style. Five bays, the trio of ground-floor windows have projecting bays recessed within round arches with concave extrados in which are carved reliefs of the building trades by *Joseph Cribb*. The behatted gentleman on the left is Denman. Tall pedimented first-floor staircase windows in the outer bays, also with canted window frames inset. Mansard roof covered in pantiles giving a Scandinavian air. Then Nos. 23–4, with a pretty pinched-up gable, and No. 26 with a front of tarred cobblestones. Beyond North Road Marlborough Place ends in a short cul de sac with Nos. 31–2, early C19 with full-height bows, and Nos. 33–6, humble and vernacular in character.

The next part of the road to the N was developed from the early C19 as **Gloucester Place** and widened *c.* 1900 by the removal of front gardens. Now there is nothing of before the C20, beginning with **Trustcard House** of 1985 by *Christopher Beaver Associates*, brick with glazed bays and applied metalwork, a reference to C19 Brighton architecture but with no

48. The former Citizen's Permanent Building Society by J.L. Denman, 1933, relief by Joseph Cribb

sense of fun. Then the disused **Astoria Cinema** by *E.A. Stone & Partners*, 1933, Art Deco, faced with white pre-cast stone blocks, shops incorporated at street level, formerly with tea lounge above, and the entrance under a contrasting vertical accent of three elongated round-arched windows. (The interior has Art Deco relief decoration around the auditorium and in the tea lounge, swirling abstract patterns in textured 'Marb-l-cote', partly obscured by later alterations.) Next the **Baptist Church**, 1903 by *George Baines & Son*, in their characteristic Free Perp style, of knapped flint with terracotta dressings. The interior is spacious, with slender iron columns supporting round arches, the central area with a star-pattern vault, and transverse plaster vaults to shallow projections off three sides. The fourth side has the deeper 'chancel'. Gothic **pulpit** with steps up from either side and a total-immersion **font** in front with Art Nouveau-pattern metalwork. Then nothing to note until Nos. 1–14 **St George's Place**, *c*. 1820, good deeply bow-fronted terraced houses, achieving a bold sculptural effect. Nos. 9–10 have fluted pilasters with acanthus capitals.

Trafalgar Street leads w towards the station and into the lively area of North Laine. Characteristic are the small-scale C19 industrial buildings and artisan housing, mostly opening directly to the street. The one exception is **Pelham Square**, opening off Trafalgar Street. This was laid out *c*. 1845 but with only the flat-fronted two-storey terrace on the w side, still in a Late Georgian tradition, with paired entrances and ground-floor rustication. The s and E sides followed after 1859, with railed front areas and canted bays. Across the N side of the square, housing, shops and a restaurant, 1998 by *Mark Hills*, sympathetic to the square's buildings but with later C20 details, e.g. big corner windows with supporting piloti and circular openings. The building is finished in stucco towards the square and red brick to harmonize with the late C19 buildings in **Pelham Street**, which include the former York Place Elementary Schools (now **City College**), established in 1870 (i.e. immediately after the Education Act) and with numerous later changes, all, up to 1937, by *Simpson & Son*, in their typical Brighton Board School manner. Red brick with stone bands. The schools were entered through a castellated **gateway** inserted *c*. 1900 between houses along **York Place**, facing Valley Gardens. (This was developed by 1808 but without uniformity and now decayed and a mixture of glazed black mathematical tiles, cobble fronts and bows and later bays. Nos. 17–22 can still be recognized as elegant paired stucco villas with giant Ionic pilasters; poignant reminders that in the 1820s this was a desirable address).

The highlight at this end of the Steine and deliberately sited as its focus is **St Peter's Church** of 1824–8. Its design was won in competition (against 78 entries) by *Charles Barry* when he was still under thirty and little known. Such a prestigious competition success undoubtedly helped launch his career. It was built to relieve the overcrowding at the old parish church of St Nicholas (p. 158) and located closer to where much of the town's expansion was taking place (Brighton doubled its population in the decade before 1824). The builder was *William Ranger*. The church is large and impressive. It is still entirely pre-archaeological, in a loose Perp style familiar in Commissioners' churches but with none of the weakness associated with such churches. Barry's design is bold and remarkably inventive. Goodhart-Rendel said of it, 'No better Gothic church than this was designed during the first quarter of the C19.' The tower has to its broader pinnacled lower parts open giant arches with pinnacled ogee hoodmoulds with the windows and doors recessed. Elaborate zigzag parapet with pierced quatrefoils. The slender upper part, with flying buttresses connecting to the pinnacles of the lower part, incorporates a clock stage and tall two-light bell-openings beneath a crocketed ogee with panel tracery in the spandrels and, once more, pinnacles and a pierced quatrefoil parapet. Barry designed a spire in 1841, but this was never built. The nave is Perp too, and here the Commissioners' conventions are unmistakable. Buttresses with pinnacles. Tall Perp windows of three lights divided by transoms with panel tracery below, to conceal internal galleries. Narrow two-light clerestory windows. The (liturgical) E bay of the nave, the chancel and adjoining chapel are by *Somers Clarke & Micklethwaite*, begun in 1889, delayed

49. St Peter's Church, 1824–8 by Charles Barry

50. Nos. 5–13 Adelphi Terrace, Ditchling Road

until 1892 for lack of funds and not completed until 1898 (chapel) and 1906 (chancel). The style is again Perp but more archaeologically correct than Barry's, and in a sandstone ashlar that sets it apart jarringly from Barry's white Portland stone; the intention had been to reface the whole church in sandstone. Memorial **hall** attached to the NW, 1927 by *E.P. Warren*.

The **interior** is large and somewhat austere. The piers are thin and the aisles are high; the removal of the galleries radically altering the sense of space. Barry's church was symmetrical in plan with apsidal ends, that at the (liturgical) W end remaining. Plaster rib-vaults, quadripartite to the aisles and sexpartite to the nave with foliate bosses. The galleries and box pews were removed in 1873. The lack of any division between nave and chancel accentuates the vastness of the space. The nave arcades are continued into the chancel to modified detail, separated only by corbelled-out rood stairs. The shallow canted roof is panelled, with bosses and painted emblems, the latter due to *Denman & Son*'s restoration in 1966. Magnificent eleven-light (liturgical) E window. The SE chapel is of four bays with four-light windows. **Stained glass**. The earliest is the brightly coloured glass in the clerestory, 1834, by *William Collins*. Otherwise mostly by *Kempe*, from 1880, including the E window, Christ in Glory, flanked by saints and prophets, a portrait of Queen Victoria (in whose memory the window was installed) at the bottom right-hand corner, 1906. The Jesse window in the N aisle, 1936, by *Hugh Easton*. **Monuments**. A group of good C19 wall monuments at the W end including Joseph Allen d.1831 by *W. Pepper the elder* (also by Pepper a small Gothic tablet to Mrs Crozier). Bust and drapery. Caroline Lancey d.1897, yet still the motif of the angel carrying her heavenward; only now it is done in small detached figures. Fine **organ case**, 1966, by *Denman & Son*. **Triptych** painted by *Fellowes Prynne c.*1918, incorporated within the reredos in St George's chapel.

s of the church a **drinking fountain** in the form of an obelisk, 1871, by *Robert Kierle*, erected by the Metropolitan Drinking Fountain Association.

N of the church is **St Peter's Place**, formerly Prospect Place, a terrace of *c.* 1825, part of it rather grand with giant Ionic pilasters. It lies between London Road (NW) and **Ditchling Road**, which was originally known as Brunswick Place North. No. 3, on the corner of Queen's Place, is a modest cottage of *c.* 1815 with a latticework veranda and louvred shutters to the top window, a feature sometimes used by the *Wilds*. Nos. 5–13, Adelphi Terrace, also early C19, is composed as a group with a central pedimented gable. Bow windows, almost describing a semicircle, with central mullions. Decorative ironwork to a continuous first-floor balcony with covered veranda to all but the outer houses. An enjoyable mix of the rustic and the elegant. Behind, in **Queen's Place**, a surviving row of six tarred cobble-fronted cottages of *c.* 1815. For buildings to the N and along London Road *see* p. 181.

We have now reached **The Level**, largest of the open spaces along the valley floor. Preserved from development and presented to the town by Thomas Kemp (*see* Topic Box, p. 145) and other landowners in 1822, it was formally laid out by *A.H. Wilds* with landscape gardener *Henry Phillips* (*see* Topic Box, p. 121), though little of their scheme survives. On the E side of The Level is **Hanover Crescent**, built *c.* 1814–23 by *A.* and *A.H. Wilds*. Twenty-four houses set back behind a private garden. The composition was never consistent. Blocks mostly of three houses each, those towards the centre the least altered. 2–3–2 bays, the centre part with fluted Corinthian pilasters beneath a pediment. The block to the left has the Wilds' trademark, the ammonite capital. The block to the left again is much smaller and has a plain façade with the fenestration set within slightly recessed panels under shallow segmental arches on plain impost bands. Single-storey pedimented lodges have temple fronts with Doric columns distyle *in antis*.

By 1823 there was almost continuous building on the E side of Valley Gardens from the seafront N to Elm Grove (for buildings N of Hanover Crescent *see* Walk 9). S of Hanover Crescent is **Richmond Terrace**, built speculatively from 1818 by *A. & A.H. Wilds* with a mixture of villas and terraces. Nos. 16–18 are linked, a semi-detached pair and a single house set behind generous front gardens. Shallow pitched roofs with overhanging eaves and wreathed pilasters. Then Nos. 11–15, busy with detail; only No. 15 has a bowed front, the rest flat-fronted, just two principal storeys with cornice and a bold triglyph frieze. The centre part has rustication to the ground floor and a bracketed balcony with arched cast-iron balustrades. Panelled piers to front area railings with arched tops and shell niches. Next the former **Municipal Technical College**, the centre part of 1895–6 by *Francis May*, Borough Surveyor; N wing 1909 and S wing 1935, all consistently treated with red brick and buff terracotta, in a Free Jacobean manner. The centre section has the windows set in linked terracotta surrounds, those in the middle under an all-embracing round arch beneath a pedimented gable with polygonal turrets on either side. It is an overbearing neighbour to No. 7, originally a single house, three bays under a hipped roof with pairs of incised pilasters with Corinthian and ammonite capitals. Nos. 4–6 have been much restored but were a single house first occupied by, and perhaps built for, Lord Combermere, George IV's Lord Chancellor. It is a piece on its own, a little raised by steps, and very prettily handled. Three bays, narrow, wide, narrow; beneath a broad shallow pediment with arched antefixae. Rusticated ground floor with broad segmental central recess, the first-floor windows with elaborate decorative cast iron verandas with tent canopies, the supports treated as columns with Ionic capitals and supporting a fantastically ornate entablature. The centre window has mullions treated as fasces, repeated in the window above. Lunette windows to the attic. Either side of the steps, big cylindrical piers carrying lanterns with crowns on top. Nos. 1–3 Richmond Terrace are probably a few years later; rusticated stucco ground floor but yellow brick above, with full bows and the entrances generously set between.

Tucked behind in **Phoenix Place**, the former **Phoenix Brewery offices** of 1893, possibly by *C.H. Buckman*, who earlier designed the brewery's copper house and several pubs. Italianate with a phoenix carved in the pediment – a lone survivor of Richard Tamplin's brewery established here in 1821 following the destruction by fire of his Southwick brewery.

The University of Brighton **Phoenix Building** is a brutal intrusion (1976 by *Fitzroy Robinson Miller Bourne & Partners*) destroying almost entirely **Waterloo Place**, laid out in 1819 with a terrace of fourteen houses of which Nos. 1 and 2 alone survive. No. 1 in red brick with a shallow bow and No. 2 with a covered first-floor veranda. In **Richmond Place** all is quite irregular, early C19 except for **St Peter's House**, 1986, by *Hibbert Andrews Partnership*, pallid Regency revival, with a heavy gable at one end and an awkward lozenge-shaped window. Boldly turning the corner into Richmond Parade, the former **Richmond Hotel** (now Pressure Point Bar), rebuilt in 1931 by *J.L. Denman*. Red brick, nicely composed and detailed Neo-Georgian, with very tall round-arched first-floor windows.

The next stretch s is **Grand Parade**, part of the Steine's late C18 development and again developed in small groups of terraces so that there is a mixture of glazed black mathematical tiles, tarred cobble fronts, bows and later canted bays; Nos. 18–19 are treated more grandly, with an arcade of giant pilasters. Much of the variety is from house to house, probably reflecting the incremental nature of development here, where open fields abutting Valley Gardens were in multiple ownership, but also in the nature of later embellishments. No. 39, of diminutive scale, with a castellated parapet (perhaps a refronting of an earlier building); No. 44 with the later Victorian version of the full-height bay window and first-floor veranda; and No. 46 with pretty ironwork. No. 47, 1840, attributed to *Charles Barry*, continues the Regency bow-front tradition but the façade (which alone survives) is much wider and, with its raised quoins and balustraded parapet, is Victorian Italianate.

On the corner of Kingswood Street and Grand Parade the **University of Brighton** (Grand Parade Annex) [51], built as the Brighton Polytechnic Faculty of Art and Design, 1967, by *Percy Billington*, Brighton Borough Architect, with *Sir Robert Matthew & S.A.W. Johnson-Marshall* as consulting architects. *F.E. Green*, college principal, is also said to have had input in the design. One of Brighton's better postwar buildings and remarkably considerate to its site. Concave front following the curve of Grand Parade with glazed ground floor set behind pilotis. Two bands of fenestration above, articulated in a rhythm which reflects the width of the Regency terraced frontages which follow. Angled clerestory. To Kingswood Street four projecting bays of windows, slanting back at the top.

At Edward Street, No. 80 Grand Parade, flats of 2000 by *Moren Greenhalgh*, turns the corner in a quadrant of smooth render with vertical fins and recessed balconies. Two set-back upper floors with overhanging canopy pierced by circular holes. Evocative of the stream-lined style of the 1930s but without the elegance. We are now in **Pavilion Parade**, historically also known as Town Parade, where houses were erected by 1788. Many with balconies, some with verandas but the most enjoyable of the lot are Nos. 3–4 [52] with tarred cobbles, painted brick dressings and doorcases with segmental pediments, and No. 5 with its stucco front of channelled rustication and a delicate first-floor tent-roofed veranda (replaced in replica in 1957). The last of this group faces **Pavilion Street** where closing the view with some panache are the former **Parochial Offices** (now flats) on **Prince's Street**, 1894, by *Nunn & Hunt*. Tudor-Gothic, red brick with stone dressings and polished granite. Gatehouse-style centre with an oriel above the entrance.

51. University of Brighton (Grand Parade Annex) of 1967 by Percy Billington, Borough Architect, with Sir Robert Matthew and S.A.W. Johnson-Marshall

52. Nos. 3–4 Pavilion Parade, houses erected by 1788–9

A short terrace of late C18 houses survives to its right. Opposite, **The Glass Pavilion**, 2006 by *3W Architecture*, has its main front towards the Royal Pavilion with balconies behind a crisp steel and glass screen. The façade is angled around the corner to abut two surviving Georgian houses facing the sea: No. 3 **Old Steine**, 1790, the façade of tarred brick with painted brick dressings, the entrance with engaged Doric columns; and No. 4, stuccoed, with a late C19 bracketed veranda with elaborate cast-iron railings. Nos. 6–12 all date from 1786 (erected as the North Parade) but all have been refronted at various dates. Good run of Tuscan doorcases with open pediments. Nos. 9–10 have attractive first-floor verandas with ornate ironwork and trellis-like supports at No. 9, and original front doors, panelled and studded with button motifs. The final group of terraces down to the sea (Nos. 19–31) were built as South Parade in 1786 but are now quite irregular and include a Late Victorian dark red brick Jacobean front; No. 20 has a front of *c.* 1825, a broad bow with two tiers of balconies; No. 26, probably by *A.H. Wilds*, with a busy façade with giant pilasters on high socles and with ammonite capitals; No. 28, with a first-floor veranda, its pitched roof curiously wrapping around the full-height bow; and No. 30 with bowed front and pilasters supporting a round-arched arcade, once more probably by *A.H. Wilds*.

The Seafront:
West of the Pier

The seafront w of the Pier is everyone's picture of a resort with its almost continuous run of hotels and palaces of entertainment, although the thrill of the townscape preserved in Victorian and Edwardian photographs has been diminished by numerous crass postwar insensitivies.

Before the C19 the buildings of Brighton's Old Town extended down to the cliff edge and there was little or no development w of West Street until the last decades of the 1790s. After 1800 Thomas Kemp began to acquire land in the West Laine, selling or leasing in blocks to builders and developers. This enabled development of a generous and consistent layout with a series of squares facing the sea, beginning with Bedford Square in 1801, followed by Regency Square [10] in 1817. Seafront development was otherwise sporadic until property on the West Cliff rose in value but by 1820 stucco terraces and squares extended inland to Western Road and beyond. The road along the cliff edge was improved as a broad promenade (renamed King's Road) in 1818–22 and extended

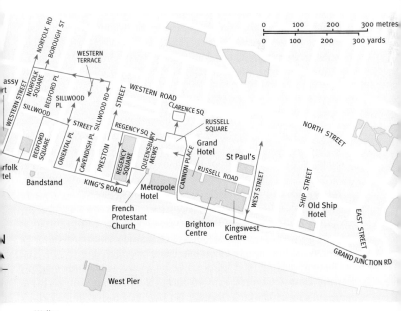

53. Walk 3

w to Hove in 1834 (work supervised by *A.H. Wilds*) but only linked to the Steine and Marine Parade to the E in 1829 with the construction of Grand Junction Road. This not only enabled the resort's elite to parade in their carriages from Kemp Town to Brunswick Town, a distance of over two miles, but also promoted the seafront as the preferred destination for wealthy visitors, both to hotels and lodging houses. From the 1860s the advent of the Victorian super hotels and the piers drew, as now, the day-trippers and holidaymakers but since the later C20 their visitors are as likely to be brought here by the conference trade.

King's Road has encroached onto the beach several times, notably in 1883–7 when *Philip Lockwood*, Borough Surveyor, created the **Upper Esplanade**. This is raised on a series of distinctive red brick vaults that face the beach. Of this date, also the decorative cast-iron **railings** and **shelters**. The ornate lamp standards cast by *Walter Macfarlane & Co.* (*Saracen Foundry*) were added in 1893 when the esplanade was extended w of the Metropole Hotel as far as the Hove boundary. The widening of Grand Junction Road in 1929–30 is by contrast utilitarian. The **Lower Esplanade** was updated in the 1920s by *B.H. Maclaren*, Superintendent of Parks and Gardens, with paddling pools, gardens etc. in an attempt to keep the resort up to date. This work has in turn been replaced from 1993 with new landscaping and attractions designed by *Fiona Atkinson*, due for completion in 2009, and incorporating several artworks, notably *Afloat* (near the East Street groin) by *Hamish Black* and *Passacaglia* (near the Fishing Museum) by *Charles Hadcock*, both of 1998.

The walk starts on **Grand Junction Road** at the monumental, faience-clad **Grosvenor Casino**, built as the Savoy Cinema in 1930 by *William Glen*. Strongly vertical entrance held within a frame, its big corner entrance in East Street classically detailed with fasces but all in freely Art Deco style. This was among the largest cinemas in the town, seating up to 3,000 and with basement parking for 300 cars. After this the tone of the road is Victorian, beginning with **Clarendon Mansions**, formerly the Clarendon Hotel of 1870 by *John Giles*, which nicely turns the corner into East Street. No frills other than decorative balconies and balustraded parapet. Then the larger **Queen's Hotel**, originally opened in 1846 in the centre part of the street block which it subsequently expanded to fill, taking in the neighbouring properties. Consequently there is no unity of design, and the hotel is dominated by the ungainly five-storey section, with three pairs of canted bays and giant pilasters whose entablature embraces one pair of bays. Meagre and self-conscious SE corner turret added in 1986 by *Michael Blee*. The more ordered w elevation, with cast-iron porte cochère, was built as the Markwell Hotel in 1870, on the site of Mahomed's Baths (*see* Topic Box, p. 70). The **Thistle Hotel**, part of the dreary Bartholomew Square redevelopment to the N (*see* p. 72) of 1984–7 by *Michael Lyell & Associates*, adheres to the prevailing roof-line of the seafront but with meaningless stunted gables and a relentless run of canted bays in metal and glass, thin and lifeless.

54. Old Ship Hotel, Assembly Room of 1761 by Robert Golden

w of Black Lion Street, however, is the **Old Ship Hotel**, the oldest inn in Brighton. Established before 1600 in Ship Street to its w, it acquired a plot facing the sea in 1794 (the present entrance) and gradually expanded w and e towards Black Lion Street, culminating in its bold and taller corner block, a stylish and sensitive rebuild of 1963–4 by *Denman & Son*; its side windows are set in an overall frame and angled for sea views. But the hotel is memorable because of the first-floor Assembly Room and Ballroom designed for the landlord John Hicks by *Robert Golden* in 1761 to rival those of the Castle Inn. Golden, a London surveyor, also redecorated the card and other rooms at this date. The **Assembly Room** (now Regency Room) is in the Adam style, segmental-arched ceiling with figure panels and wreaths, and looking more 1780s than 1761. Window bay in the long wall flanked by fluted Composite columns, and an Adam-style chimneypiece opposite with calyx orna-ment. The **Ballroom** appears to have been altered but retains a coved ceiling with dentil and modillion cornice (probably of 1761) and a later c18 gallery at one end on marbled Doric columns and a second half-oval cantilevered gallery or balcony on the long wall. Its n wall is timber-framed and clad externally in painted weatherboard.

The next seafront block is varied but of little interest except perhaps Nos. 42–3 – early c19 with black glazed mathematical tiles and later canted bays. Beyond Middle Street is a barrack-like block of student housing, 1997, by *Project Consultancy Group Central*, the proportions all wrong with squashed floor heights and insubstantial corner turret, though clearly trying to emulate the nearby Victorian hotels. Genuine Victorian on the corner of West Street: **The Belgrave Hotel**, by *Lainson & Sons*, dated 1882, high and in the Queen Anne style of Sir Ernest George, busy with recessed balconies, shaped gables, classical detailing with statues in niches and a domed corner turret. The uniform painting of the walls has deprived it of its effect, originally of red brick dressed with terracotta, manufactured by the *Tamar Terra Cotta Co.*, in two shades of red. The building makes best use of the corner site and is the first to break from the norm of canted bays.

Turning inland from the Belgrave Hotel, **West Street** has no architectural coherence but rather a series of different periods overlaid. The first is represented by No. 77, on the right (the lone survivor from the era when West Street was a desirable residential address), an elegant Late Georgian two-storey town house with a wide symmetrical façade of two broad bows either side of a flight of steps to the entrance. Original area railings. Towards the seafront Nos. 79–81 (Walkabout Bar), was built 1897 by *W.J. Miller* as Chatfield's Hotel, with a Baroque polygonal corner turret rising to a cupola, with blocked columns at the angles giving a distinct and bold outline. Brick with stone dressings but now all painted. **Avalon**, flats of 2004–6 by *Lawrence & Wrightson* (job architect *Christopher Richards*), fills a substantial plot and also has a frontage to Middle Street. A rounded s-facing wing boldly opens into the inner courtyard, matched by a curved front, firmly departing from C19 urban conventions. Dramatic gates by *Christian Funnell* with a large sunflower in the centre. Pavement in front by *Fiona Atkinson*. West Street's upper part was widened on the E side in 1868. No. 57 (Heist Bar) has a narrow, darkly painted Free Renaissance Late Victorian front with a gable, turret and an oriel window with lush carving, the details reminiscent of *Treadwell & Martin*. Inside, stained glass (not *in situ*) with a depiction of the West Pier. The whole of the w side of the street was widened between 1928 and 1938 with what the *Brighton Herald* described as a 'rising tide of tall buildings', and a run of enervating stripped classical façades remain from this period, including **Bostel House**, 4–3–4 bays and **Atlas Chambers** (by *Clayton & Black*), both originally insurance company offices.

The seaward end of the w side has been redeveloped more recently with big and worthless commercial buildings (e.g. Oak Hotel, 1990) but between these an architectural gem remains: **St Paul's Church**, one of the great churches of Victorian Brighton. 1846–8 by *R.C. Carpenter*. Paid for by the Rev. Henry Wagner but strongly influenced in its design by his son Arthur, the curate from 1850, (*see* Topic Box, p. 101) who paid for much of the interior work and the bell-tower. Carpenter, who chose 'Middle Pointed' (i.e. Dec) Gothic, was in tune with the views of the Cambridge Camden Society, and the church was greeted enthusiastically by *The Ecclesiologist*: 'At last Brighton is to have its proper place in the revival of church architecture, and its hideous chapels are to be shamed by a real church.' Brick-faced externally with knapped flints and Caen stone dressings. The church is hemmed in on all sides except at the chancel end, with the tall tower attached to its N side. A stone broach spire had been intended but instead a lead-covered timber bell-stage was added in 1873 by *R.H. Carpenter*. Whether the change of heart was driven by economy or by fear for stability (the spire at Chichester Cathedral had dramatically collapsed in 1861), the result is a unique and imaginative solution, and a most distinctive beacon in Brighton. Octagonal bell-stage with tall corner pinnacles set on octagonal bases which rise from the tower buttresses. Each face of the bell-stage has a

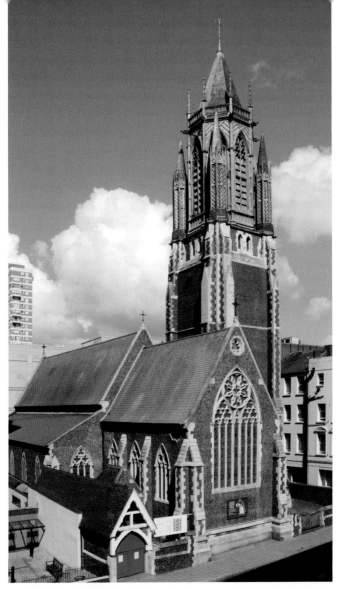

55. St Paul's Church, 1846–8 by R.C. Carpenter, the upper part of the tower added in 1873 by R.H. Carpenter

tall two-light window with shafts at the angles, rising to eight smaller pinnacles around the pierced parapet at the base of the shingled spire. The tower below is large and plain, of three stages of sheer flint without openings, apart from the richly moulded arch of the original main entrance at the base. Tympanum over, divided into roundels carved with scenes from the life of St Paul. St Paul himself under a canopied niche. Impressive seven-light E window with a small sexfoil window in the gable. A long, plain wooden passage along the s side leads to the entrance to the narthex added by *Bodley* in 1874. This has its roof at right angles to the church in order not to obstruct the nave w window. Inside this is a rectangular room with a row of four cusped two-lights within an arcaded niche on the w side. Off the narthex the **Fisherman's Vestry**, intended as a community centre and library for the fishermen of the district, lit from high up and with an enormous hooded stone fireplace as if in a medieval hall.

The interior of the church is simple. No fuss, no enrichments, just a subtle gradation in detail emphasizing the greater significance of the chancel, but otherwise an understated backdrop for the stained glass and furnishings. Six-bay arcades, quatrefoil piers, hollow-chamfered arches, bare spandrels. No clerestory and hence rather dark; most of the light comes from the immense E window and the five-light w window. Tall and sharply pointed chancel arch, with moulded orders decorated with painted motifs and carried on shafted responds with foliate capitals. Steep nave roof, with high arched braces and two tiers of wind-braces, the corbels carved with angels holding musical instruments. Painted wagon roof to the chancel, the painting added in the 1870s by *Bodley*. Angel corbels holding scrolls. The chancel is long and was intended for ritual, as the Cambridge Camden Society recommended. Plain octagonal **font** but with one inset painted panel and an elaborate canopy by *R.C. Carpenter*. Brass **lectern** [12], 1888, a superb piece made by *Hardman, Powell & Co*. Inspired by the Apocalypse, it has, around the base and projecting forward from flying buttresses with crocketed pinnacles, free-standing angels with their swords, holding back the four winds. Above, supported on a bracket, is an angel issuing from the clouds, originally holding a censer. Above, around the cylindrical stem, an upper tier of eight small angels, one bearing the cross, the other seven with trumpets, and above again, supporting the lectern itself, two cherubim with interlocked outspread wings. The piece took a year to make and cost £1,000. **Pulpit** by *R.C. Carpenter*, hexagonal with carved and gilded tracery panels, the tester *c.* 1960 by *Denman & Son*. **Screen** by Carpenter, with fan-vaults supporting the loft and rood, added by *Bodley*. The figures by *McCulloch* of Kennington. Painting by *Daniel Bell*. The screen was completed in 1911 by *H.C. Ingram*. **Paintings**. The retable behind the altar by *Burne-Jones*, of 1861, i.e. when Burne-Jones was still very young, was sold in 1993. The retable in the s aisle probably formed the outside panels of a triptych of *c.* 1515–20 and has been attributed to the Cologne workshop of *Barthel Bruyn the elder*. Retable in the N aisle, The Deposition, Flemish, early C16, school of *Rogier van der Weyden*. **Wall painting** above the chancel arch executed by *George Parlby* to designs by *Daniel Bell*, *c.* 1880, a dramatic piece with Christ in Majesty at the apex and angels ascending either side of the arch. **Choir stalls**. Carved misericords with mythical beasts and figures. **Communion rails**, to the nave altar. *c.* 1700, with richly carved panels. French, but brought here from St Andrew by the Green, Glasgow, in 1979. Also probably early C18 French, the communion rail or low screen

E of the nave altar, with heavy balusters, painted and gilded. **Stained glass**. A unified iconographic scheme, with one exception, of nineteen windows, its incomparable significance is as the most complete set of glass for an Anglican church designed by *Pugin* and made by *John Hardman*, soon after Pugin had persuaded Hardman to set up his glass workshop in Birmingham. Pugin's two principal helpers were *Powell* and *Oliphant*. The E window came first (1849), the rest installed by 1853, by when Pugin was suffering from ill health so we do not know to what extent the design of the great w window, with figures of saints in richly coloured glass, is Pugin's or Powell's. E and w windows were restored by *Meg Lawrence*, 1990. Also glass by *Kempe*, 1887–8, in the SE chapel and in the narthex, and by *Alfred Bell*, s aisle central window, *c.* 1855. **Monuments**. *William Bainbridge Reynolds*, the Arts and Crafts metal-worker, d.1935, and wife (s aisle). No doubt by himself. An angel holding a banner and a coat of arms in coloured enamel. Alabaster tablet to Rev. Arthur Wagner d.1902 (chancel N), by *Bodley*.

Arthur Wagner and Ritualism

Father Arthur Wagner (1825–1902), stout, genial and very rich, was educated at Trinity College, Cambridge. Ordained deacon in 1848 and priest in 1849, he was provided by his father, the Vicar of Brighton, with the church of St Paul, West Street, the first church in Brighton to reflect in its design the revival of ritual in Anglican worship of a kind associated with the medieval Catholic church (renewed use of chancels with altars, sung services, vestments, etc.). Wagner's pronounced views on ritual and ecclesiology were influenced by his father-in-law, Joshua Watson, a leading Tractarian, and by thinking on Christian piety and the symbolism of churches within the Church of England and at the two universities of Oxford and Cambridge. His 'activities' at St Paul's soon attracted controversy which brought Wagner to the notice of the Victorian public, and Parliament, including his establishment of the Community of the Blessed Virgin Mary and the Anglo-Catholic tenor of some of his services, as well as his insistence on the privacy of the confessional during the trial of the child murderer, Constance Kent. All raised ultra-Protestant ire. One of Wagner's circle, the Rev. John Purchas, was actually prosecuted. As author, with J.M. Neale, of *Directorium Anglicanum* (1859), on the 'rites, functions, Offices and Ceremonies of the Church', he was charged with using rites and vestments which were unlawful in the Church of England. Anti-Tractarian agitation in Brighton continued for the rest of the century and as late as 1902 the followers of 'the Protestant agitator' John Kensit first tried legally, and then forcibly, to remove 'various adornments' from the Church of the Annunciation, Washington Street (*see* p. 188), one of the important series of churches erected in Brighton under Wagner's influence.

Now back to the seafront where one can't ignore the intrusively aggressive **Kingswest Centre**, the first phase of the massive postwar Churchill Square development by *Russell Diplock Associates* (*see* p. 161), clearance for which began before the Second World War but was not complete until 1968. The low, windowless corner building opened in 1965 as Brighton Top Rank Suite (converted to a cinema in 1973 by *DHD Design Group*). Emphatically horizontal with striking origami-like roof-line of bronzed aluminium to glitter in the sun. The adjoining site was intended to have a residential tower but in its place the same firm's **Brighton Centre** of 1974–7. Grim, monolithic Brutalism, with slab-like horizontals and verticals of textured concrete. Polygonal tower bays either side of a stepped polygonal centre, the first cantilevered over the pavement, and a red brick box rising from the top, containing the conference hall. The placing of these inward-facing blocks on the seafront is perverse.

After this unpleasant interlude, however, comes the earliest and best of the swagger Victorian hotels, erected during the boom of the 1860s: **The Grand** of 1862–4 by *J.H. Whichcord* of Maidstone, who also designed The Clarence Hotel at Dover (demolished) around the same time. These were among the first of the big luxury hotels to be built outside London*; the cost was £150,000, double the amount raised in the initial share flotation (raised principally from Londoners); as *The Builder* commented, 'the hotel will be one of those immense establishments which are rapidly springing up in the metropolis and our larger provincial towns, and which seem to be now thoroughly accepted as a public necessity.' A stuccoed Italianate pile, of eight storeys with corner eminences and balconies in six tiers, which originally towered over its neighbours by several storeys. With 150 bedrooms it was the largest hotel in Brighton and the first hotel outside the capital to have hydraulic ram lifts (by Messrs *Easton, Amos & Son*), for the water cisterns which were held in the towers. *The Building News* for 1865 was not complimentary: 'vulgar and evidently important in its own estimation behind its enormous screen of balcony railings which seem hung out in rows like gilt gingerbread at a fair'. Inside, separate coffee rooms were provided for ladies, smoking and billiard rooms for gentlemen, gas lighting throughout and running water in all the bedrooms.

The **interior** still has grand reception rooms arranged along the frontage, with Corinthian scagliola and marble columns and coved and panelled ceilings with ornate plasterwork. To the N, a grand open-well **staircase** [56], galleried to the N with marble Corinthian columns, rising the full height of the building and lit by a roof lantern (renewed). The structure is cast iron, with thin columns and pierced strings and balusters, the lightness of which marries awkwardly with the stone stairs, heavy handrail and ponderous architecture. The combination

---

*The Great Western Hotel, Paddington (1851–3) started the hotel boom which rapidly spread to other large towns over the next twenty years.

56. Grand Hotel staircase

of metalwork construction and conventional ornament shows the influence of Owen Jones and 'design reform' of the 1850s. The **Albert Room** (former ballroom) has a coved and panelled ceiling with decorative plasterwork. The Grand Hotel Company mostly chose London firms for the building and fittings, e.g. *Glentons* of Blackheath (builders), *A. Gamble* of Westminster (internal carving), *R. Warren* (scagliola) and *Signor Galli* (paintings for the main rooms and staircase). Following the IRA bomb attack in 1984 the hotel was refurbished by *Yawetz (Igal) Associates* and reopened in 1986. The work was mostly internal but included the enclosure of the seafront-facing terraces. By the same architects the w wing, opened in 1992. The West Battery, part of the Napoleonic War defences, stood on the front here until 1858 and Artillery Place was set back behind it, a set-back retained for the hotel forecourt.

The **Hotel Metropole**, *Alfred Waterhouse*'s 'monster hotel' of 1888–90, for the Gordon Hotel Co. (one of Britain's first hotel chains), eclipsed The Grand in scale and was the largest hotel in the country outside London. It is typically Waterhousish, using his characteristic vivid red brick (from Rowlands Castle) and terracotta from Burmantofts for the front and elsewhere from *Joseph Cliff & Sons* and *Gibbs & Canning*. The sheer size and Waterhouse's rejection of stucco for the seafront shocked contemporaries, though the *British Architect* considered it 'a wonderful relief to come upon the hotel with its warm colour, picturesque skyline, and variety of light and shade'. The mansard roof had a central turret and spire rising out of the pyramid roof and taller pavilion roofs at the ends with finials, but these were removed and replaced in 1961 by a roof of lumpen excrescences destroying utterly Waterhouse's romantic skyline. This work is by *R. Seifert & Partners*, who also designed the wing to the E and, in 1966, bland and windowless exhibition halls behind, extended in 1972. The original arrangement was an H-plan front range (open to W and E) with an Italian-style terraced garden behind, with a fountain and tennis courts, enclosed by W and E annexes. Not only were there 305 bedrooms but also several suites, including a state suite on the first floor, public rooms including a library and Moorish-style Turkish baths in the basement. Public rooms, furnished by *Maples*, were arranged either side of the entrance hall which ran from front to back, widening towards the rear for the staircase and a lounge overlooking the garden, with three interconnecting dining rooms to the E, with a music gallery and smoking room, library, reading and other reception rooms to the W. In order to avoid columns in these rooms the upper floors are supported on massive inverted queenpost trusses (by *Handyside* of Derby), 41 ft by 14 ft, with the corridors running through them. The hotel was lit throughout by electricity. The **interior**, following the 1960s remodelling, is disappointing and retains little of its extravagant opulence. Main staircase towards the rear of the original building, around a square well. Between ground and first floor all is marble and palatial but then (as most guests now used the lifts) the staircase narrows and has a lightweight iron balustrade. **Dining Room** with Jacobean-style ceiling. At the NW corner the **Clarence Room**, a commodious ballroom with shallow barrel-vaulted ceiling on paired Corinthian pilasters separating the high-level windows.

Cannon Place runs between the two hotels. It was begun in 1809 but today has the character of a service road, except for the early C19 building on the corner of **St Margaret's Place**. To Cannon Place this is a house with two four-storey bows, but around the corner it becomes the symmetrical frontage of *A.H. Wilds*'s **Royal Newburgh Assembly Rooms**, 1833, built for Charles Wright, bookseller and librarian, as a social centre for the emerging residential neighbourhood in this part of the town. It has a pediment with two columns *in antis* that have Egyptianizing capitals. Opposite, Nos. 2–3, with Ionic pilasters, may be by *Wilds & Busby*. The view W down St Margaret's Place was originally closed by St Margaret's Chapel, *Charles Busby*'s finest church. But this was demolished in 1959 for *R. Seifert & Partners*' redevelopment of the area behind the Metropole, including the appalling **Sussex Heights** flats (completed 1966), at twenty-four storeys the tallest building in Brighton, which so damages the skyline, especially from the N. From what remains of St Margaret's Place it is possible to imagine how delightful it must have looked, an indictment of the insouciance of so much 1960s town planning regarding scale and good neighbourliness.

At the top of Cannon Place is the partly preserved **Russell Square**, a long, narrow rectangle, developed from 1809 and complete as a square by 1825, with nice Regency verandas, especially on the W and S sides; S side of ten bays, symmetrical with Corinthian pilasters in pairs, decorative ironwork balconies and a central pediment. The W side is just four bays wide. The N side is more piecemeal and the E side has been lost to the Churchill Square development (*see* p. 161). Constable stayed here in the 1840s (*see* Topic Box, p. 174). **Clarence Square** to the N was begun before 1810 and is associated with the contemporary developments along Western Road but the three-storey terraces with canted bays are a later remodelling.

From the SW corner of Russell Square a pedestrian way leads through to the set piece of **Regency Square** [10], one of the best of Brighton's seaward-facing squares. Built between 1817 and 1830 and attributed on stylistic grounds to *Amon Wilds* and his son *A.H. Wilds*, the square provided houses large enough for entertaining. It is all bows and verandas, though not uniform, probably reflecting the protracted construction. The site was Belle Vue Field, used for fairs and shows, when it was acquired by a developer, Joshua Hanson. He laid out the square garden and divided the surrounding land into seventy plots for sale to various builders, insisting that each conformed to his overall design, though there was evidently much deviation. The N side has ground-floor bows only and is treated as a kind of palace front, the centre section in brick, tripartite, the parapet with antefixae and forming a shallow pediment in the centre, with the name in incised lettering, a feature which Pevsner thought 'not enough of an accent to pull the square together'. Quasi end pavilions have parapets stepped up to shallow pedimental form. The long sides of the square are quite different. On the w side, from the seafront, six houses have three-storey bows with a continuous covered veranda to first floor. Then sixteen houses with shallow bowed fronts to the parapet, three in the middle stepping up and two towards the northern end standing out as the upper parts are in brick. The covered verandas are less consistent. The E side is more varied though there is some discipline with a parapet stepping up in the centre and to unequal 'pavilions' to either side. Near full-height bows only to the centre three houses and, curiously, just one of these is in exposed brick. The covenants reveal that stucco was only to be used for the lower parts of the façades, thus the majority, which have stucco throughout, are in breach of the original covenants, rather than the other way round as one might have guessed. The central gardens were taken over by the Corporation in 1884, and in 1969 were re-created in a stepped arrangement over an underground car park, a convenient response to the need to provide for the motorcar but visually damaging.

A short detour across the northern end of the square takes us into **Preston Street**, where uphill on the right is **The Royal Sovereign** pub, a conventional Regency front with shallow bows but with a low, lively Late Victorian addition on its corner with Regency Mews. Slightly downhill on the left is the diminutive No. 79, 1820s, with a single, rounded bow, slightly recessed, with pretty ironwork and, unusually, with casement windows rather than sashes. Open parapet with an elongated guilloche pattern. No. 5, on the other side, has the remains of a *c.* 1840s shopfront with engaged Corinthian columns.

Now back to Regency Square and the front, where, aligned on the square but marooned out at sea is the forlorn wreck of *Eugenius Birch*'s **West Pier** (1863–6; *see* Topic Box, p. 21), built to serve the w end of town but strongly objected to by the residents of the square at the time of its building. Will they care any more for the **i-360**, a 150 metre-high steel shaft with ascending viewing pod, by *Marks Barfield Architects*, approved in 2007? Facing out to the pier at the s end of the square's gardens is The Royal Sussex Regiment **Boer War Memorial** of 1904, by *John Simpson*. Tall rectangular plinth, the main faces tapering to pediments and with four shell cases at the top corners. Freely modelled bronze statue, by *Charles L. Hartwell*, of a bare-headed bugler, in greatcoat striding up a mountainside.

Just off Regency Square's E side, in **Queensbury Mews**, is the tiny **French Protestant Church**, built by and for Brighton's French-speaking community, 1887–8 by *J.G. Gibbins*, and one of only two such purpose-built churches in England. Tucked in the lee of the towering Hotel Metropole and Sussex Heights, it is dwarfed but still dignified. Steeply pitched roof with lantern and Gothic window on the w side rising into a gable. Circular window over the entrance with bold quatrefoil tracery. Plain interior with round arch dividing the nave from the chancel apse.

Now for the seafront w of Preston Street, where the next block is regrettably filled by the lumpen and grey **Holiday Inn** of 1967 by *R. Seifert & Partners*, a development which also included the seventeen-storey **Bedford Towers**, with a craggy and restless outline of overlapping, cantilevered balconies wrapping around the corners. This is the monstrous replacement of the Neoclassical Bedford Hotel of 1829 by *Thomas Cooper*, described by Pevsner as 'something special at Brighton', but destroyed by fire in 1964 and one of the most grievous postwar losses to the seafront. It adjoined **Cavendish Place**, into which Seifert's hotel and tower now brutally intrude and conspire with the corresponding tower of flats to the w to conceal. This street was conceived originally as a seaward-facing 'square' with terraces on each side and, at the head of the square, a new house for the landowners, the Count and Countess of St Antonio. *Charles Busby* was the architect and a print of the scheme to raise interest was published in the *Brighton Gazette* in 1825. Development began from the following year. The venture was initially unsuccessful and the mansion was not built, its place eventually taken by a large six-bay astylar house. The sides of Cavendish Place are flat-fronted (apart from some later added bows and canted bays) with giant Corinthian pilasters. At the s end only the block on the w side remains, with a six-bay front set back facing the sea. On the esplanade opposite is the Alfresco café, built as a **bathing pavilion** in 1953 but converted in 1957 and much altered. Brick, with much glazing and rounded corners, in the style redolent of the Festival of Britain, for which it was a belated project.

Further w on the seafront **King's Hotel**, three houses of the 1820s with porches of coupled Greek Doric columns. Converted into a hotel *c.*1864, the giant Corinthian half-columns are awkwardly squeezed between later canted bays. This is the only part completed of Oriental Terrace, which was planned concurrently with the development of **Oriental Place** [57], into which it continues with a façade of giant Corinthian pilasters above an enclosed cast-iron conservatory. The street was planned by *A.H. Wilds* with *Henry Phillips*, landscape gardener, as the approach to a subscription garden, with an outlandish iron and glass Athenaeum (conservatory and literary institute) at its centre. Work began in 1825 but lack of funds led to the abandonment of the proposed gardens in 1827. The completed houses form long, broadly symmetrical terraces with pedimented centrepiece and pavilions, and are typical

57. Oriental Place by A.H. Wilds and the Athenaeum by Henry Phillips, engraving of *c.* 1825

Wilds, with ammonite capitals and shells in blank window arches. But the richness and grandeur of the composition are difficult to appreciate in such a narrow street. Oriental Place's continuation N is **Sillwood Place**, developed in 1827–8 by *Wilds* for Sir David Scott, a director of the East India Company and local magnate, on the land originally reserved for Phillips's botanical gardens. It is terminated at the N end by Scott's Sillwood House, of four bays and three storeys with canted bays and balconies running right through on two storeys. Of the two facing terraces, only the E one remains and these houses have mostly been altered (their entrances are now from the rear), although they retain a largely unified composition. Nos. 1–8 have a slightly irregular rhythm of giant Corinthian pilasters framing the centre and outer bays, but classical order is delightfully interrupted by No. 9, which has polygonal pilasters and Moorish cusped pointed arches (influenced no doubt by the Pavilion) and other oriental details to the ground floor. Nos. 10–11 have narrow first-floor windows with alternating pediments. Both Sillwood House and the terrace on the E side of Sillwood Place were drastically restored *c.* 1990 and have no surviving original interior features. The 1970s **Osprey House** opposite is a banal neighbour completing the 'square'.

Heading w, Sillwood Street crosses Montpelier Road to **Bedford Place**. On the right this is a street of mostly bow-fronted houses but facing an unusually varied group on the other side, notably the **New Venture Theatre** (built as Christ Church Schools). Two parts, both with shaped gables, but of different dates. The modest cobblestone building to the fore is dated 1841 but its much larger red brick range behind dates from *c.* 1890. Christ Church (1838, by *George Cheesman Jun.*, dem. 1982 after a fire) stood to the left, and **Christ Church House** by *Michael Blee* stands on the site. Two residential blocks with frontages to Bedford Place and Montpelier Road and a courtyard between. The Bedford Place frontage is set back, with a filigree of steel access balconies, evoking the Regency, but with a prominent International Modern polygonal stair tower rising from a central pier. To the right Nos. 22–3, 2001–3 by *Ivars Gailis*, two houses facing an internal courtyard. Clad steel frame carried over an open terrace to one side, making the street a prominent rectangular opening enclosing both the large window to the first-floor living room and the terrace. Simple bold forms.

Bedford Place leads s into **Bedford Square**: the second of Brighton's squares, begun around 1801. It was well away from the town and perhaps for that reason only a third of the houses were complete by 1814, the rest by 1818. No single developer was in control so it is a square without programme. Nos. 27–31 in the NE corner form the best group, with bows and enough space between them for coupled pilasters. One or two pointed arches with Gothick glazing bars. Associated with this square are Nos. 146–8 **King's Road**, at the square's SW corner on the seafront, which have an Ionic colonnade carrying a cast-iron veranda. Opposite, on the Lower Esplanade, is the **bandstand** erected in 1884 as part of the seafront improvements (*see* above); it was then connected to the Upper Esplanade by a bridge. Now forlorn and neglected, due for restoration by 2009. Cast iron, by *Walter Macfarlane & Co. (Saracen Foundry)*, Glasgow. Loosely Indian style, with a squashed onion dome on round arches with trefoil cusping. Octagonal stone basement with banded rustication.

The final group of buildings along the Brighton seafront begins with the former **Norfolk Hotel** (now Ramada Jarvis), of 1864–6, by *Horatio Goulty*. French Renaissance style, in imitation of E.M. Barry's London hotels, i.e. Cannon Street (1861) and Charing Cross (1864), with pavilion roofs. Tall, to make a show and perhaps to compete with The Grand. Inside, cantilevered staircase rising through four storeys with cast-iron balustrade. Moorecroft's 1866 guide considered it 'more beautiful than any other building in Brighton'.

After that flourish there is the cool counterpoint of the Modern Movement landmark of **Embassy Court** (on the site of Western House, one of the last private mansions on the seafront to be demolished), flats of 1934–5 by *Wells Coates,* fresh from the sensation which his Isokon Flats in Lawn Road, London, had caused. Here he uses the same vocabulary but the scale is much bigger (sixty-nine flats in total) and in the more nautical, streamlined interwar vein of Modernism. This was a private speculation for Maddox Properties, aimed at wealthy professionals: Max Miller and Rex Harrison were two notable early residents. L-shaped, with a curved corner and long elevation to Western Street, the upper storeys stepped back and with a canopied sun terrace on the roof. To front and back the floors are cantilevered out from the steel frame, providing balconies on the front and access galleries at the back. To the street these appear as long unbroken bands of rendered concrete between strips of glazing; at the rear the bands rise diagonally in tiers to express the outer staircases.

The typical floors have seven flats, the largest on the corner. All flats have a balcony and enclosed sun bay, bedrooms and living room on the outer face and service rooms on the inner, with a corridor between. Coates designed tubular steel furniture for the flats, made by *Pel Ltd*, and cabinet-work was by *D. Burkle & Son*. The ground floor originally

58. Embassy Court, flats of 1934–5 by Wells Coates, detail of the rear elevation

had five flats, a bank, foyer and waiting hall. In the latter was a mural by *E. McKnight Kauffer* using a novel technique whereby monochrome photographs were printed directly onto a light-sensitive cellulose coating. Embassy Court was restored 2004–6 by *Paul Zara* of *Conran & Partners* after decades of neglect: including major repairs but also restoring the original cream colour render, reviving the qualities which the *Architects' Journal* (1936) claimed to 'thrill one to the marrow'. But this was and is a good building in the wrong place; Pevsner's opinion of 1965 is still pertinent: '. . . well designed in itself or otherwise, a modern block, eleven storeys high, is a bad neighbour to the Regency, and it is unfortunate that Wells Coates had to demonstrate his style in the very place where the Brighton and Hove seafront becomes serious neo-classical architecture for the first time', with the beginning of Brunswick Town (*see* Walk 4).

The walk can end here or with a brief foray inland to look at more of the Regency developments between the front and Western Road. **Western Street** has just a few groups of early C19 houses including No. 5, with bow front and veranda, and Nos. 31–3 with pretty iron balconies. On the corner of Sillwood Street on the right, an ungainly and evidently altered double-fronted house set behind and above later C19 shops. Heavy cornice and bows precariously overhanging. Then paired villas, Nos. 23–9, set well back, with altered ground-floor colonnades. At the top of the street is **Norfolk Square**, to which Nos. 11–19 Western Street belong. This was completed in the 1820s and is associated with building along Western Road, to which the square is open on its N side. There is little to hold it together visually. Four-storey and bow-fronted on the W side, three-storey on the E, with continuous first-floor balconies. On the S side, Nos. 30–3 are flat-fronted with giant Ionic pilasters; No. 34 is lower with a bow. The square gardens have been clumsily municipalized with bus stops, lavatories etc. closing the gardens from Western Road.

Across Western Road, **Norfolk Road** runs N. No. 3, on the left, may be by *C.A. Busby* (who in 1827 rented land here from Thomas Kemp); two broad bows, the upper-floor windows with fasces as mullions. E, also off Western Road, **Borough Street** commemorates the creation of the Parliamentary Borough of Brighton in 1832. W side of bow-fronted terraces and on the E side the former **St Stephen's School**, 1855, by *Samuel Dawkes*, for Rev. George Wagner. Enlarged in 1895. Knapped flint with stone dressings.

The final part of the walk takes us a short distance along Western Road, past good Regency bow-fronted houses on the S side beyond Montpelier Road as far as **The Gothic House** (Nos. 95–6), built in 1822–5 by *Wilds & Busby*, though as their partnership dates from May 1823 it seems likely the design was that of *A.H. Wilds* alone. Also known as The Priory and Priory Lodge, it is fanciful and irresponsibly Gothick, with a polygonal tower with buttresses topped by crocketed pinnacles. Converted into a shop in 1898, and partly obscured at the E end by a two-storey shopfront, probably of *c.* 1920, by *Henry Ward*. Its side elevation is to **Western Terrace**, which has a good selection of the work of *A.H. Wilds* including, most memorably, his own house, aptly named the **Western Pavilion**. Built in 1831, it reveals Wilds's humour and his willingness to embrace the exotic; the Pavilion's baby brother, complete with dome and 'Hindoo' details. Map evidence indicates that there was a N wing balancing the extant S wing. The interior was altered in 1957 when both floors were incorporated into a dress shop on Western Road with a highly glazed front by *Marmorek & Weaver*. Facing is the E elevation (show front) of Sillwood House (*see* above). Here a grand palace front with three-bay pedimented centre with a raised attic and single broad end bays, advanced and with paired fluted pilasters. All the pilasters have Wilds's ammonite capitals. Its former coachhouse (No. 8a) closes the street and is by contrast rather sober, with round-arched windows and ball finials to the parapet, but with pedimented aedicules in the Greek taste to either side and to the sides of its rear extension.

Parallel with Western Terrace to the E is **Sillwood Road**, originally called Western Cottages, but renamed *c.* 1870 when Nos. 32–47 were built on the W side. Designed by *Thomas Lainson*, rather in the Osborne House Italianate of twenty years before and still with some Regency lightness. Set back, three storeys, stuccoed, with two-storey canted bays topped with ironwork cresting, a continuous ground-floor veranda, and round-arched top-floor windows beneath a heavy dentil cornice. The interiors (well preserved at No. 40) have the heavy plaster cornices of the period and elaborate cast-iron staircase balustrades. Opposite, Nos. 13–25, completed in 1828 by *C.A. Busby*, is one of his several forays into speculative development. The houses step down the hill and are quite plain, divided by thin pilasters topped with antefixae. From Western Road numerous buses run back to the city centre. For the buildings of Western Road *see* pp. 160–2.

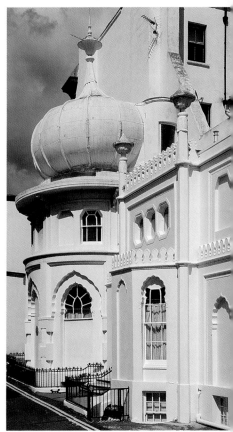

59. The Western Pavilion, Western Terrace, A.H. Wilds's own house built in 1831

Walk 4.

Brunswick Town

Well before Brighton had become a resort visitors to the town had been attracted to the neighbouring parish of Hove by the chalybeate springs discovered at St Ann's Well on the Wick Farm estate. A building was erected at the spring by 1750, replaced *c.* 1830 by a larger building with an Ionic colonnade and 'a very handsome and airy reading room

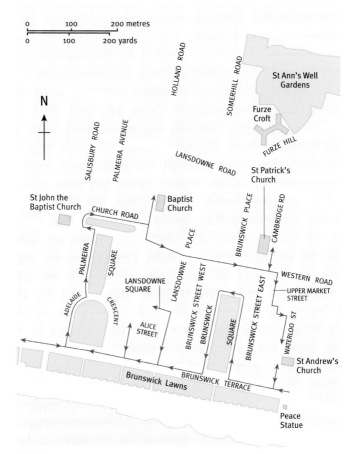

60. Walk 4

– decidedly one of the best in Brighton' (Parry 1833). In the 1820s, Rev. Thomas Scutt (whose family had purchased the estate in 1701), began to sell off much of the surrounding property, capitalizing on the insatiable demand for building land along the seafront in Brighton. The first product of this urban expansion was Brunswick Town, the idea for which may be credited to its designer *Charles Busby*, no doubt inspired by his employment at Kemp Town (Walk 6). The design, exhibited at the Royal Academy in 1825 was listed under Busby & Wilds, the only written instance in which Busby's name was given first. His scheme, largely completed between 1824 and 1830, was for four terraces of first-class housing facing the sea and set around three sides of a long square running inland, with second-class housing in streets to either side (now Lansdowne Place and Waterloo Street). A market building was provided, together with a church, hotel and baths, promising Brunswick Town a degree of self-sufficiency absent at Kemp Town. In order to manage the new estate the Brunswick Square (Brighton) Improvement Act of 1830 set up a board of Commissioners responsible for the upkeep of the garden, policing, drainage, lighting, paving and rate collection. The act, still in force, stipulates that the houses be finished in Parker's Roman cement (i.e. stucco), painted a stone colour every three (now five) years and required owners to erect a balcony without a veranda. The Commissioners appointed a surveyor, first *Thomas Clisby*, a former clerk to Wilds & Busby and, from 1832, Busby himself, to ensure that the terms of the act were complied with. Further plans were made for a series of three small squares to the w, but this was only partly realized by 1833 when Busby finally overreached himself and went bankrupt. He died a year later. Brunswick Town, unlike the more remote development at Kemp Town, was a success from the outset because Busby was in closer control of its execution and ensured that the infrastructure was provided. In addition, being in Hove parish, Brunswick Town's residents did not have to pay Brighton's taxes.

In 1825 the *Sussex Advertiser* reported that Thomas Kemp had plans for a 'Kemp Town west' and was negotiating purchase of the rest of the Wick Farm estate from Thomas Scutt. Instead the land was sold to the broker and financier Isaac Goldsmid. He commissioned *Decimus Burton* to prepare plans for a single crescent (Adelaide Crescent) facing the sea (design exhibited at the RA, 1831) [63], but this was later modified to include a square (Palmeira Square) and not completed until the 1860s. Concurrently with this development, the area between Western Road and Lansdowne Road was laid out as a grid of streets, and from 1851 the whole of the new development was brought under the management of the Brunswick Town Commissioners. Wick Hall at Furze Hill, close to St Ann's Well Gardens, was rebuilt for Goldsmid by Burton in 1835–8 and Burton then drew up proposals for a picturesque village of nineteen villas set in an Arcadian landscape NE of St Ann's Well. Six or seven houses were built but very little survived redevelopment of this high ground from the 1930s with large blocks of flats.

61. Hove seafront, Peace Statue of 1912 by Newbury Abbot Trent

A walk which follows the principal developments within Brunswick Town should start on the seafront at Embassy Court (*see* p. 108) where Walk 3 turned inland along Western Street and King's Road becomes **Kingsway**. Between the road and the esplanade are **Brunswick Lawns** with the historic boundary between Brighton and Hove marked by the **Peace Statue** of 1912 [61], erected by both towns in memory of Edward VII. A stepped sandstone pedestal with moulded segmental-arched top, surmounted by Peace, a bronze angel holding an olive branch, by *Newbury Abbot Trent*.

The introduction to Busby's Brunswick Town is Nos. 1–6 **Brunswick Terrace** with many characteristic features but quite different from the main terraces of his scheme. Symmetrically composed as five units, of eighteen bays overall with a wider centre of five rather than four storeys. The ends and centre have fluted giant Ionic columns through two storeys, the centre bay with a pediment. The intermediate bays are recessed with bow fronts, not a successful composition.

A short detour can be made here to take in **St Andrew's Church** of 1827–8 (now in the care of The Churches Conservation Trust). It was provided not by the developers of the estate but a prominent local clergyman, Dr Edward Everard, to designs by his friend *Charles Barry*. It is just three years later than Barry's St Peter (*see* p. 88), but how different in style and learning. Barry here turns to the Italianate style for which he became famous with the design for the Travellers' Club in London, but that was begun only in 1829. So St Andrew's is the first-fruit of this change from Antiquity to the Renaissance, which was to have such universal effects. As in the Travellers' (and Attree Villa, *see* p. 191), Barry takes his cue from the Quattrocento. Later, in the Reform Club, it was from the Cinquecento. The façade is quite modest, of three bays only, and basically on the Georgian scheme with giant pilasters, and a square turret on top. But the portal and the bell-openings are without any doubt Quattrocento. All the emphasis is on the façade, stuccoed, with all-over rustication. The church is squeezed into a constricted site and the rear parts are plain and of brick. The interior was a typical Regency preaching box, with just a w gallery, to which *Charles Barry Jun.* added the apsidal chancel in 1882. This has a circular central part under a saucer dome, with large round-headed arches, free-standing Ionic columns and a shallow apse with panelled ceiling and a semicircular skylight. Round arches to either side open into the organ chamber and a s chapel. The nave has a coved ceiling and Barry Jun. inserted skylights at either end to striking effect. The church was rendered yet more Italian by the addition of the **baldacchino**, with a shallow pediment on fluted Corinthian columns, and other furnishings in 1925 by *W.H. Randoll Blacking*. Delightful **font**, a marble pedestal with three timber supports and elegant painted cover, set beneath another baldacchino, flat-topped and squeezed in under the w gallery. **Stained glass**, mostly by *Hardman (John) & Co.*, c. 1869 and 1882, and good. Figures of saints re-set in clear Venetian glass roundels, with sparing use of strong colours. Especially attractive the angel musicians in the roundels of the E window behind the organ. In the s chapel E windows excellent glass by *Christopher Webb*. Nativity scenes in the upper window, 1938, and a beautiful Annunciation of 1927 in the roundel

Houses in Brunswick Town: Planning, Function and Decoration

Although most of the houses in Brunswick Terrace were lodging houses, many of the houses in Brunswick Square were for owner-occupiers. Both conform to the Georgian formula of 'First Class' houses, a plan type that can be seen at No. 13 Brunswick Square (the **Regency Town House Museum**). The entrance opens to a hall and staircase. Dining room and parlour on the ground floor, a waiting room and water-closet occupied the first half-landing leading onto the first-floor drawing room, usually two rooms that could be thrown together. Bedrooms occupied the upper storeys and the basement housed the servant accomodation, with separate access from the front area and rear coach-house. Most houses have timber open-string staircases (a few grander ones have cantilevered stone stairs) and pilasters supporting an entablature to the first-floor landing. Typical details, as at No. 13, are marble chimneypieces, acanthus cornices and a pretty dome on the first landing. Much grander, the interior of **No. 33** (now Nos. 33 and 33a) occupying a large plot in the square's NW corner, which has a generous square staircase hall lit by tripartite windows and with a cantilevered stone stair around a large open well. Elegant alternating iron balusters, two per tread. Interior decoration was left to individual householders but in 1824 Busby reprinted his *Modern Embellishments*, perhaps intending it as a guide to new owners. The decorative wallpapers preserved at the Regency Town House Museum and Royal Pavilion give some idea of the likely appearance of interiors at this time. **No. 14** has a delightful vestibule with Ionic columns and Soanian shallow-vaulted ceiling, although this may be of 1918 when the house was converted to flats.

below. **Monuments** to Lord Charles Somerset, d.1831, and Sir Charles Dallas, d.1833, by *John Ternouth*, both with an allegorical figure.

Then, w of Waterloo Street we are immediately upon Busby's great set piece of the two principal blocks of **Brunswick Terrace** (1824–6), each of thirty-nine bays, and **Brunswick Square** (1825–30) between. What distinguishes these from the Kemp Town development (Walk 6) is that the accents have sufficient strength to articulate long rows of windows. Both of the ranges of Brunswick Terrace are of three, not four, storeys and have a centre of ten giant Corinthian half-columns, and only above this an extra storey as an attic instead of a pediment. The end accents are giant pillar–column–column–pillar and an attic too, and in between all has giant pilasters. That gives enough relief – in both senses. Bruce's 1834 *Brighton Guide* considered Brunswick Town 'the handsomest spot in Brighton' and superior in elegance to Kemp Town.

The square tries the same, not so successfully. The N side is open in the centre and has flat-fronted terraces to either side, angled at the corners, with giant Corinthian pilasters and attic windows beneath blind semicircular arches. The long sides of the square are stepped and form a mirror image of each other in groupings if not in detail: three groups of three in the upper part, with bow fronts and balustraded parapets, then a run of bows in two groups of four, all with giant Ionic columns (w) but three with pilasters only (E), i.e. irregular. Then a group of five, where alternate bows have giant Ionic columns. Closest to the sea, smaller double-fronted houses, of reduced depth as here the square abuts the rear parts of Brunswick Terrace. Towards the top of the square the bows have no orders at all. Squeezed in between these blocks are four much narrower frontages (Nos. 7, 12, 47 and 52) which may be the consequence of Scutt selling plot widths by the linear foot, as desired by purchasers, without consideration for Busby's overall design. The balconies are given varied treatment too, straight runs across the groups of three at the top of the square, elsewhere either with straight runs across single houses or with individual window balconettes.

Back to the seafront now where Nos. 20–32 **Brunswick Terrace** form the matching western arm of the composition. No. 26 was the home of Philip Salomons who added the pepper-pot cupola on the roof as his private synagogue. The staircase at No. 28, perhaps later, has elaborate iron balusters. No. 32 has its entrance on Lansdowne Place, set back behind Greek Doric columns as at No. 1 Brunswick Square. Its plain but generous staircase is lit by a circular lantern with tapering sides.

The continuation of development by Busby from 1827 is represented by Nos. 33–42 Brunswick Terrace, w of Lansdowne Place. More simply treated, thirty identical bays, no central or outer emphasis, just a continuous run of giant pilasters and a first-floor balcony. Begun in the same year were the four bow-fronted houses on the w side of **Lansdowne Place** (at that time Wick Road, Stanhope Place and Lansdowne Place, all renamed in 1834). No. 1 is wider and double-fronted but only one room deep. The others have unusual doorways

62. The w side of Brunswick Square, 1825–30 by Charles Busby

guarded by bearded herms. On the E side, the **Lansdowne Place Hotel** was built as Lansdowne Mansions in 1854. Still like a Regency terrace in character but with subtle changes: a higher proportion of glazing, faceted bows and rounded corners to the upper and lower windows. Converted to a boarding house in 1878; the round-arched entrance is of 1911 by *F.C. Axtell*. The plain bow-fronted houses further N were built by Busby in 1829, No. 2 was his own house, with rear stabling and his draw-ing office (now Brunswick Cottage) with pedimented gable to the street.

Opening off the street's w side is **Lansdowne Square**, completed by 1833, the only square realized of the three projected by Busby for the second phase of Brunswick Town. Little more than a wide street, but with a palace front on the w side with a central pediment on Corinthian columns and symmetrical side ranges with plain giant pilasters. Either side of the square's entrance, facing Lansdowne Place, are symmetrical paired villas, with full-height bows with ground-floor balconies and covered verandas to the first floor. A late introduction by Busby, and his last buildings, they perhaps indicate a desire among purchasers for a more suburban environment and relief from the ubiquitous long terraces. Two further pairs have a balustraded Ionic colonnade uncom-fortably placed across the front, perhaps a later addition or perhaps the whim of the builder completing the development after Busby's death in 1834.

Holland Road (named by Goldsmid after Lord Holland, an advocate of Jewish emancipation) defined the w limit of Brunswick Town in 1830. Here only **The Brunswick** pub of 1938 is worthy of detour, set back and dominated by a steeply pitched tiled roof and two elegant semicircular projecting bays. Ashlar surround to the entrance continued above with fluted pilasters between the windows. A subtle combination of the traditional and the modern. It was built by Tamplins Brewery; their usual architect was *Arthur Packham*.

No sooner was Brunswick Town complete than Isaac Goldsmid commenced his ambitious development of the rest of the Wick Farm estate to the w and N. For the part closest to the sea he commissioned *Decimus Burton* as architect. **Adelaide Crescent** began to emerge in 1830 but only ten houses were complete before building halted in 1834. When work resumed *c.* 1849–50 Burton's plan had been abandoned and a revised scheme adopted (by an unknown designer) with the crescent opening into a square, as at Kemp Town. It was not completed until the 1860s. Of the original scheme is the corner block (Nos. 1–3), facing the sea with a terrace up steps. It is monumental but of a different character to Brunswick Town, away from the Regency to the Neo-Renaissance. Eleven bays only, i.e. a mansion rather than a terrace, a raised pediment in the centre with a frieze of garlands below. The first-floor windows have heavy balustraded balconies and some windows are pedimented. The top bracketing also points to the Neo-Renaissance, indeed the bracketing shows at once that we are on the way to the Victorian Age. The symmetrical elevation to the crescent (a misnomer for the sides begin straight), is treated similarly: 3–5–3 bays, without a pediment over the centre. It was extended after 1850 in matching style but there is no companion piece to this on the w side, and the other terraces of that period, stepping uphill in blocks on both sides, are more uniform and simpler in their details, e.g. lighter dentil cornices and continuous cast-iron balconies. The two sides of the crescent do not quite match (the terrace blocks of different sizes and those on the w with heavy porches), but this does not notice in an overall appreciation of the composition

63. Decimus Burton's original scheme for Adelaide Crescent

64. Adelaide Crescent

and, unlike Kemp Town, the transition from crescent into square is most elegantly handled in a double curve. The best of the **interiors** is No. 34, which has a large drawing room with a most enjoyable plaster ceiling in the English Rococo style of the 1730s with flower baskets and **C**-scrolls, foliage trails with squirrels and rabbits, cherubs and figures of Ceres [65]. The rather controlled pattern and the contrast between the flatwork and the more three-dimensional forms is unmistakably Victorian, and the ceiling probably dates from the 1880s when the house was occupied by Harry Gordon, a wealthy stockbroker. Of about the same date are the entrance hall embellishments at No. 15, a Moorish arch and an elaborate decorative frame or achievement with trophies, guns and a shield, probably introduced by Colonel Robert Goff who served in the Crimea, retired in his early forties to devote himself to landscape painting and lived here from 1891. Also a fireplace with Aesthetic Movement tiles with allegorical figures of the virtues of truth and moderation. No. 10 has a plaster relief of King Midas judging a musical contest between Apollo and Pan. No. 11 had minor internal alterations carried out in 1933 for Dr Beresford by *Raymond Erith*, including a first-floor chimneypiece with heavy tapering fluted half-columns and capitals with a kind of stylized acanthus decoration.

The land N of Adelaide Crescent was originally reserved for the ill-fated Anthaeum glasshouse (*see* Topic Box). Construction of **Palmeira Square** (Goldsmid had been created Baron Goldsmid of Palmeira in 1845 by the Queen of Portugal) began in the mid 1850s but was incomplete until *c.* 1865. The square continues the façades of the crescent and shows the transition into the Italianate as clearly as contemporary work on the same scale N and S of Hyde Park in London. Here the designs have rusticated quoins and windows in tripartite groups. Canted bay windows to the first floor. The two terraces are symmetrical and identical, the central house having a full-width colonnaded porch and a tripartite square bay through the two floors above. The adjoining houses and paired end houses are set slightly forward, with quoins and larger first-floor bays, forming a 2–5–3–5–2 composition. The treatment

65. No. 34 Adelaide Crescent, detail of drawing room ceiling, probably 1880s

Henry Phillips and the Anthaeum

Henry Phillips (1779–1840) was a botanist, horticulturalist and landscape gardener, publishing a number of books during the 1820s. He met and became friends with John Constable and in 1826 (when Constable was working on 'The Cornfield') sent him a list of flowers that would bloom in the hedgerows at harvest season. Phillips's first work in Brighton was (with *A.H. Wilds*) the laying out of The Level in 1822 (*see* p. 184), when the land was given to the town by Thomas Kemp. The following year saw his (unexecuted) design for a park surrounded by detached villas, on land between Kemp's house, The Temple [92], and Bedford Square, ambitious proposals likened by the *Brighton Gazette* to 'the cemetery of Pere la Chaise or to the city of Constantinople with its roofs and minarets encircled by trees'. In 1825 Phillips drew up a scheme (once again unexecuted and again with Wilds) for an Oriental Garden as part of the development of Oriental Place (*see* p. 106), including, at its centre, the Athenaeum: an iron and glass onion-domed conservatory and literary institute [57]. In 1828 Phillips was engaged in the layout of the Kemp Town Enclosures (*see* p. 150) and is said to have designed the conservatory for the Surrey Zoological Gardens, opened in 1831, described as 'the largest continued surface of glass in England'. His Oriental Gardens project was revived as the Anthaeum (flower house) for a site N of Adelaide Crescent, partly financed by Isaac Goldsmid. It was to be an immense dome, 65 ft-high, with a 16 ft-tall cupola, and 165 ft in diameter, covering an area in excess of one and a half acres with lake, a rocky hill, mature exotic trees and birds. *A.H. Wilds* was appointed architect with *C. Hollis* engineer. The structure was erected in 1832–3; the Duke of Devonshire's gardener, Joseph Paxton, inspected it (three years before he built the Great Conservatory at Chatsworth) and J.C. Loudon planned to visit on 12 September 1833. But when nearing completion the projectors proposed abandoning the central supporting pillar. Wilds and Hollis resigned. Before Phillips could seek an opinion from Sir John Rennie, the contractor took precipitous action and removed the temporary support scaffolding on 29 August 1833. The following day the Anthaeum collapsed and remained where it lay, a heap of twisted iron and glass, for twenty years, until cleared for the development of Palmeira Square. Phillips allegedly went blind from the shock.

of double porches and segmental or triangular pediments to upper windows also gives emphasis. Nos. 30–4 (**Palmeira Court**) were converted laterally into flats in 1910 (Nos. 15–17 Adelaide Crescent and others were similarly combined at this period). The half-width back extensions were removed and replaced by accommodation for servants in a range parallel to the main building, separated from it by a courtyard,

66. No. 33 Palmeira Mansions, Venetian glass overmantel

but linked at either end. Of note is the chimneypiece in the lift hall at No. 32 with paired baluster-like columns, Jacobean-cum-Baroque, and an aedicule overmantel with an oval recess set within a frame with lugged surround, more Baroque-looking. The two parts probably do not belong together.

At its N end Palmeira Square opens to a second garden square, actually a widened section of **Church Road**, which runs along its N side (the s side is St John's Place). Continuing the Italianate style, grandeur and scale of Palmeira Square are the two terraces of **Palmeira Mansions**, flanking Palmeira Avenue, of 1883–4 by *H.J. Lanchester*. Each has a shaped pedimented gable at the centre and outer full-height canted bays. At the w end, No. 33, on the corner of Salisbury Road, was bought in 1889 by A.W. Mason, owner of Mason's Ink, who remodelled the interior in the most extreme Victorian theatrical taste (possibly in 1899 when the first-floor conservatory was added by *S.H. Diplock*). Entrance and staircase halls lined in veined and coloured marbles including the curving staircase balustrade. The ceiling has a complex design in plaster or heavy lincrusta. Oval mirror with a heavy frame of disporting cherubs and an original light fitting with a writhing winged serpent. Heraldic stained glass in the windows, some of it set in inner secondary glazing. The front room is in a lavish Moorish style with heavily coffered painted and gilded ceiling [13], carried down at the corners onto marble columns. Doorcase and chimneypiece have flattened ogee arches. The first-floor landing has a Moorish horseshoe arch and ornate painted and gilded ceiling, carried through into the first-floor conservatory with Tiffany-style coloured glass. Also on this floor, one room with extravagant gilded pelmet, lincrusta frieze and ceiling and chimneypiece of riotous swirling motifs, almost Art Nouveau. Another room has an outstanding Venetian cut-glass over-mantel framing a mirror. In the former ballroom, an odd mixture of Adam-style and Rococo decoration and a richly coloured *Doulton* ceramic chimneypiece. Several other rooms with ornate chimneypieces, one with hearth tiles to a design by *Walter Crane*.

The view w is filled by **St John the Baptist's Church**, built for the developing area in 1852–4 by *W.G. & E. Habershon*, and for many years one of the most fashionable churches in Brighton. Large, Dec of flint with ashlar dressings. Cruciform with nave and aisles of uniform height and a tower (built *c.* 1870) set in the angle between chancel and N transept carrying a broach spire with lucarnes. The steeple forms a distinctive feature in the townscape but is rather too small in relation to the rest of the church. Tall five-light E and W windows and six-light transept windows, all with Dec tracery, going Flamboyant, a Habershon trait criticized by *The Ecclesiologist*. W porch 1906–7 by *Rogers, Bone & Cole* of London. The interior, with steeply pitched hammerbeam roofs and detailing of the earlier phase of the Gothic Revival was, as Goodhart-Rendel observed, a compromise between the auditory church favoured by evangelicals and the tastes of the Ecclesiologists, though the latter criticized the design. Luscious foliage capitals at the crossing and carved foliage relief panels below. A stone screen separates the N transept from the organ chamber. Partially converted to the Cornerstone Community Centre in 1990–2 when *Mark Hills* inserted a steel frame into the nave for three storeys of accommodation, meeting rooms, café etc. The reduced space for the church was reordered in 1994 by *John Small*. Central altar and corona lucis, with glazing inserted into the apex of the roof. **Pulpit** of stone and elaborately carved with flamboyant tracery. Octagonal **font** with sides alternately short and long and with angels at the angles and carved roundels in the panels. **Stained glass**. W window of 1852–4, Christ and the Evangelists in architectural sur-rounds, good. E window and two windows at the W end of the former N aisle, 1927, by *A.L. & C.E. Moore*. In the SE chapel three windows of the 1920s by *Ward & Hughes*.

Now back E along Church Road. Between Rochester Gardens and Holland Road, **Gwydyr Mansions** of 1890 by *Clayton & Black* in Flemish Renaissance taste. Contrasting red brick and ashlar, busy with canted bay windows, corner oriels and turrets and multi-tiered gables. The

67. Barber's shop at Gwydyr Mansions of 1890, fittings of 1936

ground floor, with Tuscan columns *in antis* either side of a pedimented corner entrance, was a bank. On the w side a basement barber's shop has an original glazed screen forming the lobby, and vitrolite fittings of 1936 [67]. The basement also originally had a sixty-seat restaurant for residents. From here we can glance up **Holland Road** to note *Lainson & Sons*' former repository for the Brighton & Hove Co-operative Supply Association – 1893, French Second Empire with steep roofs and a flourish of gables (loft-style residential conversion by *R.H. Partnership*, 2004–6) – and the **Baptist Church**, 1883, by *John Wills*; forming a group with the Sunday schools and Young Women's Christian Institute. Purbeck rock-faced stone. Gothic, with a corner tower rising to gables and pyramid roof. The chapel interior has a hammerbeam roof with trefoil tracery and trusses supported on bold foliate capitals. Gallery on slender iron columns. Brightly coloured **stained glass** with foliage patterns in the large N window and abstract patterns in the rose window opposite. The schools have an extension on the front, part of a refurbishment of 1998–9 by *dk architects*, and the Institute is in a plainer, secular style 'to avoid the appearance of uniformity, as this institute is an unsectarian enterprise', according to *The Builder*.

Then E along **Western Road** where the buildings achieve an urban scale and are predominantly late C19 commercial. One might note No. 64, on the corner of Holland Road and Church Road, the former London & County Bank, 1890 by *Zephania King* in a loosely Tudor style with a busy skyline of gables and elaborate chimneys, and the richly Italianate **Palmeira House**, opposite, by *Lainson & Sons*, 1887, for the Brighton & Hove Co-op (established here 1873). Opposite, **The Biscuit Factory**, an impressively tall Italianate corner pub of 1875, then the eccentric frontage of the former **Hill's Department Store** of 1921 by *Garrett & Son* with a series of full-height bows between paired columns – was this a radical remodelling of an existing C19 terrace or a rebuilding *de novo* in sympathetic spirit? Clearly 1920s is the emphatic and deep parapet with horizontal strips at the streamlined angles. No. 60 shows what the parade looked like before the rebuilding. Beyond Lansdowne Place (consistent bow fronts) is **Brunswick Street West**, one of Brunswick Town's original service streets. No. 64 built in 1854 as a town hall for the Brunswick Town Commissioners. Opposite, a group of three town houses (2004, by *Alan Phillips Associates*) give a C21 interpretation of the Brighton bow, boldly projecting quadrants supported on columns which run through the storeys. Dramatic glazed elevation to the inner garden. At the top of the street, **The Freemasons** has a striking restaurant frontage to Western Road added by *J.L. Denman* in 1928, and reminiscent of the Viennese Secession. Within a frame of blue and gold mosaic, including Masonic symbols, a double-height bronze and glass screen curving inwards to the entrance. Inside, plaster friezes of stylized Art Deco swags.

Then **Brunswick Place** crosses, with views to Brunswick Square and the sea to the s, and to the N bow-fronted houses continuing in the

68. The Freemasons Restaurant, Western Road, by J.L. Denman, 1928

1840s what Busby began in the 1820s. Nice run of balconies stepping up the hill and, closing the view, **Furze Croft**, a large seven-storey modern block of flats, 1936 by *Toms & Partners*, on the site of Wick House. In **Cambridge Road**, squeezed between houses on the left, **St Patrick's Church**, 1857–8, by *H.E. Kendall Jun*. Long façade to the street of rock-faced Kentish ragstone with Bath stone dressings. Dec style but idiosyncratic and thoroughly Victorian. Despite the cramped site Kendall exploits it to the full, providing a church with six-bay aisled and clerestoried nave with three-bay chancel with an aisle and a gabled transept and, to the right, the base of the uncompleted tower which was intended to have a tall octagonal belfry stage and a parapet with eight pinnacles. At the s end a porch to a narrow narthex (the original main entrance), and a curious turret, square, turning octagonal and finishing with an octagonal pinnacle. The aisle bays are divided by buttresses and have two-light windows with geometrical tracery of different designs. Two-light clerestory windows beneath gables which form dormers. The transept has a four-light window and stepped lancets in the gable, whilst the tower has heavy buttresses, one broadened to include the stair, a busily detailed porch and a three-light window with reticulated tracery. The church's other side faces private gardens. The interior has been subdivided, as a part conversion for a hostel (1997–8 by *Lee Evans de Moubray*), with a five-storey steel-framed structure inserted into the nave. The church now occupies the (liturgical) eastern parts of the building. Roof with closely set hammerbeams with faceted pendants, the spandrels pierced with geometrical patterns and decorative cresting, almost Jacobean in character. The hammerbeams stand on stone corbels carved by *Thomas Earp*. Tall chancel arch, three-bay arcade to the Lady Chapel on the (liturgical) N side and two-bay arcade to the transept. Lady Chapel remodelled by *Walter Tapper* in 1906 with a plain wagon-vault. **Font**, 1910, perhaps by Tapper. Alabaster cylinder, its **cover** a tall gilded openwork spire. **Pulpit**, *c.* 1870 by *George Gilbert Scott*. Stone, red and green marble colonnettes and saints in relief set beneath trefoiled arches. **Reredos**, 1887, by *Somers Clarke Jun.*, in red sandstone with gilding to the heads of canopied niches, with turret-like features at either end. When the church opened in 1858 it was praised by the local press for being 'truly protestant' with none of the 'colouring, gilding and emblazoning' that fuelled opposition to the Wagner churches, but this changed from 1870 with the insertion of a rich scheme of stained glass (*see* below). **Wall paintings** in the chancel, of 1890–1 by *Clayton & Bell*. Figures of saints in arcading fill the upper parts of the side walls, with the apostles and other saints in tiers below, painted in grisaille against dull red grounds. Elsewhere biblical scenes and repeating decorated patterns around the arches and piers. **Stained glass**. Main chancel window with radiant colours, 1870, by *Alexander Gibbs* to a design by *William Butterfield*. Also designed by Butterfield, the four-light window in the (liturgical) s transept, of the four Evangelists. In the Lady Chapel two windows made by *E. & C. O'Neill* and designed by *William Bainbridge Reynolds* who worked with Tapper elsewhere. In the nave more windows by Gibbs and two by *Clayton & Bell*.

Back to **Western Road**, and after the opulent Late Victorian display of The Juggler (former **Western Hotel**) on the corner of Brunswick Street East we return to the Brunswick Town of the 1820s with No. 20, which has giant Ionic pilasters and a first-floor bow window with a three-part sash. This is on the corner of **Upper Market Street**, where the view downhill, between bow fronts (w) and canted bays (E), is terminated by the principal front of the **Old Market Arts Centre**, incorporating *Busby*'s Market of 1826–8. The market closed within ten years and was converted for Dupont's Riding Academy, *c.* 1875 when Busby's building was enveloped by extensions on all but the E side. This has a plain three-bay arcade with lunette windows and there were similar eight-bay arcades to the long walls. The upper storey, together with further s extensions, are of 1997–9 and part of the conversion by *The Conservation Practice* to the current use. Inside, the concert hall preserves the main space (100 ft by 40 ft) of Busby's covered market. The roof has been raised whilst retaining in position the original trusses. An **archway** erected in 1877 for the riding academy leads E into **Waterloo Street**. This has a nice mix of bow fronts, bow and bay windows, and decorative balconies, all built in the 1820s and 1830s. Nos. 54–9, on the E side, have giant Corinthian pilasters, above which the parapet rises into funny little gablets or pinched-up pediments, a quirky, childlike motif. From here it is a short walk back to the seafront where the walk began.

The Seafront: East of the Pier to Portland Place

Brighton's East Cliff was developed before the West Cliff because it had better access to the Steine. The open fields of Little Laine and East Laine were built over from the last quarter of the C18: Marchant's map (1808), shows continuous development along the coast road (now Marine Parade) as far E as Lower Rock Gardens (Royal Crescent was an almost isolated development further E until the 1820s) and inland to Edward Street and Carlton Hill. St James's Street and Edward Street, the two main streets in the area, follow the line of field trackways. By 1814 the rentals of terraced houses on the seafront were some of the highest in Brighton, though the housing inland N of Edward Street was always of an inferior quality, and this was the subject of the largest C20 slum clearances in the city. The typical pattern of late C18 development, dictated by the breakdown and ownership of the open fields (numerous individuals owning narrow strips or paul pieces), was of narrow streets at right angles to the seafront with rows of terraces on both sides and completed by a pair of houses facing the sea, where property values were highest. Fragmented ownership militated against the building of grand squares or terraces, and as a result, much of the East Cliff development is incoherent and lacking in continuity, except furthest E at Kemp Town (*see* Walk 6).

From 1823 the Chain Pier (*see* p. 18) provided a new attraction on the seafront E of the Steine and in 1830–3 the massive **seawall** 23 ft thick at its base and up to 60 ft high was engineered against the cliff by *Thomas Cooper*, using an early form of concrete, made with slaked lime mixed with cold water and cast into blocks using wooden frames. The wall permitted the widening of Marine Parade and from 1838 was extended E to the seawall at Kemp Town. As along the western seafront, the present appearance, so redolent of Brighton, was set down by late C19 improvements beginning with cast-iron **railings** with dolphin motifs (dated 1880) and **shelters** of 1883 by *John Brunnell & Co.* of Westminster. They are to the same design as those along the Western Esplanade; so too the **lamps** installed in 1893.

A tour should commence at **The Aquarium**, between Madeira Drive and Marine Parade. This was opened in 1872, the idea of its designer *Eugenius Birch* (*see* Topic Box, p. 21), and originally set on the approach road to the Chain Pier (1823). The Aquarium was among the growing number of attractions for Victorian tourists [70] along the seafront

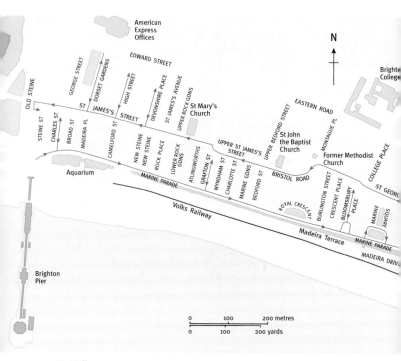

American
Express
Offices

N

Brighton
College

69. Walk 5

before construction of the Palace Pier (1899; *see* p. 59). Its sea frontage, extended in 1876, is nearly 900 ft long. The original entrance was at the E end, in line with the Chain Pier, but Birch moved this to the W end in 1874, adding an attention-seeking clock tower, gateway and lodges; at the same time he created a series of roof terraces for a roller-skating rink, terraced garden, smoking room, café and music conservatory. Sadly none of this High Victorian work survives outside, following complete rebuilding in 1927–9 by *David Edwards*, Borough Surveyor, in a Louis XVI style, faced in white artificial stone. The main entrance is set in a sunken plaza with a flight of steps descending from the two square kiosks with eye-catching tent roofs. Balustraded parapets enclose the roof terraces which Edwards laid out as gardens but which are now filled by restaurants and (at the E end) a nightclub in a rotunda, 1998 by *The Colman Partnership*; a mix of stripped-down Regency with more contemporary forms. The 1870s work remains inside, based around an aisled hall twenty-one bays long with double aisles in the centre part, all with quadripartite rib-vaults on polished granite columns with capitals carved by *Henry Pinker* with naturalistic forms and representations of sea life.

Madeira Drive (the name dates from *c.* 1918) originated in 1823 as the short esplanade and carriageway along the base of the cliff to the Chain Pier. In 1872, as part of the development of the Aquarium, it was extended eastwards (as Madeira Road) to a ramp at Duke's Mound where

70. View of the interior of the Brighton Aquarium from the *Illustrated London News* following the opening in 1872

it rejoins Marine Parade. It was further extended to Black Rock in 1895 and resurfaced in 1905 for the annual motor car speed trials inaugurated in that year. Its backdrop for almost half a mile is the superb cast-iron **Madeira Terrace** by *Philip Lockwood*, Borough Surveyor; built in stages *c.* 1889–97.* Set out against the early C19 seawall, it is of two storeys with a wide, open promenade above a continuous arcade (Madeira Walk) whose filigree pierced spandrels provide a sun screen for promenaders. The keystones alternately depict Venus and Neptune. Towards the mid point is a large **shelter** (now café) incorporating a **lift** to Marine Parade, its brick shaft with pagoda-like roofs.

Also running the length of Madeira Drive is **Volk's Railway**, an enduring monument to the inventor and engineer, *Magnus Volk* (*see* Topic Box, p. 131). Opened in 1883, it was the first public electric railway in Britain and at first ran for just 300 yds between the Aquarium and the Chain Pier, but with extensions in 1884 and 1901 Black Rock was reached, a distance of 1.1 miles. There are three stations, but their simple buildings were demolished during the Second World War. The line reopened in 1948 with a tram shelter as The Aquarium station and a rebuilt Black Rock station.

Now for **Marine Parade** (also from 1908 known as King's Cliff, in honour of Edward VII who often stayed in Kemp Town), where building was commenced in the fourth quarter of the C18. Its start is unpromising and it is the side streets that we must look to for earlier buildings, e.g. Nos. 9–12 and 20–3 **Charles Street** with full-height bows

---

*A competition for 'improvements to Madeira Road' was won in 1883 by John Johnson of London, but nothing seems to have come of his designs.

and mathematical tiles. But in Marine Parade the themes are familiar, bows and balconies chiefly. Only occasionally a feature strikes one as out of the ordinary. One such is Nos. 13–14 at the corner with Broad Street, which has a semicircular bow to the seafront and a long side elevation with advanced pedimented ends with Venetian windows on one side and the lower windows on both sides encompassed within a semicircular headed recess. Characteristic is No. 18, with a balcony under a tent roof with pierced timber valance. Further E, the **Van Alen Building**, flats of 1999 by *PRC Fewster* (project architect *Peter Rutter*), hark back to the streamlined traditions of the 1930s seaside with three attached blocks stepping out towards the street, with curved bays, porthole windows, fins between the balconies and glazing in strips.

There is more of consistent interest further on, beginning with No. 37 Marine Parade, attributed to *Wilds & Busby*, *c*. 1825 – certainly characteristic is the narrow five-storey bow front with Tuscan pilasters rising through three storeys – and then **New Steine**, which is one of only two squares along the eastern seafront until Kemp Town is reached. Houses 'with black rustic tiles' (i.e. mathematical tiles) were standing by 1790 and by 1795 the square was railed off. If the late C18 houses were of a uniform appearance this was not maintained in the addition of stucco fronts *c*. 1825, and there is now little to unify them except the repeated motif of paired entrances under segmental pediments with sunburst decoration. Enclosing the garden, robust iron railings reinstated in 1996–7 to the original Victorian design.

Facing the sea E of the square, Nos. 41–4 have Tuscan pilasters linked by blank round arches and paired porches with three fluted Doric columns with bold entasis, the fluting only carried part-way down. Nice decorative ironwork to the first-floor balconies, though this draws attention to the changes in level. No. 48 (much rebuilt in the 1970s) has a Tuscan colonnade with later infill trellis with pierced spandrels. Giant pilasters and a full entablature with metope frieze. The façade to **Lower Rock Gardens** has an enclosed six-bay castellated corridor decorated with a mixture of classical and Gothick features which might be reused from Rock House which stood on the site from 1788; at the time in an isolated position. The street was developed soon after, originally as a narrow cul-de-sac garden square known as Rock Buildings. Nothing now looks earlier than *c*. 1825; the garden was removed in 1879 and the land regraded to join St James's Street.

Marine Parade E of Lower Rock Gardens has the usual stucco terraces, varied and unexceptional. No. 53 is of interest for the survival inside at the rear of a picture gallery, one of six built *c*. 1865 for Captain Henry Hill, a military tailor and pioneer collector of the works of Degas, to house his collection of contemporary French and British paintings. The surviving room is large and rectangular, approximately 19 ft by 22 ft, with curved ends, coved ceiling and a two-tier dome. Nos. 54–5 are taller, bow-fronted on the left, with giant fluted Corinthian pilasters and full entablature with two further storeys above, also divided by

Magnus Volk (1851–1937)

Son of a German clockmaker, Magnus Volk was born in 1851 and lived most of his life in Brighton. Around 1879 he established the first telephone link in the town and the following year wired his own house for electric light, taking advantage of two recent inventions: Bell's telephone (1876) and Joseph Swan's incandescent electric light bulb (1878). In 1883 he fitted the Royal Pavilion with electric lights, illuminating the grounds the following year. The same year saw his best-known achievement, the first public electric railway in Britain. In 1887 Volk designed a hydraulically operated 'time ball' for the North Street Clock Tower (*see* p. 162) and an electric 'dog-cart', which led to an order from the sultan of Turkey, delivered by Volk to Constantinople, in person, in 1888. Serious financial difficulties led him to move with his family to London where he installed and managed the charging stations for an electric launch service on the Thames. Volk returned to Brighton in 1892 and the following year devised his second wacky project for the town, the Brighton & Rottingdean Seashore Electric Railway, which ran nearly three miles along the coast on 18-ft gauge rails that were submerged underwater most of the time. The passenger car, powered by an overhead cable, was supported on four 24-ft legs, earning it the nickname 'Daddy-Longlegs'. This bizarre creation, offering a 'Sea Voyage On Wheels!', had a short life, from 1896 to 1901, but carried amongst other notable passengers the future King Edward VII. Volk also took part in the Emancipation Day car rally (the first London to Brighton run) in 1896. Though he lived until 1937 Volk never again enjoyed such fame as an inventor after the closing decades of the C19.

71. Volk's railway advertisement *c.* 1896–1900

pilasters. The unusual front extension on the right was probably a shop, added, one imagines, not long after No. 55 was built (attributed to *Busby*). It has to the street a three-bay arcade with Composite pilasters. This is repeated with differing details at No. 56 on the other side of Atlingworth Street. **Atlingworth Street**, developed in the 1820s, has a nice rhythm of bow windows.

Back to **Marine Parade** and some interesting variety, e.g. No. 58, remodelled in 1901 in yellow brick with polished granite Composite columns to the upper-level bay window. To the rear of the main building an impressive galleried staircase hall lit by a lantern with Italianate round-arched windows. Nos. 62–3 have pretty balconies and a return elevation to Grafton Street in a self-consciously mid-C19 Italianate, with pedimented windows and a bowed oriel rising from a corbel of a bearded Neptune. No. 12 **Grafton Street**, beyond, has ogee-headed ground-floor windows recalling the Mughal-inspired detail of the Royal Pavilion. No. 69 Marine Parade has its entrance in Charlotte Street with a bold round arch with a Doric prostyle porch and Greek key frieze. Breaking with the stuccoed tradition is **The Lanes Hotel**, dated 1844 but thoroughly transformed in a Norman Shaw style by *Col. Robert Edis*, from 1880. Knapped flint and red brick with tile-hung gables – *The Building News* described it as the only building 'in which coloured materials are used along the whole three miles of sea frontage at Brighton'. Informal and picturesque to Charlotte Street where the staircase tower has a tile-hung gabled roof and a projecting bay on the left oversailing a canted bay. Nice balcony on the seaward face but the centre part spoilt by a late C20 balcony insouciantly grafted onto the front. The interior has panelling, decorative plasterwork, leaded lights with coloured glass and a pretty fireplace, set in a recess, with Aesthetic Movement tiles and mirrored overmantel.

Between here and Royal Crescent a varied sequence of stuccoed houses, reflecting incremental development by a multiplicity of owners, together with later modifications. Nos. 73–4 return to the bow-front theme but No. 74 steps forward assertively and is altogether larger. Gothic railings at No. 75, Victorian Italianate at Nos. 76 and 76a and delicate Victorian cast-iron colonnade across the full width of No. 77 with filigree panels, while No. 78 has a timber Regency tent-roofed veranda. Only No. 79 is obviously different, its squatter proportions and gambrel roof suggesting C18 origins. Then a little more order is imposed. Nos. 80–3, a somewhat ungainly terrace of four bow-fronted houses, their façades divided by a strong horizontal band at second-floor level, rusticated below and with pilasters linked by round arches above. Two porches on sturdy Greek Doric columns. Nos. 84–9 appear mid C19, with full-height canted bays, with segmental pediments to the second-floor windows and a canopied balcony across the front.

Now we have reached **Royal Crescent**. Built 1799–1802 for J.B. Otto, a West Indian plantation owner, as lodging houses to be let during the season. It stood alone when built. This is the earliest unified architectural

72. View of Royal Crescent built for J.B. Otto, 1799–1802

composition among Brighton's terraces, a crescent because of Bath and Buxton, and the earliest demonstration of a sympathy with the sea. Otto may have built grandly in order to attract visitors to what was then a peripheral location. It is set well back from Marine Parade, the end houses parallel to the street but those in between arranged in a shallow curve; all with timber-framed fronts faced in glazed black mathematical tiles. They have four storeys, canted bays (replacements of the original bows), first-floor verandas and doorways mostly with open pediments. In 1802 Otto erected a *Coade* stone statue of the Prince of Wales by *John Rossi*, probably to curry favour, but the statue deteriorated in the exposed position, the prince was evidently angered, and it was removed in 1819. To its E, set forward and alone, is **Royal Crescent Hotel**, opened in 1857. Five storeys with a busy front of closely set full-height bay windows, the outer ones canted, the middle with curved sides, and three storeys of balconies applied across the front. Nos. 102–4, once more well set back, make quite a grand composition of three bow fronts with fluted Ionic pilasters squeezed between and heavy moulded entablature and cornice, all repeated on the side elevation; the style very suggestive of *Wilds & Busby*. Spoilt by the later two-storey cast-iron porch and balconies. Comically diminutive neighbours at Nos. 105–6, probably indicative of earlier origin.

Two more formal groups on the seafront follow. First **Bloomsbury Place**, developed after 1810 with stucco terraces, originally with two-storey bows, but still with consistent runs of balconies along both sides. On Marine Parade, pairs of bow-fronted houses face a semicircular garden enclosed by railings with distinctive openwork piers of Chinese character (reinstated in 1996). Then **Marine Square**, built in 1823–5 for Thomas Attree, the N side raised above the flanking terraces, with the outer houses set slightly forward. Bows only on the side ranges, to afford views of the sea. Continuous first-floor balconies throughout, though with much variety. One house even has balconies on three floors.

The next group is more consistent and belongs with the development of **Portland Place**. This was begun in 1824 as the first speculation for new building between Royal Crescent and Kemp Town, on land owned by Major Villeroy Russell. His architect was *Charles Busby*, who had just gone into partnership with *A.H. Wilds*. Work began with Russell's house at the top of Portland Place, with views both to the sea and E to Busby's St George's Church (*see* p. 145). The house had a dome, pedimented portico and lavish accommodation but was destroyed by fire during construction. A plainer building was erected in 1847 but what we see today is a dull stucco façade, retained when the site was redeveloped in 1971–3 for the St Dunstan's Institute. Lining Portland Place are terraces articulated, as on Marine Parade, with giant Corinthian pilasters in three-bay 'pavilions' with attics and individual splayed balconies to each first-floor window. Plainer sections between with continuous first-floor balconies. The return elevation to St George's Road reproduces the design of giant pilasters but in polychrome glazed bricks, an amusing solecism.

The walk may conclude here, with buses back to The Aquarium, or return to Old Steine along **St George's Road** which runs parallel to Marine Parade. Unsurprisingly the character is quite different from the seafront; here was the service accommodation and the lesser-quality housing, e.g. Nos. 29–33 on the right, modest stucco terraces of the 1830s, two storeys over a basement, with flights of steps up to round-arched entrances. But the principal buildings of interest are the later C19 and

C20 ones, e.g. the **John Nixon Memorial Hall** at the corner with Crescent Place. Built 1912 in Free Style with an inventive skyline, chequerboard gable and broad shallow-arched windows. This was the hall to St Ann's Church in Burlington Street (1862–3, by *Benjamin Ferrey*, dem. 1986). The Hall was converted to flats in 2002 by *Deacon & Richardson*, who also designed the three town houses in Crescent Place behind, an essay in simple unadorned forms and stepped planes, the middle floor projecting as a floating white-rendered square

73. John Nixon Memorial Hall, St George's Road, 1912

panel, complementing the modest *c.* 1825 paired villas opposite. Opposite the hall, in **College Road**, the former **Kemp Town Post Office**, built in 1887 but extraordinarily old-fashioned, with a Tuscan pilastered arcade and the first-floor windows with shell fans in their tympana. w at the corner with Montagu Place, No. 2 has a glazed terracotta shopfront with floral and fretwork panels dating from a remodelling in 1908 for the Sussex Dairy Co. by *M. Mellor*, surveyor. On the opposite corner is a former **Methodist Church** (Brighton College annexe), 1873 by *Thomas Lainson*. High Victorian polychromy in a debased Italian Romanesque style. Gabled front with lean-to arcaded porch flanked by a stair-turret on the left and a tower on the right with large round-arched windows. The side elevation has paired windows under relieving arches and with a continuous stone sill with a frieze of stylized flowers.

Here the street opens into an informal square and turns left and then right, and for this short stretch becomes **Bristol Road**. On the N side, as far as Upper Bedford Street, is an important group associated with the church of **St John the Baptist** (R.C.) which was erected here in 1832–5. Built by *William Hallett*, who was probably also the designer, and based on John Newman's St Mary Moorfields, London (1820). Three-bay temple front with pediment and giant Corinthian columns *in antis*. Hallett's church was a plain rectangle with giant Corinthian pilasters carried around the sides with the plain square-headed windows set high up. N extension for sanctuary and side chapels, in classical style, by *G.R. Blount*, 1875. *S.J. Nicholl* exhibited plans for a radical remodelling at the Royal Academy in 1887 but nothing came of this. Inside, Blount's sanctuary is the width of the nave and divided from it by three round arches, the centre arch wider and taller. The side arches lead into chapels with two-bay arcades to the sanctuary. Corinthian capitals. The sanctuary extends one bay further than the side chapels but all are barrel-vaulted with panelled arches. The sumptuous **wall paintings** and decorative scheme are of 1890 by *Nathaniel Westlake*. Christ in Glory, above the high altar; the panels in the nave depicting the life of St John the Baptist, a memorial to Father Johnston, date from 1917–21. **Pulpit**. 1898, by *F.A. Walters*. At the (liturgical) w end Hallett's **gallery** supported on two cast-iron columns with capitals of acanthus and palm leaf. Delicate wooden screen above with thin turned colonnettes on high socles supporting a nine-bay arcade of cusped round arches: 1898 by Walters. Filigree iron railings. The **screens** between the sanctuary and side chapels probably also by Walters. In the baptistery, added in 1889, with a pretty circular **font**, the former altarpiece **sculpture** of the Baptism of Christ; life-sized figures in low relief, by *John Carew*, 1835 [74]. Lit from above, it is remarkably good; in the Baroque tradition, not at all Neoclassical. Also by Carew, **monuments** to Maria Fitzherbert d.1837 (E wall), a large kneeling figure by a draped table with a Bible, and to the Rev. Edward Cullin d.1850 (opposite), with a profile at the top and palm fronds left and right below, and a big cherub's head at the foot (again Baroque, not classical). Below the windows nearest the gallery the embrasures are treated as niches with three-bay screens and figures of saints (again by Walters). **Stained glass**. 1888, by *Lavers & Westlake*.

Adjoining the church is **Bedford Lodge**, a handsome yellow brick villa of *c.* 1830, with a bow on the left and a porch with Tuscan pilasters with a frieze of wreaths. This was taken over as **St Joseph's Convent of Mercy** (R.C.) in 1858 and the surrounding site much developed for them in 1866–74 by *C.A. Buckler*. To the right of Bedford Lodge is a slightly projecting range built *c.* 1872 and set across the gable of the convent's **chapel**. This is the only survivor of Buckler's buildings which included the main convent buildings, cell block and refectory around an internal courtyard. The chapel is of five bays, nave and chancel in one

74. St John the Baptist Roman Catholic Church, Baptism of Christ, 1835 by John Carew

and no aisles. Dec style, two-light windows except for the N (liturgical E) window which is of three lights with spherical triangles in the tracery. Good **furniture** in pale wood, 2004, by *Peter Pritchett* of *J.D. Clarke & Partners*. **Stained glass** in all windows, *c.* 1892 by *Hardman's*. Strong colours. Buckler's other buildings were demolished in 1991–2 as part of a redevelopment for St Joseph's Rest Home by *J.D. Clarke & Partners*. An Early Victorian house to the E of the chapel was retained and extended in matching style. No. 13, opposite, is a plain stock brick house of *c.* 1830 set back behind a garden. Acquired by the convent in 1905; its castellated bay window may be of this time. Opposite the church a particularly urban four-storey terrace with good Late Victorian shopfronts. In **Marine Terrace Mews**, stucco, aggrandized, and **St John's Mews**, cobble-fronted, former stables and grooms' accommodation which serviced the houses on Marine Parade.

Bristol Road becomes Upper St James's Street after the junction with Bedford Street and **Upper Bedford Street**. In the latter, on the right the former **Pelham Institute**, a working men's club built in 1876–7 by *Thomas Lainson* for Archdeacon Hannah. Purple brick with red brick and terracotta dressings. High Victorian Gothic, a style favoured for Anglican slum missions. The ground floor contained reading room, kitchen, non-alcoholic bar, games and smoking rooms; lecture and mission rooms above, and top-floor bedrooms let by the night or the week.

There is little of interest in **Upper St James's Street** except on the s side and the streets off towards the sea: much of it minor variations on the buildings already seen, e.g. the **Kemp Town Brewery** with its prominent gambrel roof. **Marine Gardens** also has cottages, some cobble-fronted, others also with gambrel roofs. This street was completely built up by 1822. Set back on the w side, more cottages with gambrel roofs, that to Upper St James's Street looking entirely early C20, pebbledash with a pretty shaped gable. In **Wyndham Street**, Nos. 1a and 2 were built in 1866 as stables for Captain Hill (*see* p. 130) but converted to a fire station *c.* 1900 by *John Johnson*. Polychromed High Victorian Gothic, originally with brick finials and pinnacles.

Further w, **St Mary's Church** [75] comes into view at the corner with Upper Rock Gardens. Built 1877–9, the only church in England by *William Emerson*, a pupil of Burges, whose architectural career was mostly pursued in India (at the same time as his work in Brighton he was building the cathedral at Allahabad). It replaced *A.H. Wilds's* chapel of 1826–7, which collapsed during repairs by Emerson in 1876. St Mary's is most interesting and unexpected, a blend of E.E. and French C13 Gothic. But its red brick exterior with sandstone dressings is difficult to appreciate in its begrimed state and scruffy environs. On the left, a gabled porch of sturdy dimensions, capped off by an ugly gabled roof. It is the base of an intended tower and the composition suffers for the lack of it. The paired entrances are set beneath a hollow-moulded arch springing from groups of shafts with waterholding bases, shaft-rings and crocket capitals. Within the arch a rather incongruous row of

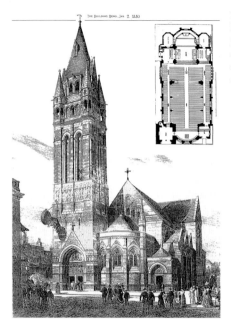

75. St Mary's Church
by William Emerson,
perspective from the
Building News of 1880
showing the architect's
original intention

Burgesian canopies and a septfoil window within a circle. The arch is
flanked by blind arcades and the gable above is decorated with diaper-
moulded terracotta tiles. In the centre of the front the curved projection
of the baptistery: three bays with two-light windows, the bays divided
by buttresses which rise to paired colonnettes supporting a corbel table
with a frieze of stiff-leaf and a plain parapet. To the right a polygonal
stair projection and a secondary porch (now used as the entrance).

The body of the church, set back behind, has a three-bay aisled nave,
shallow transepts and apsidal chancel flanked by apsidal vestries. Nave and
transept roofs are of the same height and, in the absence of a clerestory,
give a massiveness of scale. Aisles with gables and two-light windows
with uncusped main lights and a tracery sexfoil. Similar three-light windows to the transepts. Stepped lancets high up in the (liturgical) w gable.

Inside, the floor is set at a lower level, contributing to the splendour
of the interior. Three-bay arcades on conjoined double shafts (a French-
derived feature) with crocket capitals. Transverse arches from the aisles.
The arch to the crossing is similarly treated. The crossing narrows to the
chancel, a clever device which gives the latter, which is raised up, the
appearance of greater depth. The chancel has arches of similar design to
the nave on either side and the apsed sanctuary has an exceedingly tall
arcade around a narrow ambulatory. Rib-vaults to the crossing, chancel
and sanctuary and brick-faced concrete barrel vaults to the transepts. The
nave has a hammerbeam roof, an English feature. The walls throughout
are of banded brick, the floors mosaic in the chancel. Excellent chancel
fittings, including choir and clergy stalls and sedilia. Octagonal **font**,

the plinth carrying a circular granite drum and carved alabaster bowl. The granite shaft comes from the Swiss mountain where the Rev. Julius Elliott died in whose memory the font was given. **Pulpit** *c*. 1892. Caen stone with angle shafts and carved panels. **Altar** of 1893, crisply carved with a central relief panel. Lady Chapel altar, of early English pattern with riddle posts, dorsal and side hangings. **Reredos** given in 1893. **Stained glass** of consistently high quality. In the apse, 1886, by *A.O. Hemming* (a pupil of Clayton & Bell), also two windows in the (liturgical) s chapel, one in the s transept and two in the baptistery. The centre window in the baptistery, 1884, by *Gualbert Saunders*, a favourite of Burges. Luscious coloured rose window, 1878, by *G.A. Luxford*. The other s chapel window, 1915, by *James Powell & Sons*, who also did the southernmost window in the N aisle, 1897. To its right, 1880, by *Burlison & Grylls*, and to the right again, 1906, by *Kempe*. Finally, in the N transept, an Ascension by *Mayer & Co.* in the centre light, flanked by glass of 1989 by *Ann Goodman* in the upper register and of 1942 by *Kenneth Barton* in the lower register.

The w side of **Upper Rock Gardens** was developed in the early C19. The land on the E side belonged to Lord Egremont's town house and was not developed until 1879. Nos. 39–49 are Italianate but going Gothic, with ring shafts applied to entrances and windows.

In **St James's Street** what interests are the occasional lapses into the vernacular that one finds here and in the side streets built up in the late C18: e.g. Nos. 75–6 and No. 78 with central chimneystacks and gambrel roofs; the **No Name Bar** on the corner of Wentworth Street, very modest, with first-floor bow and mathematical tiles; and the entirely unselfconscious late C18 cottages in Camelford Street.

Off the N side of St James's Street, first in **Devonshire Place**, Nos. 38–9 on the right (now flats) were rebuilt in 1836 by *David Mocatta* as Brighton's synagogue. Then, the oddly named **High Street** is dominated by **St James's House**, a monstrous sixteen-storey tower block of 1966 by *K.W. Bland* of *Wates*, with *D.J. Howe* of the Borough Architect's Department and *Arup (Ove) & Partners* consulting engineers: a linked pair using Wates's industrial building system. It dwarfs **Windsor Lodge** (former Primitive Methodist Chapel) of 1886, by *W.S. Parnacott*. Papery thin front, still Gothic, with large windows. Redeveloped as flats behind the retained façade in 1987. On the left, Nos. 23–30, early Brighton Council housing, dated 1910, by *Clayton & Black*, a small but highly attractive row stepping uphill; Arts and Crafts style, with stone-mullioned windows, roughcast and half-timbered gables.

Back in **St James's Street**, Nos. 95–9 on the left is a more urban early C19 four-storey terrace with bow windows, those at Nos. 97–8 elaborated with fluted Ionic columns insubstantially supporting moulded round arches. No. 102 has a C19 shopfront with a pair of Ionic columns support-ing an entablature which in turn supports a decorative first-floor balcony.

Further w, in **Dorset Gardens**, a **Methodist church** of 2003 by *Saville Jones Architects*, on the site of the town's first Methodist church (built

1808, replaced 1884 by *C.O. Ellinson*). Terracotta cladding with bold forms, a semicircular flint-clad chapel projects at ground level, whilst the large projecting overhang above the street gives sidelight into the main worship space on the second floor. The lead-clad sail on the roof throws light onto the main staircase which rises dramatically in one straight flight to the worship area. Here, the podium furniture in oak using trapezium forms is by *Paul Fuller*. **Stained glass** by *Catrin Jones*, the glazed cross at the top of the main stair and the five etched glass panels to the worship space. The main window on the stair designed by *Shirley Veater* and made by *Opus Stained Glass*. Forming part of the same development are **flats** of 2002 by *Deacon & Richardson*. Closing the view at the end of Dorset Gardens is **Amex House** [17] of 1977 by *Gollins, Melvin, Ward & Partners*, its huge bulk softened by the use of chamfered corners and emphatic horizontality of alternate bands of white GRP and blue-tinted glass.

Return to **St James's Street**, where Nos. 107–111a, on the left, is the first of a more unified terrace group, with shallow first-floor bow windows and much of the original continuous balcony fronts remaining. On the street's N side, **Boots** has a symmetrical five-bay façade dated 1914, the centre with an open pediment and jalousie shutters giving a Mediterranean feel. Small but distinctive is No. 9 with its upper windows set back behind a giant Ionic screen. Its neighbour, **Somerfield**, 1985, makes a laudably discreet entry to the street with a three-storey façade in stripped Regency style. Downhill, Nos. 1–4 is another terrace with the same design of shallow first-floor bow windows as Nos. 107–111a, but here treated more consciously as a single composition with pilasters and the central section rising to an attic with balustrade to each side. A twitten between Nos. 4 and 5 leads into **St James's Place**, a grandly scaled w-facing early C19 terrace, unexpectedly tucked out of sight. Mostly tarred cobble fronts with painted brick dressings. Several houses have broadly similar fronts with central round-arched entrances with attached Tuscan columns supporting an entablature lintel with modillion cornice and decorative fanlight. No. 3 has a sturdy flat-arched entrance with Tuscan pilasters, frieze decorated with laurel wreaths and a studded door.

76. **No. 127 St James's Street of 1899 by Clayton Botham, detail of hopperhead**

The s side of **St James's Street** concludes with a good late C19 commercial group including No. 127 (Nobles Amusements), 1899, by *Clayton Botham*, in Flemish Renaissance style, red brick with stone dressings. Pedimented shaped gables and a florid display of windows above a first-floor balustrade, quite different to each floor but building up nicely. Barley-sugar down-pipe topped by a dragon [76]. It forms part of the larger **Steine Mansions** which terminates the view from Old Steine down **Steine Street**, a narrow lane on the left, with a tripartite arched doorway, the hood on paired brackets and a corbelled-out balcony beneath a pedimented gable. For Old Steine *see* p. 94.

Outlier

Brighton College, Eastern Road. Founded in 1845 by a group of prominent residents in order to provide 'a thoroughly liberal and practical education in accordance with the principles of the established church'. The original buildings are of 1848–9 by *George Gilbert Scott*, set back from the road, of galleted flint with Caen stone dressings, symmetrical and pretty, although Pevsner thought them 'joyless'. Four bays either side of a two-storey gabled porch with oriel window. Three-light windows below, two-light above, extending into gables. Scott's original plans provided for three ranges around a courtyard open to the s, which followed later to his designs and consistently done in flint and stone. To the E the **headmaster's house** and **dormitory** project, 1854, three-storey, a gable to the left with a prominent two-storey oriel carried on a stout pier connected to a buttress. To the w the **chapel**, 1859, originally an aisleless nave and chancel but greatly enlarged E to form a T-plan in 1922–3 by *T. G. Jackson*, an alumnus of the college and pupil of Scott. His work is very sensitively done, though he takes care to make clear distinction. Three three-light windows to the s with Geometrical tracery. The w wall has a pair of two-light windows over the modest entrance, with a circular window in the gable with encircled quatrefoils. Jackson's part has aisles, lean-to on the N and gabled to the s. The s windows follow Scott's, the E window is of an impressive five lights, with angle shafts externally. In the tracery a circle encloses four encircled cinquefoils. Inside, three-bay arcades with moulded arches on cylindrical columns. The main roof is continuous through the length of the chapel, with exposed rafters and the trusses on corbels. **Stained glass**. All but one window by *Morris & Co.*, 1922–7. Variable quality, with some of the figures rather wooden. Among the better glass is the centre window, Faith, Hope and Charity, in the s aisle, and the Nativity window, nave s easternmost. Much very attractive foliage and angels in the tracery. In the N aisle a pretty sequence of windows executed in yellow-stain and pale grey only. By *Clayton & Bell* the N window in the w wall, (*c.* 1869).

Jackson also built the school's grand s range in 1884–8, again harmonizing with Scott's work in style and materials, although the outer elevations use red brick and terracotta and are more lavishly done, especially in the treatment of the entrance gateway [77]. To the ground

77. Brighton College, Eastern Road entrance, 1884–8 by T.G. Jackson

floor a carriage arch and a pedestrian arch to one side. Above, a rich display of crocketed ogees and pinnacles forming a screen of three broader units, the centre blind, the outer two-light windows, with narrow blind arches between. Crenellated panelled parapet above with trefoiled arches and quatrefoils. A tower was intended above this.

On the college's w boundary facing Sutherland Road, the **Burstow Gallery** and **Hall**, 1913–14, by *F. T. Cawthorn*, enlarged in 1926. Perp, with two-light windows. Red brick, but to the quad flint predominates, with red brick and flint chequerwork. On the corner of Eastern Road and Walpole Road, the **Preparatory School** occupies two former stucco Italianate villas of *c.* 1860. Between 1889 and 1971, when taken over by the school, they were occupied by the Convent of the Blessed Sacrament, who added an extension to the N and the small brick chapel (now library), 1913–14, by *B. H. Dixon* of Brighton. Bellcote on the E gable, and polygonal chancel. Plain lancet windows and a rose w window.

Walk 6.

Kemp Town

Kemp Town is the first example of formal Georgian town planning applied to the seaside. Its building was a bold speculation, moving development away from the Steine, hitherto the focus of fashionable Brighton, to the town's E periphery where it was possible to offer a spaciousness of layout and provide large houses suitable for entertainment by the town's wealthiest visitors.

The planning of the estate and the design of the façades was set down for Thomas Kemp (*see* Topic Box, p. 145) by *Wilds & Busby*, but the evidence seems to suggest that here their role ceased, as the execution shows great variation from the published designs. The main elements

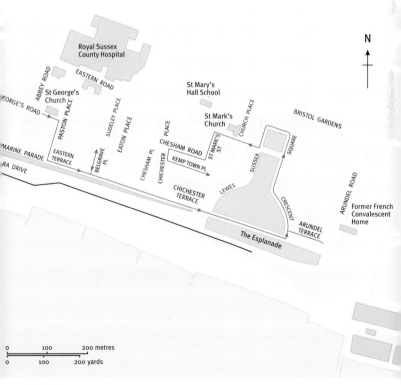

79. Aerial view of Kemp Town from c19 engraving

of the plan comprise Sussex Square at the northern end on the higher ground, opening out into Lewes Crescent (200 ft wider than the Royal Crescent at Bath) which slopes down to the coast road, where the arms of Chichester and Arundel terraces face the sea. Oddly, these terraces are of unequal length, although as they cannot be read together this matters little. The views published in 1824 show that the intention was for them to be identical, with further terraces to E and W (clearly extendable), and there were to be two more squares and further terraces behind. The concept of a crescent opening into a square was at that time unique.

Building work began in 1823, the first houses were occupied in 1826 and most of the façades were up by 1828. Completing the carcases and fitting out was left to the landowners, individual purchasers and builders, so took much longer. It was not until the mid 1840s that sufficient houses were complete and occupied to assure the future of the estate. In 1845, the Duke of Devonshire wrote that his house was still 'surrounded by the shells and carcases of the houses that compose Kemp Town'. Several contractors were employed on the construction, including *Thomas Cubitt*, the great London builder, who built about thirty-seven houses and also took up the option to purchase some of the carcases for completion and sale by himself. Generally Cubitt's houses have wide stone staircases to the top of the house and invariably a plaster relief plaque of classical scenes, often placed as an overdoor to the principal ground- or first-floor room. As early as 1828, in order to fund his development, Kemp was forced to convey land W of the estate to Cubitt in exchange for the execution of further building work. None of the terraces was developed consistently from one end to the other. Broadly, Arundel Terrace came first (complete by *c.* 1830), then the N part of Sussex Square (mid 1830s), Lewes Crescent was generally developed on the W side before the E, though again inconsistently and Chichester Terrace [81] was complete in 1855.

Although Kemp Town when begun was a mile from the town centre, with little building E of Royal Crescent (*see* p. 132), the gaps were rapidly

Thomas Read Kemp (1782–1844)

Thomas Read Kemp inherited his father's estate (including nearly half of the freehold land within Brighton parish around the Old Town, bringing with it the status of joint Lord of the Manor of Brighton) in 1817 with a fortune that enabled him to indulge his taste for property speculation. Kemp moved to Brighton in 1818 with his first wife, Frances Baring, building The Temple [92], a villa on the NW edge of the town (now Brighton & Hove High School, Walk 8). With his brother-in-law George Baring, in 1816 Kemp had formed an evangelical sect of which he was a minister and for which *A.H. Wilds* designed Trinity Chapel in Ship Street (Walk 1), but in 1823 Kemp returned to the Church of England, regaining his seat as M.P. for Lewes in 1826. As a politician, though never a party member, Kemp's sympathies lay with the Whigs. A town commissioner and freemason, Kemp became a prominent figure in Brighton society, involved in numerous ventures (e.g. Chairman of the Chain Pier Co. and a Director of the London, Brighton & South Coast Railway Co.) and a liberal patron of charity, especially the giving of land. He gave The Level to the town in 1822 and in 1826, gave the site for the Jewish burial ground off Ditchling Road and land for the Sussex County Hospital. In 1823 he began the development of Kemp Town, a bold and for Kemp unsuccessful speculation, on a forty-acre site a mile from the Old Town. Despite the poor financial return on Kemp Town he negotiated to purchase parts of the Wick Estate w of Brunswick Town (Walk 4) but unable to raise the capital sold his land-holding there to Isaac Goldsmid in 1830. Kemp's wife died in 1825 and he remarried in 1832. In 1837, under increasing financial pressure, the Kemps left England to live on the Continent, where Thomas died in Paris in 1844.

closed up by other speculations, including those on the land acquired by Cubitt in the 1820s. In 1903 Lord Rendel (an uncle of the architect Goodhart-Rendel) acquired several of the large Kemp Town houses and converted them to flats, starting a trend that continued throughout most of the C20: today only about half a dozen of the properties in Sussex Square and Lewes Crescent survive as single houses.

The walk covers the historic heart of Kemp Town, although the name now refers to a much wider area of the city's eastern suburbs. It should start at the junction of St George's Road and Eastern Road with **St George's Church**. This was the parish church of Kemp Town, originally erected as a chapel of ease to serve the emerging suburb, although placed at a surprising distance from its grand set piece. Perhaps this was to encourage investors to develop the land in between, much of which Kemp had acquired in order to extend Eastern Road eastward, gifting land for the hospital and selling the rest for development. Kemp obtained a private Act of Parliament in 1824 for erection of the church,

which opened in 1826; designed by *Charles Busby*. A typical Regency preaching box. Yellow brick, largely unrelieved, windows in two tiers and a bold, continuous entablature. A rectangular box with just a slight step-in to denote the chancel, (an addition of 1890 after the chapel became a parish church). Busby adopted his favoured Greek Revival style, with recessed giant Ionic columns *in antis* at both ends and a tall square bell-turret with paired Doric columns at the angles and an octagonal cupola. The columns at the entrance end, unusually, have winged cherubs at the top. The interior is late C19 in its details but still has the galleries around three sides that one would expect in a Regency chapel. The solid gallery front and classical columns were replaced in 1890 with thin cast-iron columns with acanthus capitals and open timber balcony fronts. Also of 1890 the boarded ceiling. The Victorian e end has three heavy round arches and a round-arched e window with bold tracery, all Romanesque in feel. The galleries were extended eastwards, over vestries. Curved upper **w gallery** with plain staircase, added in 1831 to cope with the growing popularity of the chapel. Over the w door, **royal arms** given by Queen Adelaide who worshipped here. **Reredos**. Pedimented, with paired pilasters. 1890 but similar in style to the narrower reredos that stood at the e end of the Regency chapel.

se of the church, on the opposite corner with **St George's Road** is the former **Sassoon Mausoleum** (now the Hanbury Club) [80], built in 1892 by and for Sir Albert Sassoon (d.1896), the Jewish merchant and philanthropist who lived at No. 1 Eastern Terrace. His remains, and those of his son, Sir Edward (d.1912) were removed in 1933. It is a curious little building, square with a circular tent lantern roof, originally covered in gold leaf, and Indian details including a trilobed arched entrance and blind arches of the same form and a lotus-leaf parapet. The Royal Pavilion is the inspiration, but here used for a serious purpose and by a man who could claim connection with India, which the Regent could not.

Now s down **Paston Place** to the seafront, and on the right-hand corner, the former **Bristol Hotel** of 1835 by the builder *William Hallett* (converted to flats and a pub in 1935), with the usual bow fronts facing the sea and a two-tier cast-iron balcony, probably late C19, wrapping around the corner. Hallett founded the Kemp Town Brewery which eventually occupied most of the land to the n.

Turning E along **Marine Parade** we immediately see **Eastern Terrace** (under construction in 1826), which belongs to the small series of developments that filled up the seafront between Royal Crescent and Kemp Town in the 1820s (*see* also Marine Square p. 133, and Portland Place, p. 134). It is grand, an L-shaped range set back behind a raised garden with balustraded parapet. The largest houses, Nos. 1 and 9, at each end of the terrace are double-fronted and curiously face w rather than to the sea. They are nearly identical compositions with tetrastyle porches in the centre and full-height bows in the outer bays, of which the right bow at No. 1 is continued as a great circular tower in the manner of Nash. It was converted into flats *c.* 1955. Its sea-facing neighbour also has a bowed front, with its porch placed asymmetrically on the curve, its columns distyle *in antis* but at the terrace's other end the façade (No. 8) surprisingly describes a concave curve in the angle with No. 9. In between are flat-fronted houses with deep porches, some with yellow brick upper floors. No. 8 has a surprisingly generous staircase hall with a cantilevered stone stair around an open well lit by an octagonal lantern. Good decorative balustrade with anthemion pattern. A full-height bow to the rear lights the main rooms which all face N as the house is built up against its neighbours. No. 9 also has a grand open-well stair with the same detailing and a first-floor lobby, the plaster ceiling treated with pendentives and an oval, with an arcade on fluted alabaster columns to the stair. The entrance hall has late C19 Rococo overdoors with inset painted roundels depicting mythological scenes. One ground-floor room has a compartmented ceiling and heavy late Victorian joinery, another has a marble chimneypiece with classical figures and cherubs. The staircases in Nos. 5 and 6 have oval skylights and the same balustrade detail, whilst the staircases at Nos. 2 and 3 have iron balustrades to a different pattern. The ground-floor front room of No. 2 has early C18-style bolection-moulded mahogany panelling installed *c.* 1905 by Messrs *Lenygon* of London. Similar painted panelling to the stairs.

The next group, Nos. 155–57 Marine Parade, post-date the Regency developments and are in Italianate taste, built *c.* 1850 as three houses but designed as a single composition of 2–3–2 bays, the centre three advanced. Much rustication, mostly round-arched windows and a heavy bracketed cornice. The elevation returns into **Belgrave Place**, running uphill, terminated at the top by a terrace dated 1846. This was the first development by *Thomas Cubitt* on the land conveyed to him by Kemp in the 1820s, its name a reminder of Cubitt's building of Belgrave Square, London. The street is uncomfortably narrow in relation to the height of its buildings, and the purity of the original concept is only preserved in the N terrace, which is of four storeys and seven bays, the centre three squeezed in beneath a pediment, and with first-floor windows under segmental and straight pediments. The sides are of mixed heights, however, and some with later embellishments, but held together visually by a continuous first-floor balcony; in the NW corner curiously supported on Ionic columns with entablatures.

81. Chichester Terrace, 1832–55

Cubitt also began the laying out of **Eaton Place** to the E at about this date, completed over a period of around ten years. Repeated bow fronts with first-floor balconies. Now, as we approach Kemp Town proper along the seafront, a degree of uniformity and consistency is established, at Percival Terrace and Clarendon Terrace, erected on land purchased from Cubitt by W. Percival Boxall, whose builders were the Cheesmans: *George Cheesman Jun.* may be the designer. Each terrace is set back and separated from Marine Parade by a wall with balustraded parapet, the grander of the two being **Percival Terrace** (1845–50), which comprises ten houses behind an undulating rhythm of bow fronts and first-floor balconies. The eastern end partially collapsed in 1987 and was reconstructed, with a mansard roof, 1997 by *Moren Greenhalgh*. **Clarendon Terrace** (1855–9) has a more subtle rhythm with an overall symmetry set by the flat-fronted entrance bays, the entrances with attached Tuscan columns and entablatures with triglyph and metope friezes. **Chesham Place**, running inland between the two terraces, was also begun in the 1850s, its W side at first continuing in Regency style but then with canted bays, as on the E side probably finished some twenty years later.

The change in architectural aspiration between these terraces and those at the western extremity of Kemp's town, that is the Kemp Town as originally proposed and realized, is very marked. **Chichester Terrace** heralds the beginning of *Wilds & Busby's* grand formal conception from the W but was the last to be completed, in 1855 – thirty years after work had begun – and represents the compromises of the later years. Chichester House at its w end was, however, ready for occupation as early as 1832 and for some years stood alone so its design is entirely independent of the rest of the terrace. Its stylistic features are ones that we associate with Busby, rather than Wilds. Asymmetrical elevations with a broad bow towards the sea and a much narrower one to Chichester Place, with giant Corinthian pilasters, singly and in pairs. Plain pilasters above with antefixae rising above the attic. All-over rustication to the ground floor and a porch on Greek Doric columns. Balustrade modified later to form a balcony. Individual balconettes to the first-floor windows.

In front, cast-iron **piers** mark the entrances from Marine Parade (reinstated in 1993). Also under way in the first phase of development was No. 14, at the e end of the terrace, which goes compositionally with the development of Lewes Crescent in having giant pilasters. Busby's intended composition was then abandoned and Cubitt, who developed the terrace, modified the design before building and strove instead to give emphasis by setting forward the fronts of No. 3, Nos. 6–8 (No. 7, the centre house, stepped forward again) and No. 11. On such a grand scale the visual effect is too subtle to succeed. Of the Greek Doric porches, all but one have later enclosed tent-roofed verandas. No. 14 Chichester Terrace must be considered as the beginning of the grand showpiece of **Lewes Crescent**. The 6th Duke of Devonshire purchased the shell of No. 14 in 1828 and in the following year bought that of No. 1 Lewes Crescent to which it is joined by a quadrant curve. Curiously, although inhabiting them as a single property the Duke had the houses completed (by *Cubitt*) separately, i.e. with their own staircases and fitted out in different styles. In 1853 he also bought No. 2 Lewes Crescent and linked it to No. 1 (the three houses have since been separated once more). No. 1 has the best interior: top-lit staircase hall with curved ends and an

82. **No. 16 Lewes Crescent, classical relief in the entrance hall**

elegant cantilevered staircase. On the top landing the dial of a weather-vane on the roof inserted by the Duke. The first-floor drawing room was decorated by *J.G. Crace* in 1848, a decorative scheme uncovered and restored 2002 by *Allyson McDermott*. Italian style, the ceiling with elaborate centre and rich border of arabesques and flowers enclosed within strong double-bordered frames. The walls have luscious foliage drops with birds and flowers separating bright red damask panels.

The houses on Lewes Crescent step up the slope, adding to the overall drama of the grand composition, and the balconies, which run continuously across the first-floor windows, step up in groups of three houses. The crescent's eastern arm is treated broadly the same, except that the houses have prominent porches, some paired, and many have enclosed balconies above and covered verandas, creating a cluttered effect. No. 16, on the upper corner, has a generously proportioned staircase hall set parallel to the façade at the rear of the building. Cantilevered stone stair with plain columnar iron balusters. The house was built by *Cubitt* and has three classical relief panels in the entrance hall [82].

Between the two sides of the crescent are **gardens** (known as the Kemp Town Enclosures), nearly fifteen acres in extent, which continue N into Sussex Square. They are informally laid out and planted, with perimeter paths. *Henry Phillips* (*see* Topic Box, p. 121) made plans in 1828, including shrubberies with untrimmed plantings to give an informal appearance and mounded to give privacy and weather protection for plants. Phillips was appointed and the work carried out.* At its s end the gardens drop down to a **tunnel** beneath Marine Parade, which emerges onto the undercliff **esplanades**. This major feat of engineering from Royal Crescent to Arundel Terrace was undertaken 1828–40 for the estate's proprietors by *H.E. Kendall Jun.*, who also designed the tunnel's seaward entrance, with arched openings and Tuscan pilasters, to incorporate two **cottages** either side: one for a gardener, the other for the estate constable. At a lower level a **reading room** with coupled Tuscan pilasters and a shelter known as the **Temple**, all built into the cliff face. The esplanades' immense battered retaining walls with a promenade between and a network of paths with shrub planting down the steep embankment is best appreciated from the base of the cliff.

Arundel Terrace forms the seafront arm of Wilds & Busby's scheme E of Lewes Crescent. By 1828 six of its thirteen houses were ready for occupation; the rest were finished by *c.* 1835. It is to Arundel Terrace that we must look to appreciate both Kemp's and Busby's vision, although even here the façades do not entirely follow the published design. The architecture is bolder, the only instance where Corinthian columns appear, and thus a proper building-up of effects. The ground floor is treated as a rusticated base from which the giant orders rise. The composition is of course symmetrical. The centre house projects forward of

---

*Although *Joseph Paxton*'s name is also associated with the gardens through his connections with the Duke of Devonshire, there is no evidence of any formal involvement.

any other and has a tetrastyle portico of Composite columns and a balustraded parapet. The adjoining houses set back have attached giant half-columns (unfortunately those of No. 8 obscured by ugly C20 glazed balconies), flanked by projecting fronts with attached half-columns and pilasters at the angles. These houses form the centre, those to either side with plain fronts and then end pavilions with attached giant half-columns. No. 1 was given a quasi Oriental-cum-Romanesque facelift later in the century, with Solomonic shafts to the porch, with a coved cornice above with cable moulding and nailhead, details carried across the front below the balcony. Billetted architraves to all windows. Another example in Brighton of the wish to perpetuate the exoticism of the Royal Pavilion.

Now back to the top of the Crescent to **Sussex Square**, which is cut in two by Eastern Road. Crescent and the Square are so large that one cannot read the façades together (a failing found contemporaneously in Belgrave Square, London). In Sussex Square thirteen of the thirty-four houses were taken by 1834, much of the w side completed before the E. The rhythm of every third house having giant pilasters continues around the square except on the N side. Here, to give appropriate emphasis to the centre, Nos. 24–7 project forward, fifteen bays of giant pilasters arranged 3–9–3, the nine centre bays advanced and the five centre bays rising to a parapet and shallow pediment. In Sussex Square it becomes quite evident that the covenants requiring frontages to be

83. Nos. 19–20 Sussex Square of 1829–31 by H.E. Kendall Jun., detail of staircase balustrade

covered in stucco were not enforced. The corner plots of Nos. 19–20 were purchased by the Marquess of Bristol in 1828 and a large L-plan house erected (1829–31) by *H.E. Kendall Jun*. The builder was *William Hallett*, who built several other houses on the estate. The front entrance is curiously modest but there is a Tuscan-columned porch entrance at the rear, and gardens originally extended to Church Place and Bristol Gardens. Fine cantilevered stone staircase, the cast-iron balustrade with alternate balusters like palm fronds [83]. Cantilevered stone back stair-case with plain iron balusters interjected with more elaborate balusters of angled squares. No. 22 was Kemp's own house, into which he moved in 1827, the second resident of Kemp Town. No. 32, in the NE corner, was bought in 1830 by Lawrence Peel, younger brother of the Prime Minister. The staircase hall at the rear is almost square with a semicircular s wall and a cantilevered stone stair lit by a circular lantern. Cast-iron balusters alternating on each tread between narrow paired balusters and more ornate single broad balusters with anthemion ornament. The ground-floor drawing room has an elaborate plaster ceiling and marble chimney-piece. To the rear, originally connected by a tunnel under Bristol Place, the extensive garden survives, enclosed by a high wall, on the corner of Bristol Gardens. It is the last remaining of several such gardens. In 1918 Lady Sackville bought Nos. 39 and 40 Sussex Square and commissioned *Lutyens* to make internal changes but all this work is thought to have fallen casualty to later flat conversion. No. 46 (SE side) is still a single house, built by *Cubitt* and completed in 1844. The first-floor drawing room has matching marble chimneypieces and the arch between the two parts of the room has been dressed up Pavilion-style.

That is the end of historic Kemp Town, but within its environs are a small number of other buildings associated with its development, in par-ticular the former **St Mark's Church**, on the corner of Eastern Road and Church Place, w of Sussex Square, which was paid for by the Marquess of Bristol. He had evangelical sympathies and wished to provide a church for the servant class and poor of the neighbourhood (the elite of Kemp Town worshipped at St George's). Begun in 1839, probably designed by *George Cheesman Jun.*, but completed in 1849 by *Thomas Shelbourne*, builder. Of this period the nave, with big tall lancets, and tower, with crude pinnacles and short spire, like a child's toy. The walls, surprisingly, are concrete cast in blocks to resemble ragstone. In 1891 a shallow chancel was added with vestries to the N and double transept to the s, all by *William Gilbee Scott*. The style is more Dec than E.E. but sits comfortably with the earlier work and uses Kentish ragstone. Inside, thin cast-iron clustered piers with three tiers of shaft-rings. Straight braces to the roof collars and purlins, the spandrels with pierced quatrefoils, mouchettes etc. Chancel arch on short polished granite shafts. Two-bay s transept arcade with a polished granite pier. The chancel is richly finished with Gothic arcading and marble facing; work of 1913. **Reredos** with sub-cusped Gothic arches. **Altar rail** incorporating an open-sided **pulpit**, in cast metal painted to look like stone. **Stained glass**. E window 1859, by

Lavers & Barraud. s transept windows by *Clayton & Bell*. Nave windows by *Heaton, Butler & Bayne*.

The church now forms part of **St Mary's Hall School**, which is set back in an elevated position to the NW. Built as a school for the daughters of clergymen in 1836 by *George Basevi*. Symmetrical, Tudor style, with gables and mullioned and transomed windows. Rendered and lined as ashlar. Polychrome-tiled entrance hall with open-well staircase under a rectangular lantern. The staircase was reconstructed in 1871; it is timber, partly cantilevered but with exposed timber supports. Cast-iron balusters and elongated timber newels. **Junior School** to the w, 2005–6, by *Howard, Fairbairn & Partners*.

Finally, in **Chichester Place** opposite, a 1950s block of flats, (**Chichester Close**), in brick, with full-height fluted pilasters without capitals or bases, emulating the bow fronts of Nos. 23–5 built in the late 1840s by *Thomas Cubitt*. On the right a Modernist intervention, a house of 1967 by *Fitzroy Robinson & Partners*. Down the street opposite is **Kemp Town Place**, a wide, enclosed mews entered through gatepiers. This is contemporary with the early development of Kemp Town in the 1820s but follows the more rustic treatment reserved for minor domestic buildings with cobble-fronted and tarred two-storey coachhouses with accommodation over. The walk ends here but there are a number of outliers both E and w of Kemp Town.

Outliers

Former **French Convalescent Home**, Marine Parade (now flats). Built for patients from the French Hospital in London, and paid for by the French Government. Gauche François Premier Revival by *Clayton & Black*, 1895–8, extended 1904 (E pavilion) and 1907 (w pavilion). Skyline of steep roofs and ironwork cresting, but made rather drab by later cement rendering.

Marine Gate, Marine Parade. 1937–9, by *Wimperis, Simpson & Guthrie*. A good example of the many large-scale flats built along the coast between the wars. Steel frame with white-painted brick walls, the balconies picked out in blue. Porthole bathroom windows give a vaguely nautical air.

Brighton Marina. First proposed in 1960 at the instigation of Henry Cohen, a local entrepreneur but not begun until 1971 following fierce local opposition. *Overton & Partners* produced the initial scheme with the *Louis de Soissons Partnership* as consultant architects. Harbour walls were complete by 1976, enclosing 71 acres of sheltered water, and the marina formally opened in 1979. The architecture to date is worthless, mostly executed under a revised plan of 1985 by *Module 2* architects with commercial buildings and housing aligned on a central spine road (**The Strand**) with over-prominent supermarket, multi-storey car park etc. at the w end, a 'village' square – the Octagon – and housing to the E, in an insipid Neo-Regency style, partly built onto jetties extending into an inner harbour. To this have been added in the 1990s three sheds with waveform roofs by *Design Collective* and the **Waterfront**, shops etc., 1999, by *Webb Gray*, brick and render, with a distinctive arched roof-line. In 2006 permission was given for a major development by *Wilkinson Eyre* at the harbour's sw corner. When built this will comprise eleven buildings, including a forty-storey tower and a foot-bridge linking the development to the outer harbour arm.

Royal Sussex County Hospital, Eastern Road. Founded as the Sussex County Hospital and General Sea-Bathing Infirmary on land given by Thomas Kemp, who also contributed £1,000. The first building, 1826–8 by *Charles Barry*, comprised just the centre part of the main frontage to Eastern Road: it provides a full-stop to the vista from the seafront along Paston Place. Three-bay pedimented centre flanked by very narrow bays and wider end bays slightly projecting. Expansion was needed almost at once with the frontage extended to the w (1839, by *William Hallett*) and the E (1841, by *Herbert Williams*), and further extended with projecting wings by Williams in 1852–3, all retaining overall symmetry. The **Jubilee Building** to its E is in the same spirit: 1887, by *Scott & Cawthorn* who were the hospital architects from 1872. Attached to the rear of Barry's building is the **chapel** by Hallett, 1856. This is Italianate, with channelled rustication and round-arched windows, now hemmed in by various extensions. Inside, the windows have eared and shouldered stone archi-traves and there is a panelled elliptical arch to the former chancel, part of an internal refurbishment of 1907 by *J.O. Scott*. Coved ceiling and tall lantern with ribbons and plaster swags beneath the windows. Walnut **panelling** in late C17 and early C18 style of 1907. Of this time also the w **stalls** and other joinery. **Stained glass**. The Good Samaritan, pictorial. Opposite the main building, *F.T. Cawthorn*'s **Outpatients' department** of 1896 with broad shaped gables.

Of the later extensions, the outstanding work is the **Children's Hospital**, 2004–7, by *Ben Zucchi* of *BDP*. This looms like a brooding mother hen over the front buildings and has a boat-like form, evocative of Noah's ark. The external skin is smooth, with irregular fenestration (many windows set at child height) and a set-back multicoloured top storey with balcony and overhanging roof. Also agreeable the **Audrey Emerton Building**, 2002–5, by *Robin Beynon* of *Chapman Taylor Architects*, with its bulk set back behind plain rendered walls punctuated by a Brighton motif of shallow bows. E again, **Sussex Eye Hospital**, of 1935 by *J.L. Denman*, blocky Neo-Georgian. Splayed U-plan. Symmetrical front of multicoloured brick and sparing use of stone. Entrance set back and rising to a tower-like feature. Bold projecting outer bays, subtly angled forward and with chamfered outer angles. Polygonal stair-tower at the E end. In Paston Place, on the corner of Sudeley Street, **Southpoint** is the former Royal Gymnasium and Fencing Rooms erected in 1864 by Frederick Mahomed, son of Sake Deen Mahomed (*see* Topic Box, p. 70) Stucco, lined as ashlar, the main elevation treated as a temple front with tetrastyle portico of Tuscan pilasters. The style, despite the late date, is Greek Revival.

Brighton City Centre

N

Brighton
Station

TERMINUS ROAD

GUILDFORD RD

CLIFTON HILL

DYKE ROAD

SURREY STREET

FREDERICK PL

TRAFALGAR STREET

NORTH GDNS

QUEEN'S ROAD

GLOUCESTER RD

Brighthelm
Centre

St Nicholas's
Church

WINDSOR TERR

SPRING GDNS

NORTH ROAD

HAMPTON PL

SPRING ST

DEAN ST

CROWN ST

MARLBOROUGH ST

REGENT HILL

WINDSOR ST

CHURCH STREET

Unitarian
Church

QUEEN SQ

Clock
Tower

WINDSOR ST

BOND ST

The Dome

STREET

CASTLE

STREET

WESTERN ROAD

KING PL

Theatre
Royal

NEW RD

NORTH STREET

Royal
Pavilion

Churchill
Square
Shopping
Centre

CANNON PLACE

WEST STREET

PRINCE'S PL

Chapel
Royal

PAVILION
BUILDINGS

KING'S ROAD

Old Town

SHIP STREET

EAST STREET

GRAND JUNCTION RD

0   100   200 metres

0   100   200 yards

The growth of Brighton beyond its medieval confines (*see* Walk 1) began after *c*. 1740, but by the 1820s still hardly extended N of Church Street (North Gardens was laid out *c*. 1810, and its cottages still have long front gardens, reflecting the fact that for a short time they stood alone). Subsequent expansion owes much to the coming of the railway in 1841. Within the immediate neighbourhood of the station streets of small terraces were erected (Terminus Street, Railway Street and Terminus Place of 1842–7 still give a flavour and show the enduring devotion to bow windows in houses of every class). More importantly the railway shifted the focus away from the Steine and the Old Town to the new N–S thoroughfare of Queen's Road, laid out in 1845 to link the station with the seafront via West Street. The spread of shops along Western Road and the redevelopment of North Street for banks, departments stores etc. by the end of the C19 created the commercial centre which one still sees today.

Railway Station to Western Road

A visit to Brighton still begins for many people at the **Railway Station** (*see* p. 61) from where the traveller receives a direct view s to the sea. But this thoroughfare into town was only created in 1845 (partly funded by the railway company) by clearing away a notorious slum area towards the southern end and building a completely new road in a direct line from Windsor Terrace N to the station. Before then the route to the town centre was via the newly constructed Terminus Road, which curved along present-day Buckingham Place and Compton Avenue to meet Dyke Road. Immediately in front of the station is an ill-arranged space enlarged in 1924 to facilitate access for taxis, trams and buses. The first eyecatcher is the former railway hotel, now the **Grand Central** pub, 1925 for Tamplins Brewery and hence probably by their architect *Arthur Packham*. On an appropriately ambitious scale. Baroque, ashlar-faced, the corner, with big mullioned and transomed windows, rises into a tower crowned with a bold copper-clad dome. The two side façades have mullioned and transomed windows, in shallow bows to the E, beneath shallow segmental pediments.

On any bank holiday the pavements of **Queen's Road** are thronged with pedestrians making their way between the railway station and the sea. The street was widened in 1878. Of about this date the florid façade of the **Queen's Head** with pub front, first-floor bay windows and richly decorated frieze, cornice and parapet. A more restrained stucco terrace of shops with canted bays above follows but is interrupted by the strongly vertical red brick and terracotta front of the former **Royal Standard** pub, in the Free Style of *c*. 1900, with relief decoration to its shaped gable and little octagonal, domed cupolas with columns and a finial.

Off to the left in **Frederick Place**, **Frederick House**, 1977 by *Lomax & Adutt* (job architect *Stephen Adutt*), plum-coloured brick and fortress-like, deftly handling the change in scale between Frederick Place and Gloucester Road. s of the junction the familiar Brighton bows on the right but the next building of note is **Sun Dial House** (No. 111) on the E side at the corner of North Road. Dated 1896, for the Brighton & Sussex Mutual Provident Society, in brick with stucco classical trimmings, the corner treated as a tower with an ogee roof.

Between North Road and Church Street (w side) an elevated and elegantly railed pavement fronts **Windsor Terrace**, built *c.* 1830 (i.e. before Queen's Road existed). This is long, of three storeys in stucco with big tripartite first-floor windows. Though asymmetrical, it appears to be of one build but in the middle is interrupted by the imposing if ungainly **Masonic Centre**. Originally a house (No. 25), it has four giant pilasters with honeysuckle and palmette ornament to the necking and a recessed entrance with Greek Doric columns *in antis*. The Freemasons acquired the adjoining sites in 1919 and engaged *J.L. Denman* (his offices were next door at Nos. 27–8), to make additions to either side and to the rear,

85. Masonic Centre, Queen's Road, main hall, *c.* 1928 by J.L. Denman

remodel the interior and add an extra storey. His work, in a style mixing Art Deco with Neo-Georgian, was not completed until 1928. The main entrance has a single storey to the street with the upper floors set back. This opens to a top-lit Imperial staircase with a tiered chandelier suspended from the centre of a star pattern in the rectangular skylight. A plain open-string stick-baluster staircase survives at No. 25. **Main hall** [85] at the rear on the second floor has a saucer dome painted with the stars, compartmented with bronzed ribs and symbols of the signs of the Zodiac. Coloured glass centre light-fitting as the eye of God, reflected in the patterned floor. Panelling around the walls at lower level and shallow arches on stylized capitals with Greek key and setsquare and compasses. Grand Master's chair under a kind of domed baldacchino.

Windsor Terrace originally overlooked the burial ground of the Hanover Chapel (**Brighthelm Church & Community Centre**) which became a public garden in 1884. The chapel stands at its northern end, facing s. It was built in 1824 by *Thomas Cooper*, a remarkably original version of the universal chapel theme. Four bays, giant pilasters. Bays one and four have the doorways (with Tuscan columns without bases), and pediments at the top. In the middle on the ground floor two apparently Venetian windows; in fact round-headed with columns left and right carrying an outer blank arch. It was built as an Independent chapel for the Rev. James Edwards of Petworth and from 1844 to 1972 was used by the Presbyterians. But the chapel is now no more than a shell, following a fire in 1980 and extensive rebuilding by *Wells-Thorpe & Suppel*, 1986–7, who grafted on the new community centre fronting North Road. This is robust and heavily built with a layered façade of projecting sections of ribbed concrete set against areas of yellow brick, and with ponderous fenestration, all quite harsh but suited to the generally postwar tone of North Road. In the front wall a **panel** with a pierced relief by *John Skelton* (a nephew of Eric Gill) of loaves and fishes.

Return through the gardens to see some remaining modest three-storey early C19 houses in **Church Street** (facing the gardens) and **Windsor Street**, on the corner, in red brick with burnt brick headers. In **Church Street**, on the left, downhill, is the former **Drill Hall** of the Royal Sussex Regiment, by *Edmund Scott*, 1889–90. Long, with segment-headed windows set back within their arched openings, and an exaggeratedly Baroque portal, with a broken pediment and blocked voussoirs. It is as if it stood at Salzburg and dated from the C17. Now with a deadening grey render, but originally with banded polychromy and a cupola.

Now a steep climb up Church Street and w of Queen's Road to **St Nicholas**, the original Brighton parish church. Set on the side of the hill and still with the character of a medieval village church, surrounded by a well-treed churchyard. The church itself is low, as if in defence against the weather coming off the sea. It is C14, flint, but externally only the lower parts of the low embattled tower can be called C14. Square-headed two-light bell-openings to E and s, single lancets to w and N. Tiny ogee w lancet over a moulded doorway but otherwise plain and all looking much renewed. By 1850 the church accommodated only a fifth of the town's population in spite of the usual Georgian intervention of internal galleries. It was in sad disrepair and in 1853–4 the Rev. Henry Wagner engaged *R.C. Carpenter* to restore the church, though the reality was a virtual rebuilding. Externally the body of the church is entirely Carpenter's work. He rebuilt the aisles, doubling their width, renewed all of the roofs and added a N vestry. From 1876 *Somers Clarke Jun.* undertook further works, including the addition of the clerestory (1892–3), jacking up and retaining Carpenter's roof. In 1900 *J.T. Micklethwaite* lengthened the s chapel.

Inside, the five-bay arcades, octagonal piers and double-chamfered arches are C14 (though much restored), as are the arches to the tower and the chancel, so the C14 church was probably of similar size to the present one. The two-bay s chapel arcade with typical C14 mouldings is by Micklethwaite. **Font.** Caen stone. One of the best pieces of Norman carving in Sussex. The font is drum-shaped and seems to date from *c.* 1160–70. The representations are the Last Supper, very nobly and severely composed, St Nicholas and the Ship, another scene referring to St Nicholas, and the Baptism of Christ, the latter under three narrow arches. Brighton belonged to Lewes Priory, and that may well explain the high quality of the workmanship. The style is reminiscent of North Italy (Pontile, Modena). **Screen.** Late C15, of a Norfolk type, restored and repainted in 1887. Crocketed ogee openings. Rood beam by *Kempe*, 1887, the figures 1917 by *Barkentin & Krall*. **Painting** on the w and E walls by *Kempe*, 1890–2, and very good it is, with long foliate trails, angels etc. Some sources attribute the design to Somers Clarke and state that Kempe was responsible for the execution only. The older Royal Arms on the w wall were incorporated into the design. **Pulpit.** 1867. Open ironwork design by *Somers Clarke*. **Stained glass** by *Kempe*. In the s aisle as early as 1878, pictorial and less stylized than his later work and with more colour. The rest of what he did is 1879–87, except for the tower window of 1897. **Monuments. Wellington Memorial** (w end of s aisle), in whose memory the church was restored. By *R.C. Carpenter*, and carved by *John Birnie Philip*, 1853. A towering hexagonal piece inspired by the Eleanor Crosses and executed with the highest elaboration. Frances Crosbie Fairfield d.1830 (N aisle) by *Sir Richard Westmacott*. An angel carries her up. Lady Dorothy Westmacott d.1834 (w end of s aisle). Just an antique matronly bust. By *Sir Richard Westmacott*, her husband.

Headstones in the **churchyard**, to Phoebe Hessel d.1821 (s of the s chapel): 'she served for many years as a private soldier in the 5th Regt of Foot'; and to Martha Gunn d.1815 (near the SE corner of the church), the most famous of the Brighton 'dippers': 'She was Peculiarly Distinguished as a bather in this Town nearly 70 years.' Table tomb E of the church, to Amon Wilds d.1833, possibly designed by his son, *A.H. Wilds*. The inscription reads, 'a remarkable incident accompanies the period at which this gentleman came to settle in Brighton. Through his abilities and taste, the order of the ancient architecture of buildings in Brighton

may be dated to have changed from its antiquated simplicity and rusticity; and its improvements have since progressively increased.' On the N side of the nave, a headstone to Sake Deen Mahomed, d.1851 aged 102, 'Shampooing Surgeon' to King George IV (*see* Topic Box, p. 70). NE of the church a table tomb to Anna Maria Crouch, actress and singer, signed and dated '*Coade & Sealy* London 1806'. S of the porch, a **churchyard cross** with shaft and lantern with figures of saints. The base is medieval, the rest 1934, by *Walter Godfrey*. The churchyard was extended N of Church Street in 1824 and W of **Dyke Road** in 1841. It was closed for burials in 1853. The western extension was laid out by *A.H.Wilds*. Tudor-Gothic burial vaults form a terrace on the N side.

Descending Dyke Road, below the churchyard is a charming Gothick confection: **Wykeham Terrace** of 1827–30, perhaps by *A.H. Wilds*. A long symmetrical façade sunk into the hillside with polygonal projections in the centre and at each end. Castellated parapet interrupted by gabled dormers. Unusual glazing pattern. Boundary wall with castellated gateways. At the S end the Gothic theme continues in a café front with trefoils. No. 11 (now a nightclub), opposite, was built as the **Swan Downer School** by *George Somers Clarke Sen*. in 1867. Freely inventive Flemish Gothic, with crow-stepped gable, an oriel window and lots of highly original details in the tracery.

One may descend from here to the Clock Tower, North Street and the Old Steine (*see* below) but first the walk turns into **Western Road**. The street is named after the landowners, the Western family of Preston Manor (*see* p. 205) and was developed from *c.* 1809. Piggott's map of 1822 shows some development along the new street (then called Regent Place and Western Place). Initially housing was built but as the hinterland N and S was developed with residential streets and squares Western Road assumed a service function and the front gardens were built over with shops, resulting in a narrow and increasingly congested shopping street. From 1906 the Corporation began acquiring property on its N side and in 1926–36 widened the whole road from Hampton Place to North Street. The good run of large stores appeared at this time – in 1953 Harold Clunn described it as 'Oxford Street-by-the-Sea'.

Beginning the street, in the angle with Dyke Road is a streamlined Art Deco commercial building of 1934 by *Garrett & Son*, with a long elevation to Western Road. Horizontal banding of windows balanced by stepped towers with vertical windows with chevron glazing. As part of the development the **Imperial Arcade** (1923–4, by *Clayton & Black*) was remodelled. Opposite are Nos. 81–2 North Street, the former Soper's drapery store of 1858; rebuilt with two-storey shopfronts and domed corner turrets in 1901.

Otherwise the e end is totally dominated by the **Churchill Square Shopping Centre**, a remodelling of 1995–8, by *Comprehensive Design*, of the multi-level complex of 1963–8 by *Russell Diplock Associates*, which covered eleven acres on the descending slope between Western Road and Kings Road (*see* also Kingswest Centre, p. 102). It largely obliterated the existing street pattern, with open-air pedestrian precincts (covered over after refurbishment), and incorporated car parks and an eighteen-storey tower block (Chartwell Court), one of three originally proposed in 1959 but thankfully never completed. Although the idea of a comprehensive redevelopment goes back to 1935, it was not until 1959 that the land was acquired and developers sought. The complex is a major impediment to e–w movement across the city and whilst the topography reduces its visual dominance it has a particularly unacceptable face to the w.

A little beyond the shopping centre, at the corner with Clarence Square is an earlier survivor, the former drapery store of Knight & Wakeford (see their initials in the shaped gables) with a domed corner turret and two storeys of showrooms above the street. Western Road's N side still retains its identity as an interwar shopping street with a sequence of department stores; first, on the corner of Regent Hill, built for W.J. Wade's drapery company (1928), and **Woolworths**, both in a *moderne* commercial style. On the corner of Marlborough Street, the former **Johnson Brothers** furniture store (now Topshop), *c.* 1966 by *Denman & Son*, the upper floors tiled and relieved only by a grid of tiny square windows and slits, quite different in character to the earlier stores. Then between Marlborough Street and Crown Street, the former **British Home Stores** (now Primark) of 1931 and possibly by *Garrett & Son*, much larger, Portland stone ashlar (painted in 2007, astonishingly) and in a blocky American style, with strips of windows slightly recessed and arranged in a tripartite composition. Bold decorative classical motifs in relief above. w of Crown Street, and filling an entire block, the former **Stafford's** hardware store of 1930 [87]. Rather Continental classical style with pilasters carrying bronze torchères and monogrammed cartouches. Roman-tiled mansard and square dormers with circular windows under swags. Next, w of Dean Street, is the former **Boots** store of 1927–8 by *Bromley, Cartwright & Waumsley*, an unusually palatial piece of Classical Revival. Ashlar-faced, symmetrically composed on three sides with two-storey corners building up to three in the centre of each elevation which are pedimented and have an open Ionic colonnade. Finally, **Mitre House** of 1935 by *J. Stanley Beard & Bennett*, built for International Stores and incorporating a six-storey block of flats above, very similar to mansion flats in the more middle-class suburbs of interwar London.

87. The former Stafford's hardware store of 1930 in Western Road

The stone-faced lower two storeys form a podium to the brick upper parts which are broken up by a vertical stack of balconies projecting in the centre and to left and right. Sloping uphill along the streets between these buildings are still some three-storey bow-fronted terraces of the 1820s.

Now along the s side of Western Road, where there are fewer pickings, but include in **Castle Street** a pair of houses (Nos. 33–4) of *c.* 1830, with giant Ionic pilasters. Further w on **Western Road** are two nice designs for banks: **HSBC** of 1904 by *T.B.Whinney*, with a tall, single-storey, three-bay façade in Bath stone. Rusticated engaged antae and a pair of engaged Doric columns framing full-height windows with torus mouldings and a central entrance with broken segmental pediment and garlanded oval window above. Frieze of intertwined sprays, cornice and balustraded parapet. To the w, standing alone between Little Preston Street and Sillwood Road is the neat square Portland stone pavilion of **NatWest Bank** (1925 and probably by *Palmer & Holden*). Three bays divided by pilasters, big round-arched centre windows, the outer bays with blind round arches over lintels with stepped keystones. All-over rustication above and a bold entablature with balustraded parapet.

The interwar road widening on the N side did not extend w of Hampton Place and beyond here at Nos. 140 etc. are the last reminders of how shops were built out over the front gardens of houses during the c19. From here to Montpelier Road, Western Road and the streets off still have remnants of earlier development. Now we can return to the junction with North Street to continue the walk down to Old Steine.

North Street to Old Steine

The junction of Queen's Road, West Street and North Street is the hub of commercial Brighton with its landmark **Clock Tower**, a supremely confident and showy design by *John Johnson* of London, which Pevsner harshly described as 'worthless'. It was erected to mark Queen Victoria's golden jubilee. Although a design was won in competition in 1881 by *Thomas Simpson* and *Henry Branch*, nothing appears to have come of this, and the tower was not built until 1888, at a cost of £2,000; its donor, James Willing, was an advertising contractor credited with the invention of the billboard. Portland stone with polished Aberdeen granite. Pedimented aedicules on four sides framing medallion portraits of the Prince and Princess of Wales, Prince Albert and Queen Victoria, and above these ships' prows project with directions 'to the sea' etc. lettered on the gunwales. At the corners, life-size female figures (The Four Seasons). Carving by *Baird, Harper & Woodington*. Square tower above, with banded rustication and the four clock faces at the top. Heavy dentil cornice surmounted by urns on short piers at the corners with coats of arms between. Then an octagonal section surmounted by a copper dome with gilded fish-scales. Surmounting this an open coronet with a 16-ft mast incorporating a hydraulically operated gilded 'time ball' designed by *Magnus Volk* (*see* Topic Box, p. 131) to rise and fall on the hour.

North Street was already a busy shopping street by the 1780s. It was widened first in the 1870s and confirmed as one of Brighton's main commercial thoroughfares and home to its major banks. The N side has been redeveloped with glossy commercial buildings of the last forty years, e.g. **Boots** of 1976–7 by *Comprehensive Design* (job architect *Derek Sharp*), which introduces a late C20 scale and character. Originally with its structural frame set out from the building's mirror-glazed curtain walls; a sculptural quality undermined by remodelling in 1998 by *Turner Woolford Sharp*, which accentuates the overbearing scale. It stands on the site of the Regent Cinema (1921, by *Robert Atkinson*, demolished 1974), the most impressive of Brighton's interwar cinemas. Opposite Boots is a former **Burton's** tailors (now Waterstones) of 1928, in the stripped classical style of their in-house architect, *Harry Wilson*, with giant pilasters, large areas of glazing on all levels and a deep waterleaf cornice.

88. Brighton Clock Tower of 1888 by John Johnson, detail of direction sign

The first of the grand banks that give North Street its architectural value is **Barclays** (N side), a sombre classical monolith of as late as 1957–9 by *Denman & Son*. Portland stone ashlar to the public front to give the necessary air of quality and permanence. Three tiers of tripartite windows, the upper one set behind an Italianate loggia. The long side elevations have an ashlar base and book-ends with brickwork in between. More typically postwar is the **Prudential Buildings**, immediately to the E, 1967–9, by *K.C. Wintle* of the Prudential's architects' department; strongly horizontal despite the vertical stacks of windows; successor to *Paul Waterhouse*'s offices of 1904.

On the s side Nos. 49–50 (Refuge House), 1950, by *Denman & Son*, has good brickwork, including vertical strips of moulded bricks forming giant pilasters. Beyond Ship Street, Nos. 32–6 is typical of the stripped classical Art Deco of interwar department stores: 1938 for Messrs **Vokins** by *W.H. Overton*. Nos. 30–1 (**Clarence House**) is one of the few earlier buildings and the only surviving example of the large inns that once lined North Street. Built as the New Inn in 1785 and described in 1809 as 'fitted up in a very magnificent style. It is decidedly the best Inn in Brighton.' Extended in 1811. Four storeys with a plain painted façade; the one concession to decoration is the Tuscan doorcase.

Opposite Clarence House, the entrance to Bond Street is flanked by ashlar-faced Edwardian-looking banks: **HSBC** (left), *c.* 1902, by *T.B. Whinney*, quite restrained, with an attached Tuscan colonnade, pedimented first-floor windows and balustraded parapet, and on the right the former **National Provincial Bank** (now a bar), 1921–3 by *F.C.R. Palmer* (with *Clayton & Black* as executant architects). Louis XVI style with ground-floor rustication carried into the concave window surrounds. Lush carving to keystones, around doorways etc. Good attention to detail even up to the dormers with eared architraves. Bronze doors with reliefs of the Signs of the Zodiac [3].

New Road was opened in 1806 enabling the Prince of Wales to close the part of East Street that ran past his Marine Pavilion. Much of the E side opens to Pavilion Gardens (*see* p. 42). Plots were taken for building almost immediately, beginning on the w side, and returning into North Street, with Nos. 1–10, two-bay dwellings above shops, separated by broad giant pilasters. The composition is but half of the original concept and the original detailing is best preserved at Nos. 6–7. In front of Nos. 1–7 is the Ionic **Royal Colonnade**, mostly a reinstatement in 2000 of the original colonnade designed by *Cooper & Lynn* in 1823. The **Theatre Royal** was developed at the same time as the terrace and opened in 1807, succeeding a theatre in Duke Street.* The Prince of Wales approved the designs, possibly by Messrs *Hides*, architects of Worthing theatre in the same year, for a three-bay façade with Doric colonnade. This was heightened and substantially remodelled by *C.J. Phipps* in 1866

*Plays were performed in a barn on the Steine by 1764; the town's first purpose-built theatre was opened in 1774 in North Street.

(his work still visible high up on the N side) but what we see today is of 1894 by *Clayton & Black*, who refaced Phipps's work in vivid red brick, encasing his first-floor projection, resulting in curious slots at the angles with the domed corner turrets [15]. Contemporary cast-iron colonnade with Corinthian columns in pairs. Spoiling the skyline, a glazed foyer of 1920. The theatre was also extended into Nos. 9–10 in 1894; the elaborate glazed terracotta front of the **Colonnade Bar** is probably of this date. Inside the theatre, Phipps remodelled the **auditorium** as a horseshoe form, with three tiers of galleries and two tiers of stage boxes flanked by paired pilasters; partly altered during enlargement by *Sprague & Barton*, 1927, and redecorated in a Late Louis XVI manner.

Further on, the **Unitarian Chapel**, of 1820 by *A.H. Wilds*, has an imposing Greek temple front with a tetrastyle portico of fluted Doric columns. The interior is plain and was re-fitted in the late C19. One **stained glass** window of 1888 by *Bell & Beckham*. No. 23 dates from *c.* 1815, its only distinction being the full-width first-floor veranda with lattice-pattern railings and the upright supports treated as open-fretted Ionic pilasters. For the Pavilion Theatre *see* The Dome (p. 46).

Now back to **North Street**, for the former **Royal Assurance Society** offices (No. 163) of 1904 [89], the *chef d'oeuvre* of *Clayton & Black*, an ebullient essay in Edwardian Baroque faced in pink granite and faceted around the corner, with outer towers and a central tower rising to a domed polygonal cupola open on four sides. Next is the **Chapel Royal**, in vivid red brick and terracotta, with round-arched windows (below), square-headed (above), and a square corner tower with a pyramidal roof, largely by *Arthur Blomfield*. Its history is more complex than its outward appearance suggests, and it is a refronting on two sides (carried out between 1880 and 1896) of the original Chapel Royal of 1793–5 by *Thomas Saunders* of London. That faced Prince's Place, where its refronted elevation has the original *Coade* stone royal arms, and had no front to North Street, where it was set behind buildings later cleared for a road widening. This low, stuccoed classical box was rarely used for worship by the Regent and in 1803 it became a chapel of ease to St Nicholas. Blomfield was initially engaged to remodel the interior in 1876, its highly unusual appearance indicative of the constraints of retaining the late C18 structure; with twelve double-height octagonal columns defining a square nave with galleries on three sides beneath tripartite screens. Reordered and restored by *Caroe & Partners*, 1992. **Painted decoration** (chancel ceiling etc.), 1880s by *Heaton, Butler & Bayne*. Chancel **paintings** by *Harry Mileham*, designer also of the **stained glass** window (1947), now in an office to the left of the café.

Behind the Chapel Royal is **Regent House**, 1934, by *J.L. Denman*, with patterned brickwork – a kind of *pointilliste* effect, Crittall windows and two-storey canted oriels under modishly angular canopies, curiously off-centre. Carved reliefs probably by *Joseph Cribb*. On the opposite corner of Prince's Place, **Prince's House**. Built for the Brighton & Sussex Building Society in 1935–6 by *H.S. Goodhart-Rendel*, in his own

89. The former Royal Assurance Society offices of 1904 by Clayton & Black, on the corner of North Street and New Road

inimitable response to Modernism. Steel-framed, the structure rationally expressed around infill panels but clad in coloured brickwork, blue glass mosaic and green slate in a manner at once progressive and indebted to c19 traditions. Angled corner with windows of unusual zigzag plan and a circular top at the set-back upper floor. This storey contained flats and is treated differently.

Opposite, Nos. 6–9 **North Street**, with mullioned and transomed bays through two floors, were built as the **Brighton Union Bank**, 1896, by *Arthur Keen*, built in two phases of two bays each. These buildings were absorbed by Hannington's department store; established at No. 2 North Street in 1808, the company gradually expanded to fill the entire block between North Street, East Street and Market Street, before closing in 2001.

The walk ends at **Pavilion Buildings,** a short pedestrian street leading to the Pavilion's South Gate (*see* p. 42). Before the construction of New Road, this was the continuation of East Street N to Church Street and was lined on its E side by the Pavilion's domestic ranges. These were demolished by the Corporation in 1850 and redeveloped with a terrace of shops and offices to help fund their purchase of the Pavilion estate. The group terminates s in a highly crafted bank (now **NatWest**) of 1905 by *Godfrey Pinkerton* for the London & County Bank, on the site of the town's first theatre. Ground floor with bands of red and white Mansfield stone, the windows and doors subtly recessed. The ground-floor windows have slim metal columns standing forward and sup-porting exaggeratedly overhanging tops ornamented with anthemion, like small crowns. Ancaster stone above, the first-floor windows of a quasi Venetian form with balustraded fronts and pilasters carved with scrolling foliage. The treatment, a mixture of motifs derived from the Italian Renaissance and the Greek Revival, is more elaborate on the slightly curved and recessed corner entrance bay, with emblematic figures (by *Michael Murphy*) carved in low relief flanking the upper window. Screen of paired antae to the attic flat. The refined interior has regrettably been lost though the banking hall retains its deeply compartmented ceiling and columns with stylized acanthus leaf capitals. In the NW corner an Adamesque arched recess, originally with a fire grate and lined with marble by *Farmer & Brindley*. On the opposite cor-ner, **Lloyds TSB** (former Capital & Counties Bank), in polished granite and Bath stone, by *Clayton & Black*, makes an Edwardian Baroque show

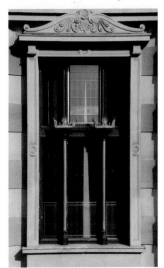

with an exaggerated open pediment enclosing a cartouche, and corner turret at the top between gables but otherwise in a conservative C17 Cotswold vernacular, with mul-lioned and transomed windows and white-painted pedimented dorm-ers. To its right, the former offices of the **Brighton & Hove Herald,** in very stylish and well-detailed Neo-Georgian by *J.L. Denman*, 1934, with bow windows attractively set in an arcade with glazed tympana. Carving by *Joseph Cribb*.

90. Detail of Godfrey Pinkerton's former London & County Bank, on the corner of Pavilion Buildings and Castle Square

Walk 8.

Montpelier, Clifton Hill and West Hill

This walk covers the early–mid Victorian suburban expansion NW of Brighton's town centre on West Hill (also known historically as Church Hill), its SW-facing slope known as Clifton Hill, and the area to the W extending towards the Chalybeate spring at St Ann's Well, known as Montpelier. Dyke Road, climbing N from the town, was turnpiked in 1777 and had a small cluster of buildings close to its route by the 1820s including Vine's Mill (*c.* 1810, dem. *c.* 1850) and the town's workhouse. But most of the area to the W was open ground for sheep grazing and held by Thomas Kemp (*see* Topic Box, p. 145), who in 1818 had erected his own house (The Temple [92]) in this isolated setting. Piggott's map of 1826 shows development creeping N from Western Road and building proceeded rapidly over the next twenty-five years with a boom period in the 1840s (e.g. Montpelier Place, Terrace, Villas etc.), no doubt encouraged by the opening of the railway station N of the town centre. The architectural traditions of Regency Brighton were slow to decline, only gradually giving way to the Early Victorian Italianate styles, often in concert with the favoured palette of bows, tented verandas etc. The only significant interruptions to the stucco orthodoxy of these streets are the two major Anglican and Roman Catholic churches built for the suburb in the 1860s, and the Children's Hospital on Dyke Road, built in 1880. Despite the similarity of street after street of stucco villa and terrace, the wealth of variety and detail and the exceptionally complete character of the area is its enticement.

For ease of orientation and walking a tour should start at **Seven Dials**, the junction of seven roads by the mid C19 including Montpelier Road which runs SW from here to the sea. Its upper parts, beginning with **Vernon Terrace**, have been renamed. Here we immediately arrive at the one great showpiece of the area, **Montpelier Crescent** [9]. This surprises because of the grand scale adopted away from the town centre and because it faces NW, away from the sea towards the Downs. It was erected by *A. H. Wilds*, 1843–7, but not to one design, and is hard to appreciate as a single composition. Building probably started from the centre where there is more consistency. The crescent is arranged in a series of ten linked pavilions, mostly of five bays, with pediments over the middle three bays, the entrances well set back in the links between. Towards the extremities the pavilions are seven or even nine bays wide and here, where the entrances are not set back as far, the effect is much flatter.

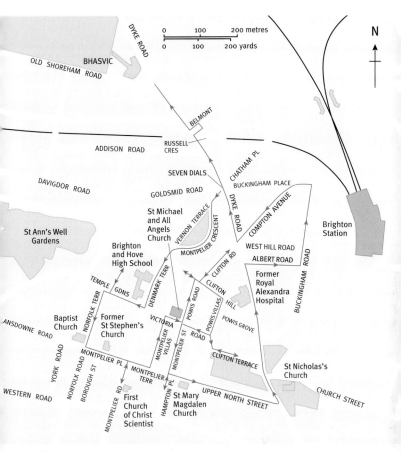

91. Walk 8

Giant Corinthian pilasters (some fluted, others with Wilds's ammonite capitals) support the pediments and in some cases extend across the whole of the projecting part. The interiors are not grand, with timber staircases and moulded detailing typical of the period. At the sw end the crescent continues in a convex curve with an unusual pattern of wreaths around the upper windows. The four-storey houses along **Vernon Terrace** were built up opposite in 1856–7, obscuring the view from the crescent, with a mixture of broad bow fronts and slightly later canted façades and a middle group of six stepping up an extra storey.

Vernon Terrace leads into **Denmark Terrace** with houses on the left of comparable height but in their heavier Italianate detailing more obviously of the 1860s, with full-height canted bays, distinctive paired porches with Gibbsian blocking and a continuous first-floor iron balcony (some pairs of houses also have linking balconies at the upper floors). The land opposite remained undeveloped until the first decade of the c20 and has cheery red brick Edwardian houses standing out amidst the stucco.

92. Thomas Kemp's The Temple (now Brighton & Hove High School) of 1818 drawn by G. Earp in 1835, with Henry Phillips's Athenaeum on the left (*see* Topic Box, p. 121)

At the s end of Denmark Terrace is **Brighton & Hove High School**, which occupies The Temple, Thomas Kemp's house of 1818. He moved to Kemp Town in 1827 and the house became a school. Probably designed by *A. H. Wilds*, it is certainly exotic enough for his taste. Kemp was a prominent freemason and the measurements of his house were said to be taken from King Solomon's Temple (the 'inner house', said to have been a nine-metre cube), considered the birthplace of masonry. It is square and had on the ground floor to all sides colonnades of coupled columns (only preserved on the N and E sides). The columns are of bizarre form, engaged and tapering, with turned capitals like stoppers, but carrying normal round arches. The sw wing was added in 1891 and the building's crowning dome was sadly removed in 1911 and replaced by an overscaled mansard (designed by the headmistress and art mistress) as part of other alterations. To the right a drab classroom block of the 1960s and more recent administration block by *Morgan Carn Partnership*. The Temple stands back from the road in its own grounds enclosed by flint walls with massive pepperpot-domed piers and gatepiers with antefixae and lions' heads. The house stood alone in 1834–5 when the **vicarage** (now the High School's sixth form) was built nearby for the Rev. Henry Wagner by *Cheesman & Son*. This survives on **Temple Gardens** to the s, set back on the left. Rendered, austere Neo-Tudor. Inside, heavy open-well staircase with tall obelisk finials. In front of it a pair of Late Victorian/Edwardian houses and the school's **sports hall** of 2001 by *Morgan Carn Partnership* – unexceptional.

On the N side of Temple Gardens more distinctive suburban Edwardian houses, continuing round into **Windlesham Road** (notably Nos. 14–16, dated 1903). On the corner, **Temple Heights**, the former **New Sussex Hospital** for women, moved here in 1921 into a house of the 1840s much altered by *Clayton & Black*. Extensions to the w of c. 1930 by *Adams, Holden & Pearson* were replaced by a block of flats, (**York Mansions**), 2001, by the *Graham-Watts Partnership*. Then left into **Norfolk Terrace**, developed from the 1850s. On the right, Nos. 1–13, by *Thomas Lainson*, Italianate, flat-fronted and divided into paired pavilions, slightly advanced, the nine-bay centre treated with groups of round-arched windows and a big central staircase window breaking through the floors. Then a four-storey bow-fronted terrace and **Belvedere Terrace**, opposite, built *c.* 1852 for Mary Wagner at the rear of her own home, Belvedere House (1837; dem. 1965). Being closer to the sea, **Norfolk Road**, s of Montpelier Place, was built up from the 1830s at its s end but probably not complete at the N end until the 1860s: see the terraces on the E side with their unusual, and not very elegant, canted bay windows whose face breaks forward (of a type seen also at King's Hotel, King's Road).

c20 interlopers are rare in this area, but on the corner of Norfolk Terrace and **Lansdowne Road** is the **Baptist Church** of 1966 by *E. Joseph Wood*, on the site of the Emanuel Reformed Episcopal church of a century earlier. In isolation not without merit, but too low and spreading for this urban context. Two broad shallow gabled bays with incised brick strips enclose a courtyard closed to the street by an arcade of slabs of brickwork with a sawtooth overhanging roof reminiscent of Coventry Cathedral opened five years earlier. Hall on the right, church on the left, with a plain unadorned space. Standing up, on the corner of York Road, the vibrant red sentinel Queen Anne Revival-style **Mercia House** of 1880 by *H.J. Lanchester*. However, here we turn E and Lansdowne Road immediately becomes **Montpelier Place**. On the left the former **St Stephen's Church** (First Base Day Centre for homeless people) erected in 1851 by *George Cheesman* on land given by Mary Wagner. Behind its blind pedimented façade with an octagonal bell-turret (as if destined for the Colonies) is the remains of the ballroom of the Castle Inn, designed by *John Crunden* in 1776. George IV bought the inn in 1821 and converted the ballroom for his private chapel (preferring it to the official Chapel Royal (*see* p. 165). It was re-erected here after the Corporation purchased the Pavilion in 1850. It is surprising, given the date and the personalities involved, that a classical interior was faithfully re-created for ecclesiastical use. It is oblong and has a coved ceiling and arched windows. In the middle of each side is a recess or alcove, distyle *in antis*, recalling Crunden's contemporary work for Boodle's club in London. The pilasters are crisply decorated. The style is classical without anything of the Rococo. The church was closed for worship in 1939.

Our walk now brings us to the area around Montpelier Road which was considered one of the best residential areas of Early Victorian Brighton, reflected in the quality of the housing laid out *c.* 1830–50 in the streets to the E. **Montpelier Road** itself is now a busy thoroughfare making it difficult to appreciate this once fashionable address, but a short detour to the right includes some of its best houses: notably Nos. 53–6, on the right [93], by *A.H. Wilds* with all his hallmarks in abundance, fluted pilasters, ammonite capitals and shell-hoods above the first-floor

93. Nos. 53–6 Montpelier Road by A.H. Wilds

windows, this and more packed into narrow two-bay façades. No. 90, on the left, is double-fronted and mid Victorian but still with shallow bows. Late Victorian decorative iron and glass porch of an elliptical arch on slender columns with foliage capitals, the panels with arabesques and stained glass. Lining the E side of the street are *c.* 1830 stucco terraces, Nos. 91–6, treated as paired villas with five-bay fronts, louvred shutters and entrances set back with Ionic columns. On the W side Nos. 48–52 have first the narrow bow windows but then broader bows incorporating two windows, whilst Nos. 36–42 are bow-fronted in gault brick. On the opposite side is the **First Church of Christ Scientist**, originally a house of *c.* 1850 but substantially remodelled and enlarged for its current use in 1921 by *Clayton & Black*. The façade has a richly decorated pedimented entrance bay on the left with all-over rustication. The chapel to the right with two tiers of windows divided by giant pilasters. The interior is simple with a gallery and panelling around the raised readers' platform and forming enclosures to the readers' rooms to either side.

Now heading E, Montpelier Place becomes **Montpelier Terrace**, which starts on the N side with a grand three-storey group (Nos. 1–5) of *c.* 1830, with Ionic pilasters through the upper floors dividing each house. Opposite, **Montpellier Hall** and **Montpelier Lodge** (No. 16) are five-bay detached houses. The former of 1846 by *A.H. Wilds*; round-arched windows and heavy Italianate cornice, L-shaped entrance hall, staircase running parallel to the façade, with cast-iron balustrade. It still retains a large garden facing S, overlooked by full-height windows to the reception rooms with external louvred shutters interlocking when open. The latter house, *c.* 1830, is, unusually for this area, in red brick, with Doric doorcase and pretty fanlight.

Then climbing uphill on the left is **Montpelier Villas**, *c.* 1845, possibly by *A.H. Wilds*, which introduces a looser suburban scale of generously spaced paired villas, especially charming. Building started simultaneously from the SE and NW and was completed over about three years. The later houses are more generously proportioned and have simpler detailing but the differences are not obvious. Here the Regency is giving way to the Victorian Italianate but still with pretty bow-verandas and full-height bows to the sides. Rusticated ground floor, taken up as quoins to the deeply overhanging cornice on moulded brackets.

The view uphill from Montpelier Villas is along **St Michael's Place**, with big terraces of 1868–9, impressive in their length, height, and consistent rhythm of canted bays and continuous balconies. The canted bays have the centre section advanced and crowned by a pediment. The original area railings complete the ensemble. These followed the building of St Michael and All Angels, the finest of Victorian churches in Brighton and Hove (*see* p. 48), which fills the entire frontage between St Michael's Place and Powis Road to the E, its scale enhanced by the fall of the land.

94. Montpelier Villas, *c.* 1845

Powis Road forms one side of **Powis Square** but is slightly later than the other three sides which were built up *c.* 1850 around a garden now filled by mature trees. The name derives from one of the developers, John Yearsley, who came from Montgomery in Powys. The square is unusually intimate and does not have a seaward aspect, with bow-fronted houses stepping up the hillside and curving in at the top of its E side where Powis Grove leads off.

Powis Road's N end leads into **Clifton Hill**, developed in the 1840s evidently piecemeal and without any overall control. To the left, Nos. 1–2 have quoins, bracketed cornice and entrances in set-back three-storey towers, like an Italian villa. To the right a double-fronted villa (No. 7), essentially the same but without the towers. Then a brief foray along

Constable in Brighton

John Constable stayed with his family in Brighton on several occasions between May 1824 and 1828, visits prompted by his wife Maria's poor health. At first they stayed at 'Mrs Sober's Gardens' (Sillwood Road) and the following year in Russell Square, both then on the NW edge of the built-up area. Constable was not enamoured of Brighton during this period of unprecedented growth and complained that the beach was like 'Piccadilly by the sea-side'. Despite his initial dislike the recently opened Chain Pier became the subject of one of his great 'six-footer' paintings, exhibited in 1827. The painter also made excursions up Church Hill into the open countryside, at that time dotted with windmills. Parry in 1833, says that Church Hill 'commands a magnificent view, and has very fine air' but Constable found the Downs 'hideous masses of unfledged earth called the country'. He nonetheless found subjects enough for his studies, frequently annotating them with temporal and meteorological details and leaving a record of an area that over the next decade was transformed into the suburb of Montpelier.

95. John Constable, *The Gleaners, Brighton*, 1824

Clifton Road, a street of some variety. Nos. 1–4, 7–8 and 9–10 are of the 1840s with tripartite windows and balconies with cast-iron railings and tent canopies. Nos. 7–8 have giant Doric pilasters. No. 26, opposite, detached and set back, the main front just two bays flanked by Ionic pilasters. For proper contrast, Nos. 18–25 of 1903–4 by *Denman & Matthews*, red brick and render, a long quasi-symmetrical group, with shaped gables, turrets and big arched dormer windows all very characterfully detailed.

Returning to **Clifton Hill** and turning left, Nos. 10–11 on the left has a rusticated ground floor and a full-width first-floor balcony, the tent canopy with fretted valance. From here we can turn right into **Powis Villas**, contemporary with Powis Square, with a mix of detached and semi-detached houses and a terrace of three with a continuous tent-roofed veranda. Opposite Victoria Road, **Vine Place**, a twitten cutting through to Dyke Road, has well-hidden single- and two-storey detached cottages, mostly of the 1850s and later. Those at the Dyke Road end may date from about 1810 when this was known as Mill Place. All is well screened and a detour is not recommended. On the s side of Vine Place are the rear gardens of **Clifton Terrace**, completed by 1851. Its houses are treated as broad, double-fronted villas, yet in terraced form with the centre stepped up and the whole terrace elevated above a raised pavement overlooking a private garden on the site of the Clifton Mill (moved across the valley to Albion Hill in 1837).

Before dropping back down the hill we should return to **Victoria Road**, as far as St Michael's Church, past Nos. 14–15 (N side), a symmetrical pair of *c.* 1834 with giant Ionic pilasters, the outer ones awkwardly terminated by the entrances. Awkward too the ground-floor windows with springing band forming a Venetian window and set within a larger blind arch. They face down Victoria Street to the steeple of St Mary Magdalen (*see* below). **Montpelier Street**, descending steeply, was laid out in the mid 1840s. On the corner at the bottom of the hill, Nos. 8–13 **Montpelier Terrace** is contemporary with Montpelier Villas (*see* above), with the same heavy bracketed cornice, and with continuous first-floor balconies with fretted valances. In **Hampton Place** opposite, developed in the 1820s, Nos. 12–26 are especially pretty houses, just one window wide, with paired fluted pilasters [96]. They were built by *William Hallett* who lived at No. 7, and the grand façades belie the modest interiors.

Turning E, we come to the group of **St Mary Magdalen** (R.C.) of 1861–4 by *G.R. Blount* and its associated school (1871) and presbytery of 1891, by *F.A. Walters*, filling most of a street block. The second church to be built for Brighton and Hove's Roman Catholic community. Blount is one of the lesser-known Roman Catholic architects. He died aged fifty-eight and was not prolific. Decorated Gothic, described by *The Builder* as being in 'the Modern Florid Gothic style'. Red brick with stone dressings and bands of black and glazed blue brick. Nave and chancel are side on to the street but set back behind the almost detached tower and broach spire aligned on Victoria Street. It has angle buttresses and

96. Hampton Place, built in the 1820s by William Hallett

a polygonal stair-turret. In niches either side of the entrance, figures of St Joseph and St George, 1962, by *Joseph Cribb*. The school adjoins to the w and the presbytery to the E, both projecting forward to the street. Vestries fill part of the gap in front of the main body of the church. Altogether a very satisfying compositional group. The lofty interior has five-bay arcades and a two-bay chancel, the roof trusses supported on corbels with carved angels. The piers have big stiff-leaf capitals whilst the E end has richly carved and painted altars and reredos. However, the applied colour is later, as Blount relied for an overall richness of effect on the quality of the carving (of which there is much), a riot of High Victorian naturalism, and the contrast between stone and coloured marbles. Good **stained glass** of 1864–9 by *Hardman's*, mostly in the chancel but also two windows in the N aisle and one in the s aisle, 1887.

We are at the point where Montpelier Terrace becomes **Upper North Street**: Nos. 73–89 is a terrace of *c.* 1842 with houses arranged in pairs with linked entrances and divided by fluted Ionic pilasters. On the s side, Nos. 42–3 are also of similar date, the fronts built to the edge of the pavement, modest yet grandly treated. From here it is a short walk to St Nicholas's Church and the city centre.

The walk can be extended back to Seven Dials and further N along **Dyke Road**. For St Nicholas's Church and the associated burial grounds *see* pp. 158–60. Overlooking the western burial ground on the left, **St George's House**, *c.* 1840, with an Italianate tower.

Facing down the road at the corner with Clifton Hill is the former **Royal Alexandra Children's Hospital**. The first purpose-built children's hospital opened in Liverpool in 1851; Brighton's opened in Western Road in 1868 and moved to the present site in 1871. The present building is of 1880–1 by *Lainson & Sons*. Queen Anne style, the main elevation of the administration block facing E, asymmetrical with a Dutch gable, two prominent first-floor bays with an oval window between and cut and moulded decorative red brick and terracotta. Elaborate cartouche commemorating the royal opening. The larger projecting wing to the N was added in matching style in 1927. The gabled s façade has prominent chimneystacks and, at the far end, twin octagonal turrets (facing w) with elegant pepperpot cupolas. In between, a two-storey colonnade of (originally) open-air balconies of 1906 by *Clayton & Black*. A two-storey N wing, set back, was added in 1927–8, by *W.H. Overton*, with a row of gables, half-timbered to the E and tile-hung to the w. To the rear a two-storey block in a more friendly domestic style with mullioned and transomed bay window under a jettied timbered gable, and a short square tower. This was built in 1905 as an outpatients' department. In **Clifton Hill** on the left the **coachhouse** of 1852 to No. 5 Powis Grove, with *Coade* stone embellishments.

The area E of Dyke Road is **West Hill**, where streets quickly dive down steeply on the eastward-facing slopes of the ridge towards the station. Unsurprisingly, development came hard on the heels of its opening in 1841. Opposite the hospital in Dyke Road stood the town workhouse, opened here in 1822 and relocated to Elm Grove in 1867 (*see* p. 180). Its site was taken for mostly large semi-detached bay-fronted villas, thoroughly Victorian in character, and mostly laid out along broad tree-lined avenues, e.g. Leopold Road, Albert Road and the southern end of Buckingham Road. **Albert Road**, on the right, leads to **Buckingham Road**, where Nos. 45–58 are representative of the larger houses, with big square bays (identical to Nos. 16–20 Ventnor Villas, Hove). **Compton Avenue** to the N also has a nice uninterrupted early 1850s terrace (Nos. 2–54), with heavy bracketed eaves and neat bay windows with pretty balcony fronts, arranged generally in pairs with the paired entrances set back. The middle section steps up an extra floor. The opposite side of the street was developed from 1865 and has a curious group, Nos. 17–21, which have a bit of fun with dentil pediments and barley twists to the first-floor window mullions. An Edwardian overlay to the ground floor of Nos. 19–21 further adds to the confusion.

Back on **Dyke Road** at the corner with Clifton Road, is a former *cottage orné* (now **Brighton Dental Centre**), an uncommon style in early C19 Brighton. It originally stood alone, its front garden later built up with shops. Opposite is a crass block of flats on the site of the Dials Congregational Church, 1871, by *Thomas Simpson*. Its tall tower was a landmark on the Brighton skyline. The **Tin Drum**, to the right, may be a much older building, given its modest proportions and its not being aligned with other buildings. N of Seven Dials, to the right in **Buckingham Place** are 1840s terraces on either side grouped in pairs.

Heading N into **Dyke Road**, the character is more varied as we approach the limit of the 1850s suburbs. On the left parades of shops with flats in a well-detailed Early Georgian style. Nos. 131–37, 1929, by *E. Wallis Long* and Nos. 139–145, 1929 by *William Overton*. On the right **Pacific House** (No. 126), with a pediment, is an inappropriately grand building of 1985 in the style of the 1850s. Nos. 128–130 is a fragment of Peel Terrace built in the 1850s, two storeys, the bay windows with a canopy on each floor. Magnus Volk (*see* Topic Box, p. 131) lived for the latter part of his life at No. 128. **The Good Companions** stands alone. 1939, for Tamplins Brewery and so probably by their architect *Arthur Packham*. Well detailed in a style which owes much to the late C17 English Renaissance, tall and with a big roof, but the brickwork detailing, especially around the entrances and the tapering windows, clearly 1930s. **Russell Crescent** has more houses like Peel Terrace. **Belmont**, on the right, is a grouping of five large houses of flint; developed in the early 1850s on the site of Hove windmill, a post mill, moved in 1852 to Clayton, N of Brighton, where it still stands. Beyond were two generously spaced villas of *c.* 1840 (demolished *c.* 1970), which marked the built-up limit of Brighton and Hove at mid century.

Old Shoreham Road was the borough boundary until 1873. At the junction, the **Brighton, Hove & Sussex Sixth Form College** (BHASVIC), 1913 by *S.B. Russell* of London. Neo-Early Georgian. Red brick. The main block, V-plan, is placed at an angle, facing down Dyke Road. Giant pilasters and a modillion cornice; stone doorcase with broken pediment. Big roof with elongated cupola. Disabled access ramps and steps adroitly, though boldly, handled, 2005 by *Nick Evans Architects*. The connection between centre and wings by staircase links all with circular windows. Extensions and alterations of 1934–5 by *J.L. Denman*. Assembly hall, behind the main entrance, with nine murals of 1913–39 by *Louis Ginnett*, an old boy of the school. They illustrate the history of man in Sussex.

Walk 9.

London Road, Lewes Road and Hanover

This walk covers the large area where the London, Ditchling and Lewes roads fan out from the N end of the Steine. Ditchling Road climbs Round Hill which separates the two valleys along which the main roads pass; prone to flooding by the winter bournes, including the Wellesbourne, the situation much improved by the laying of a drain from Preston Circus s in 1827–8 and the construction of the Patcham waterworks in 1889.

London Road (known as Queen's Road until *c.* 1826) was the main approach for visitors from London to the town from the 1770s. The Ditchling Road (to Lindfield and Cuckfield) and the Lewes Road, running either side of the area of common land at the floor of the valley, known as The Level, were turnpiked in 1770. Each retains their separate and strong character. Elm Grove, off Lewes Road, led E out of town to the racecourse, established in 1783 and still active today, but there were few other buildings by 1795 when the Hanover Almshouses and, further out, the Preston Barracks were erected along the road to Lewes. From *c.* 1808 the spread of fashionable housing began along London Road and on the valley floor on the Ditchling and Lewes Roads. Most of the area remained predominantly rural, however, with only a few villas on the sw-facing slopes after 1838 and a windmill atop Round Hill (built 1838, demolished 1913). N of New England Road lay the Prince of Wales's dairy. The Level was preserved for public use in 1822 (Hanover Crescent which overlooks it was developed at the same time) and ten acres of open ground to its N laid out in 1823 by James Ireland, a draper, as the Royal Gardens with cricket ground and pleasure gardens, including a canal, a Gothic tower and an aviary.

But from 1841 the railway with its station and extensive works and the railway viaduct [100] (1846) cut across the N and w parts of this area and affected the character of developments around London Road where an artisan suburb now emerged (largely cleared in the 1960s and in the early C21 once more undergoing major change). Attempts to introduce smart housing continued, however, into the 1850s N of The Level where after the decline of the Royal Gardens the surrounding area was partly redeveloped for Park Crescent. But more humble terraces became the norm in the 1860s and 1870s, to serve which St Martin's Church was built on Lewes Road in 1867, the first of an important group of Anglican mission churches in this part of the town, including St Bartholomew.

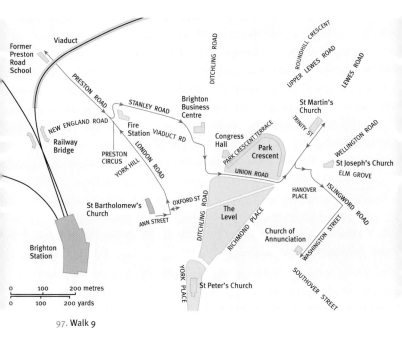

Former
Preston
Road
School

Viaduct

PRESTON ROAD

NEW ENGLAND ROAD

STANLEY ROAD

Fire
Station   VIADUCT RD

Railway
Bridge

PRESTON
CIRCUS

YORK HILL

LONDON ROAD

Railway
Bridge

Brighton
Station

St Bartholomew's
Church

ANN STREET

OXFORD ST

DITCHLING ROAD

Brighton
Business
Centre

Congress
Hall

PARK CRESCENT TERRACE

Park
Crescent

UNION ROAD

The
Level

RICHMOND PLACE

YORK PLACE

St Peter's Church

Church of
Annunciation

HANOVER
PLACE

DITCHLING ROAD

ROUNDHILL CRESCENT

UPPER LEWES ROAD

LEWES ROAD

St Martin's
Church

TRINITY ST

WELLINGTON ROAD

St Joseph's Church
ELM GROVE

ISLINGWORD ROAD

WASHINGTON STREET

SOUTHOVER STREET

0   100   200 metres
0   100   200 yards

97. Walk 9

At about the same time the workhouse (1865–7, by *J.C. & G. Lansdown* of London with *George Maynard* of Brighton; now Brighton General Hospital), was built at the top of Elm Grove on the NE edge of the urban area. Residential development also took off over Round Hill, mostly of unexceptional sweeps of terraced housing with the exception of Roundhill Crescent (*c.* 1865) which attempted a little grandeur in the Regency mould. The streets N of New England Road were developed in the 1870s on the site of the Prince of Wales's dairy, those between Viaduct Road and the railway to the N with middle-class housing served by St Saviour's Church (1886, by *Scott & Cawthorn*, dem. 1983), on Ditchling Road. By the end of the C19 the suburban districts extended as far as the town's extra mural cemeteries, laid out from 1853 on the steep-sided valley opening off Lewes Road. Much was sacrificed in the poorer areas to slum clearance and postwar redevelopment, especially w of London Road where in the early C21 the former railway lands offer new opportunities for rebuilding (e.g. New England Quarter, phase one, bounded by Cheapside, Fleet Street and New England Street, by *Chetwood Associates*, completed 2007, free-standing blocks set around hard landscaped spaces, the architecture standard developers' fare of the early C21), but good villas were also swept away on the sw-facing slopes for replacement by large blocks of flats. The area's architectural character is accordingly mixed but includes late flowerings of the Regency era development and some of the best Victorian churches in Brighton.

The walk starts on the higher ground w of London Road in **Ann Street**. Here is **St Bartholomew** (*see* p. 52), the most important church of Victorian Brighton, built in 1872–4 to serve the residential district associated with the arrival of the railway in 1841. Although most of the streets of artisan housing over which the church once towered have been cleared, the mighty scale of St Bartholomew's, no doubt intended to be awesome among the surrounding terraces, is forcefully preserved.

Dropping down the hill we arrive on **London Road**, a shopping street with a strong and somewhat scruffy character, incoherent architecturally but surprisingly rewarding for those who enjoy a bit of detective work. Here and there are clear reminders of its earlier role as a smart residential street on the approach to the town, e.g. on the w side, s of the corner with Ann Street, two early C19 survivors, obscured by later shopfronts built over their long front gardens: Nos. 9–12, two pairs of stucco villas with giant Ionic pilasters, and Nos. 13–17, similar style but terraced and not aligned with London Road. Also on this side, N of Ann Street, Nos. 22–5 are early C19 and have bows contained beneath the deep overhanging eaves.

That the Late Georgian style persisted well into the late C19 is indicated by the **chapel** in **Oxford Street**, just E of London Road. It is dated 1890 but not at all what one expects, for it is still in the C18 tradition. Symmetrical stucco front of tall paired round-arched windows either side of the round-arched entrance. The parapet ramps up at the ends and in the centre. Only the heavy mouldings around the openings seem Victorian. Back in **London Road**, starting N of Oxford Street with Nos. 114–15, a jolly Edwardian terrace filling an entire block, red brick and roughcast with white painted woodwork, dated 1904. Just beyond, on the corner of Marshall Row, the very humble proportions and catslide

98. St Bartholomew's Church, 1872–4, by Edmund Scott, dominates its surroundings

roof of Nos. 107–9 must suggest it is the remnant of once agricultural buildings.More early C19 survivors opposite (e.g. villas with fluted Ionic pilasters, modest brick terraces with bows, others larger with chunky detail and one with glazed mathematical tiles), but more typical of the street is **Woolworths**, with streamlined *moderne* façade of 1936 with coloured tiles between the glazing; it corresponds in scale with the former **Co-op** store, opposite, built as a large department store in 1931 by *Bethell & Swannell*. Pompous but stripped classicism, extended at both ends in the 1950s.

On the corner of York Hill (w side) the **Branch Tavern**, 1908, by *Clayton & Black*, with timbered gables and a square turret with ogee roof. Two more pairs of stucco villas, grander this time, follow at Nos. 54–5, with Corinthian pilasters, and Nos. 56–7 with a variant of the ammonite capital, *A.H. Wilds*'s hallmark, together with bold petal motifs in the tympana over the windows and a very unusual frieze of iron grilles set in front of the attic windows and flanked by laurel wreaths. But the best surviving house of this period in London Road is No. 87, still residential and retaining its front garden. Symmetrical and just three bays wide, with fluted Ionic giant pilasters. Buff-coloured stucco. Banded rustication to the ground floor, beneath a guilloche band, the ground-floor windows set within blind round arches. Pretty fretwork porch, perhaps later.

We are now at **Preston Circus**, a meeting of five roads, widened on the E side for tramlines in 1901 when Longhurst's brewery was demolished. The corners provide some opportunity for display e.g. the **Hare & Hounds** pub, rebuilt in 1905 by *Denman & Matthews*, and **Lloyds TSB**, 1934–5 by *W.H. Woodroffe*, bank with flats and offices over, in a Neo-Georgian Art Deco style with eccentric detailing, nicely turning the corner. **Barclays Bank** is by *Clayton & Black*, in a more routine Neo-Georgian, whilst the former **Stanford Arms** faces S, upright, brick, Italianate of *c.* 1870. A more streamlined curve, in unrelieved brickwork

99. Nos. 56–7 London Road, perhaps by A.H. Wilds, detail of the upper part of the façade

100. C19 engraved view of the London Road viaduct

with minimal detailing, is described by the **Fire Station**, won in competition in 1938 by *Graeme Highet*. Restrained Modernism, but with traditional motifs such as a tented canopy over the staff entrance, shallow projecting architraves to the first-floor windows and nice symbolic reliefs by *Joseph Cribb* to the engine doorways. Its neighbour in **Viaduct Road** is the former **Railway Mission**, 1876, by *James Barnes*, symmetrical with a bold trio of lancets flanked by entrances that just project to look like porches. Curious parapet with machicolations like a toy castle. Viaduct Road was originally known as Montpelier Road East and marked the northern limit of the parish and borough until 1873. Stucco terraces of the 1850s, on the s side with Ionic pilasters.

The view N from Preston Circus along Preston Road and Beaconsfield Road is dominated by the towering railway **viaduct** of 1846 by *John Rastrick*, engineer, for the Lewes line. Yellow brick with red brick around the arches and stone impost bands to the piers, cornice and balustraded parapet. 400 yds long, with twenty-seven semicircular headed arches and one elliptical arch (67 ft high) over Preston Road, all the piers pierced laterally with the round-arched tops mirrored at the bottom. It is all the more impressive for being built on a long curve but can no longer be taken in as a whole as was possible in 1847 when *The Builder* commented: 'the appearance of the town on approach, instead of being injured by the railway . . . is immensely improved. The effect of the curved viaduct . . . threading the Downs, with the clustering houses seen behind, is exceedingly striking.'

As the line crosses New England Road, w of Preston Circus, it is carried on a **bridge** which on the E side dates from a widening in 1852–4 and consists of four parallel cast-iron segmental-arched ribs with openwork spandrels. Behind this (i.e. a little further up the hill), is an earlier **bridge**, of 1839, also by *Rastrick*, carrying the London line into the station. It is in the form of a triumphal arch, brick with stone dressings. On Preston Road just N of the viaduct stands one of the town's excellent Board

Schools – **Preston Road School** by *Simpson & Son* (1880), brick, with steep roofs, tall chimneys and flamboyant pedimented gables.

Back to **Preston Circus**. On the N side of the Fire Station, but angled northwards, is the **Duke of York Cinema**, an early and well-preserved example of 1910, by *Clayton & Black*. Baroque with plenty of enrichments. Rusticated pilasters form tower-like features on either side of the central porch treated as a Palladian arcade with ornate Ionic columns with cartouches instead of keystones. Inside, the walls of the auditorium are divided by Doric pilasters, the proscenium arch has a concave architrave decorated with stars, possibly part of redecoration in 1937. Stanley Road runs E along the side of the cinema and leads back to **Viaduct Road** and the **Brighton Business Centre**, the large Gothic former Anglican Diocesan Training College for Schoolmistresses built in 1854 by *W.G. & E. Habershon*. It stands in a fine elevated position facing S. Knapped flint, symmetrical E-plan S elevation with plate tracery and oriel windows elaborately corbelled. Extensions to the rear, 1886, by *Scott & Cawthorn*. Diagonally opposite is the red brick former branch of the **Brighton, Hove & Preston Dispensary**, opened in 1885, in a plain Queen Anne style, very domestic.

From here **Ditchling Road** drops S and runs along the W side of **The Level**, the large area of former common land which became the focus of the townspeople's fairs and games after the enclosures of the open spaces along the Steine in the C18 and early C19 (*see* Walk 2). It was given to the town in 1822 by Thomas Kemp, laid out by *A.H. Wilds* and *Henry Phillips* (*see* Topic Box, p. 121) and in the same year **Union Road** was constructed across it linking Ditchling and Lewes Roads. On its N side **gatepiers** with niches, entablature with triglyphs and guttae and surmounted by a seated lion and lioness – all that remains of Ireland's **Royal Gardens** of 1823. The venture was a failure and its cricket ground became the private gardens to **Park Crescent**, begun in 1849 by *A.H.*

Wilds. Forty-eight houses arranged around more of a horseshoe than a crescent. Italianate with heavy bracketed eaves with wreaths between the brackets. A busy and awkward composition facing the gardens of four-bay hipped roof pavilions with set-back two-bay towers between with top-heavy gabled roofs. Taking its cue from their design is the **Brighton Congress Hall** in **Park Crescent Terrace** of 2000 by *David Greenwood* of the *Salvation Army Architects Department*, replacing the hall of 1883. Octagonal with a central clerestory lighting the main worship space.

Facing the end of Union Road is **Hanover Place** and the **Percy & Wagner Almshouses** which stood in open country when first erected in 1795 for six poor widows of the Church of England. Yellow brick, castellated, Gothick with Georgian sash windows; originally eleven bays but extended at both ends, in a matching style, in 1859, paid for by the Rev. Henry Wagner and his sister Mary. The rest of the Royal Gardens to the N, between Upper Lewes Road and Lewes Road, were taken for development in the 1860s and 1870s and laid out with streets of artisan housing. The Rev. Arthur Wagner bought some of the land and advanced money to builders to develop houses that were to cost no more than £120. He founded a mission church for the district in 1867 and its rebuilding in 1872–5, as **St Martin's Church**, was paid for by Wagner and his brothers in memory of their father the Rev. H.M. Wagner (d. 1870). This is the first major work by *George Somers Clarke Jun.*, whose father (a solicitor) had been a close friend of H.M. Wagner. It is almost exactly contemporary with St Bartholomew but yet larger, indeed the largest church in Brighton. E.E. style. Yellow and red brick, big forms, almost ruthless. Long nave and chancel of uniform height and width [103], with a long row of clerestory windows, windowless aisles, and a w front with large lancets. A broad saddleback tower the width of

102. Park Crescent, begun in 1849 by A.H. Wilds, view of the garden front

103. St Martin's Church, Lewes Road, by George Somers Clarke Jun., 1872–5, view of the chancel

the chancel and rising from it was designed but never built and the temporary bellcote remains. Lofty interior with octagonal stone piers and brick arches. The baptistery at the w end set at a higher level to increase dramatic effect. Large clerestory windows set in recesses linked by a wall passage. The aisles below with altar recesses. Panelled wagon roof to the nave painted with the coats of arms of Anglican sees in the Colonies and America; vaulted chancel. The breathtaking magnificence of the interior derives from the cathedral-like scale but also in great part from the quality of the fittings, conceived by the architect and executed under his direction. **Font**, 1875, Sussex marble with other inlaid marbles, souvenirs of Henry Wagner's travels. **Cover** elaborate and baldacchino-like canopy designed by Somers Clarke but not installed until 1907. The **pulpit** of 1880, carved by *George Trollope & Sons*. Dwarfed by the 55-ft high **canopy** carved by *J.E. Knox*, a towering edifice of tracery and pinnacles, inspired by the Sacrament House in the church of St Sebald, Nuremberg, and higher than the canopy over the Bishop's throne in Exeter Cathedral. *Knox* also carved the **lectern** and the figures on the **rood**, the two outer ones added in 1909. The **organ case** was designed by *Somers Clarke*, not as a screen but to show the various parts of the organ. The massive **reredos** with tiers of Aesthetic Movement paintings, is the *chef d'oeuvre* of *H.E. Wooldridge*. The architectural carving is by Knox and the sixty-nine carved statues by *Mayer & Co*. A fantastic display, crowned by a profusion of canopies and pinnacles. **Stations of the Cross** in *Della Robbia* ware. Aesthetic Style painted tile **war memorial** (N aisle), commemorating the Nile Campaign and probably by *James Powell & Sons*. **Stained glass** all made by *Powells*. E window designed by *Wooldridge*, 1874, w window with the canopies by *Somers Clarke* and the figures by *Wooldridge*. Clerestory windows 1886. Two small windows (s chapel and s aisle w) designed by *Henry Holiday*, 1875. Terracotta **relief** above the s door, by *John Birnie Philip*.

Returning down Lewes Road now and into **Elm Grove** where facing downhill is **St Joseph's Church** (R.C.), a soaring design on a prodigious scale. Begun in 1879 by *W. Kedo Broder*, replacing an 1860s mission chapel. The original design (*see The Builder* 1880) was meant to be more richly detailed, with a nave, polygonal chancel, transepts with apsidal chapels and a tall w tower and spire. What there is is most ambitious, although only the chancel and nave were complete before Broder was killed by a train in 1881. After that *J.S. Hansom* added a s transept and chapel in 1885. The w front was finished in 1901, by *F.A. Walters*, who also built the N transept and chapel and enlarged Hansom's s transept to Broder's original intentions. The completed church finally opened in 1906. The style is C13 Gothic, built of Kentish ragstone with Bath stone dressings. What impresses is the sheer height, outside and in, with few distracting details [104]. The transept chapels form five sides of an octagon, so they actually project beyond the transept end walls and interfere with the polygonal chancel, a very busy effect. The transepts are as deep as they are wide and the nave has no more than passage aisles, all contributing to the dramatic verticality. E.E. rib-vaulted interior with Bath stone ribs springing from high shafts and vaults of white Beere brick. The width of the transepts is divided by a tall round pier with foliage capitals: several of the other capitals and responds remain uncarved.

Islingword Road leads into Hanover, an area of tightly packed terraced housing laid out in a grid of streets either following the contour or climbing the hill steeply from Lewes Road to Queen's Park Road. Streets closest to Lewes Road were developed from the 1820s but the area mostly flourished in the 1860s. A little way up on the right is

104. St Joseph's Roman Catholic Church, Elm Grove, 1879–1906, by W. Kedo Broder and others, view of sanctuary

Washington Street where halfway down on the right is the **Church of the Annunciation**, begun in 1864 by *William Dancy*, a local surveyor. This was one of Rev. Arthur Wagner's first benefactions and, like his St Mary and St Mary Magdalene, Bread Street (by *Bodley*, 1862, demolished 1950), very modest; not yet with the overwhelming scale of St Bartholomew [98] and St Martin. The steep change in levels enabled the school to be built at a lower level, accessed from Coleman Street (domestic windows below, groups of plain lancets in the trio of gables above), with the church, on Washington Street, on top. Proposals to remove the floor and rebuild the church more grandly were abandoned in favour of enlargement, work carried out in 1881 by *Edmund Scott*, with the addition of a N aisle, similar to the nave, and remodelling of the church, including the reuse of a three-light window with Geometrical tracery of 1853 by *R.C. Carpenter*, originally at St Nicholas's church. The tower by *F. T. Cawthorn*, 1892, has simple shouldered-arched bell-openings and gableted lucarnes in the tiled pyramid roof. The materials are brick and flint throughout, all very modest and set into the tight grid of terraced housing such that it is not visible from afar. The **interior** is modest too, with whitewashed brick walls and two rows of wooden posts with struts supporting the roof – almost like a Colonial pioneers' church. However simple, the furnishings are exceptionally rich. **Stained glass**, (liturgical) E window by *Morris & Co.*, designed by *Burne-Jones*, 1866, in memory of Elizabeth Attree. The W window is the earliest known surviving design by *J.R. Clayton* (made by *Ward & Hughes*), 1853 and praised by *The Ecclesiologist* as 'singularly destitute of that vulgarity which is so apt to cling to English specimens of glass painting'. Other windows, 1884, by *Heaton, Butler & Bayne*. *Martin Travers* refurnished the sanctuary in 1925. His is the Spanish-style **reredos**, cleverly incorporating the Morris window, though it clips the stained glass rather too closely. **Altar**, **tabernacle** and gilded hanging **canopy**. To either side he provided Baroque frames for two *Della Robbia* plaques installed in 1908. **Font**, *c.* 1870 and French. An unusual piece of wood and terracotta, square base and octagonal bowl with domed top surmounted by figures of Our Lord baptizing John the Baptist.

The walk ends here, with a descent back to Valley Gardens with buses to all parts of the city.

105. Church of the Annunciation, Washington Street, 1864 by William Dancy, remodelled in 1881 by Edmund Scott

Walk 10.

Queen's Park and Carlton Hill

Queen's Park opened as Brighton Park in 1823. Like Ireland's Royal Gardens of the same date (*see* p. 184), it was placed beyond the built-up area where space was plentiful and land cheaper. A subscription pleasure garden, it was advertised as having a pump room in 1824, but was not an immediate success and its owner decided to raise capital by building villas around it. Designs were drawn up possibly by *Wilds & Busby*. This too was unsuccessful and the park was sold in the late 1820s to Thomas Attree, local solicitor and Town Clerk, who enclosed it in 1830 and changed the name in honour of Queen Adelaide in 1836. Attree also promoted, unsuccessfully, a scheme for building villas around the park. Eventually the park was presented to Brighton Corporation and reopened in 1892. Of that date **Park Street Gate** by the Borough Surveyor, *Francis May*, who also designed the present layout. A central triumphal arch with flat-arched pedestrian entrances to either side. Bold dentil cornice and attic bearing an inscription. The **Egremont Arch**, the sw entrance, is similar but a little more elaborate, its pedestrian

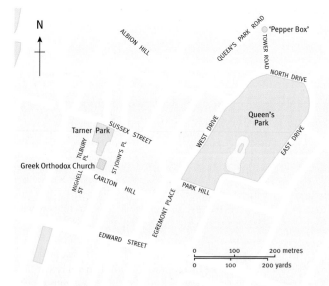

106. Walk 10

107. Queen's Park, Egremont Arch, 1892 by Francis May, Borough Surveyor

entrances arched and pedimented and topped with finials in the form of a Byzantine reliquarium.

Inside, to the left of the Park Street Gate, is an Ionic portico, all that remains of the **Royal Spa** built for Dr F.A. Struve in 1825 for the sale of his artificial mineral water. The architect is given as one *Lorraine*. Struve had opened similar spas in Dresden, Berlin and Leipzig. His royal warrant was obtained in 1835. The pump room was closed in the 1850s and all but the portico demolished in the 1970s.

The centre of the park is a small combe or valley, made more dramatic as part of the design by *May* and the borough's head gardener *George Ward*. This included the **lake** with **island** and rocky waterfall at the head of the valley, the network of paths and extensive planting. Following the path to the E of the lake the **clock tower**, 1915, by *Llewellyn E. Williams* of London, won in competition, stands in an elevated position away to the right. Red brick and Portland stone, a somewhat stolid design lacking in vigour. N of the lake a red brick and terracotta **drinking fountain** of 1893 by *May*; a curious medievalizing piece with panel tracery, octagonal corner turrets and a central turret or lantern but with Renaissance console brackets and turret tops going onion-shaped.

The original plans for a suburb of villas in the manner of Regent's Park were unrealized and the encircling roads of **West** and **East drives** are now lined with cheerful Late Victorian and Edwardian red brick villas. On the park's N side, Attree commissioned two houses from *Charles Barry*, one for himself: known as Attree Villa [108] it was designed in

108. Queen's Park, Attree Villa, mid-c19 engraved view showing the Garden Temple and the 'Pepper-Box'

1829–30 and demolished in 1972. Its site, E of Tower Road, is occupied by **Carn Court**, depressing 1970s housing, but two of Barry's garden structures remain: an Italianate **Garden Temple** with shallow pyramidal roof and the '**Pepper-Box**', visible at the top of Tower Road, a water tower/observation tower. Octagonal base and a tall rotunda with eleven attached Composite columns. Upper stage with pilasters and rich entablature beneath the domed top crowned by a shallow urn or tazza.

By the mid c19 the area between the Park and the Steine was developing as **Carlton Hill**, an artisan district for which the Rev. H.M. Wagner provided the third of his new churches for Brighton: **St John the Evangelist** [11] (now Greek Orthodox). Built 1839–40 by *George Cheesman Jun.* A strangely bleak classical s front with a recessed blank centre with giant Doric pilasters. Pedimented small entrances in the outer bays. Big metope frieze, not quite a pediment, and tiny bell-turret. The entrances lead into staircase lobbies with a vestry between and the church behind set at right angles so that the altar faces E. Galleries around three sides (deeper on the s) on cast-iron Greek Doric columns. Low chancel flanked by pilasters. Restoration 1879 by *Scott & Hyde*. In **Mighell Street**, almost opposite, **Mighell's Farmhouse** is an early c19 cobbled building with a pedimented Tuscan porch, a surprising survival in an area extensively redeveloped in the c20. Nos. 1–5 **Tilbury Place**, opposite Mighell Place, are another fragment of early c19 Brighton. No. 1 was St John's Lodge, facing s over a large garden, with ground-floor veranda. It was for many years the home of Edwin Tarner, a wealthy merchant, and his wife Laetitia (née Tilbury). Its gardens are now **Tarner Park**, which contains a flint and brick **lookout tower** of two cylindrical stages, the upper one smaller to allow an intermediate walkway.

Walk 11.

Hove

Hove 'lies one mile to the west of Brighton, from whence it is a pleasant walk in summer, over the fields' (J.D. Parry, *The Coast of Sussex*, 1833). Although first mentioned in 1288, the small settlement had a population of only about 300 in 1825 (by which date the population of neighbouring Brighton exceeded 25,000). The Manor House (demolished 1936)

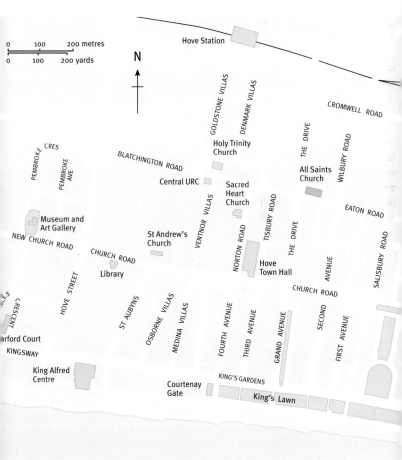

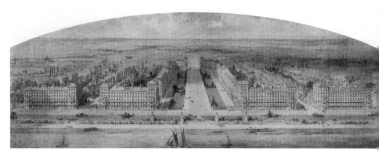

110. Watercolour perspective after Sir James Knowles of the Stanford Estate showing Grand Avenue in the centre

and a few houses and cottages were situated in Hove Street running down to the sea, with St Andrew's Church away to the NE. Housing spread over the parish boundary from Brighton from the 1820s with building on the Wick Estate, first at Brunswick Town and then Adelaide Crescent (*see* Walk 4). There were small pockets of Late Georgian development further w close to the seafront but the first significant suburban scheme was the Cliftonville estate E of the old village spreading from the seafront N to the railway station (which took its name when it opened in 1865). According to Charles Fleet, writing in 1858, Cliftonville 'sprang into existence with the rapidity of a Trans-Atlantic town', but this was nothing compared with what was to follow.

The single largest landholding in mid-C19 Hove belonged to the Stanfords of Preston Manor (*see* p. 205). Unrealized development schemes were drawn up for the seafront w of Adelaide Crescent in 1825 by *Charles Barry* and, in 1826 or 1827, by *Charles Busby*. Under the terms of the will of William Stanford (d.1853) the estate land could not be sold, effectively preventing development until unlocked by the Stanford Estate Act of 1871. *The Building News* reported in 1872 that 'the Stanford Estate . . . propose building one hundred houses a year for the next fifteen years'. The number of houses in Hove roughly trebled before 1880 and by 1884 550 acres of the estate had been sold or were under a building agreement. It seems likely that the Stanfords took a close interest in the way their lands were developed as there is a consistency in the character of buildings on their estate both in Hove and in Brighton. Indeed, the *Brighton Times* commented in 1881 that West Brighton was laid out under Vere Benett-Stanford's 'personal direction'.

The prime seafront parcel of land s of Church Road was taken by the West Brighton Estate Company in 1872 (Ellen Stanford's uncle was a Director). The company's first architect was *Sir James Knowles*, who drew up a masterplan for a grand N–S avenue flanked by lesser avenues. Subsequently several other architects were engaged on the estate, notably *H.J. Lanchester* who moved to Hove in 1870 and had already designed villas in Denmark Terrace and elsewhere. From 1875 the major developer was *William Willett* (father and son), established London builder-developers. 'Willett-built' houses had a reputation for quality and by the late 1880s the Willetts had erected numerous large detached and semi-detached houses and terraced houses. There was, however, strict control over design, and the architecture of the new suburb was quickly criticized for its uniformity, especially in the use of gault brick – there is 'no attempt even to Queen Anne-ise the estate, no Gothic work of any character', 'Benham white facing bricks are used throughout . . . producing a cold monotony' and 'we are obliged to ask if any architectural supervision exists, or if builders are allowed to do anything that pleases them' (*Building News*, 1877 and 1878). This was rectified in the more picturesque designs of the 1880s and 1890s by architects such as *G.M. Jay* (Fourth Avenue, E side N end) and by Willett's in-house architects *H.B. Measures* (from 1884 to 1891) and (from 1891), *Amos Faulkner*.

The influence of the Domestic Revival is more consistent in the character of the suburbs created w of Cliftonville after *c.* 1890 by *Lainson & Sons* and from 1895 by *Clayton & Black* on the Vallance estate, N and s of Brooker Hall (*see* Hove Museum and Art Gallery, p. 197), where broad, curving tree-lined streets such as Pembroke Avenue and Crescent have large houses in red brick with half-timbered gables.

Hove still maintains quite a different character from its more urban and raffish neighbour, spaciously laid out and still predominantly low-rise – a certain gentility prevails. Owing to its size only the most important buildings of Hove are described, followed by the seafront and the key aspects of the suburban developments of Cliftonville and the Stanfords' West Brighton estate.

Major Buildings

St Andrew's Church, Church Road. The parish church of Hove until 1892, its character still that of a village church, but much rebuilt by *George Basevi* in 1833–6. Neo-Norman, heavy and uninspired. Coursed flint with stone and Roman cement dressings. w tower with higher stair tower. The chancel is E.E. in style, probably genuine but heavily restored. The medieval church seems to have been largely early C13 as indicated by the chancel and, more convincingly, by the four easternmost bays of the nave arcade. These have round piers with waterholding bases and much-restored stiff-leaf capitals. Pointed arches of two orders, the inner with keeled roll mouldings. Heavy, rustic-looking kingpost roof to the nave, incorporating medieval timbers. **Stained glass**, E window by *Wailes*, 1851. **Monuments**. Mrs Yard d.1836. In a medallion an angel carries her heavenwards. Lt Henry Sanderman d.1852. Baconish in style. Two kneeling female figures with a portrait medallion. George Basevi d.1851 – not the architect, who died in 1845 when he fell from scaffolding at Ely Cathedral. A Gothic tablet by *W. Pepper the elder* of Brighton. **Lychgate**. 1953, with a neat hipped roof of Horsham stone.

All Saints (*see* p. 55)

Sacred Heart (R.C.) Church and Presbytery, Norton Road. Dignified and grand E.E. Gothic, in spite of the cramped site. 1880–1 by *John Crawley*, who died a few days before its opening. By him the polygonal apsed sanctuary with a busy and arresting outline, the eastern three bays of the nave and aisles and the presbytery. Crawley's practice was taken over by *J. S. Hansom* who extended the church w in 1887. Assertive Lady Chapel, N side, 1915, by *F.A. Walters,* with a five-light window under a depressed four-centred arch set high up. The delightful interior surprisingly little altered. Six-bay arcades, the westernmost narrower, clustered piers with eight shafts and octagonal capitals and bases. Hollow-chamfered arches and oversized angels playing musical instruments at the springing points. At the w end a canted stone gallery with a spherical triangle window above. The clerestory has single lancets with stone wall-shafts between, supporting a keeled timber roof. The sanctuary is stone-vaulted on shafts. Sumptuously decorated with vault paintings on canvas by *Westlake*, a continuous arcaded **reredos** around the apse, heavy and ornate **communion rails** of white and red marble, carved stone and mosaic **pulpit** and **high altar** and tabernacle, also of marble. Now free-standing **altar** with sculptured relief of Christ's burial. The **baptistery** has carved panels with inset sculpture reliefs of baptismal scenes. Alabaster **font** carved with traceried panels and the symbols of the Evangelists. **Stained glass**. In the sanctuary, 1881, by *Mayer & Co.*, in the s aisle from the E, 1897 by *Powell (James) & Sons*, 1920 by *Lavers & Westlake*, one signed by Mayer, 1909 by *Paul Woodroffe*, 1907 by *Hardman's*, 1928 by *Margaret Westlake* and the roundel over the w door, 1921 by *Nathaniel Westlake*, his last work. Lady Chapel E window, 1917 by Westlake. In the N aisle more glass by Mayer and Lavers & Westlake.

Hove Town Hall, Norton Road. 1970–3 by *Wells-Thorpe & Partners*, on the site of *Waterhouse*'s Town Hall of 1882, considered 'so red, so Gothic, so hard, so imperishable' by Pevsner (but destroyed by fire 1966). A public building of its time, as different to its surroundings as its predecessor; though the scale seeks to fit in to the suburban neighbourhood. Spreading irregular plan, set back and with no separation between the street and the open space around the building. Tough exterior of ribbed natural aggregate panels combined with broad areas of glass curtain walling, a gentler form of Brutalism than might have been expected at an earlier date. Main entrance of monumental scale, set back behind four faceted giant columns supporting a deeply overhanging roof and from which a yet deeper canopy is cantilevered. Council offices at the N end around an enclosed courtyard (now infilled) and towards Church Road, council chamber, mayoral suite and committee rooms on three levels. The Great Hall is cantilevered out over a public piazza. A clock tower at the SE corner announces the town hall in views along Church Road. Grand entrance **foyer**, but not intimidating, totally glazed on the two outer sides and originally with a luxuriant internal 'garden' over the main entrance. The main **staircase** sweeps up in two flights which unite

111. Hove Town Hall, by Wells-Thorpe & Partners, 1970–3, detail of Great Hall ceiling

and return as a broad single flight to the first floor, treated as an open platform with views down on either side. Panels of Wych elm; over the lift doors these form square light boxes, like organ pipes. The **Great Hall** has a dramatic ceiling of angular acoustic diffusers, like a geometric egg box, which appears to float within a glazed border (now blacked out).

Hove Public Library, Church Road [16]. A highly inventive design of 1907–8, won in competition by *Percy Robinson & W. Alban Jones* of Leeds. Edwardian Baroque. Ashlar front, the central entrance emphasized by a full-height recessed arch beneath a pediment. On the ground floor to either side, groups of three large windows under egg-and-dart-moulded entablature with cherubs' heads as capitals. Above, triplets of circular windows framed by ribbons, garlands and swags. Lower, service entrance to the left, the tympanum over the carriageway carved with two cherubs squeezed in. Spatially interesting interior, e.g. the first floor with shallow, almost Soanian arches and pendentives supporting a shallow dome. At the rear, the circular library within a rotunda whose upper part was originally open at the rear as a reading garden.

Hove Museum and Art Gallery, New Church Road. Formerly Brooker Hall, built in 1877 for John Oliver Vallance by *Lainson & Sons*. Drab Italianate. In the garden an exotic alien, the **Jaipur Gate** [121], given to Hove in 1926 but designed as the entrance to the Indian Art Ware courts of the 1886 Colonial & Indian Exhibition held at South Kensington. Designed by Colonel *Samuel Swinton Jacob* and Surgeon Major *Thomas Holbein Hendley* and carved in Shekhawati, Rajastan, from Bombay teak. Above the gate is a kiosk, representing the Nakar Khana, the chamber above the gateway to a temple where musicians played.

The Hove Seafront

Barford Court, No. 157 Kingsway. A large house occupying an entire street block, of 1934–7 by *Robert Cromie*, the cinema architect, for an eccentric iron millionaire from Newcastle, Ian Stuart Millar. An odd placement on the seafront to which it contributes little for it is set back in a sunken garden enclosed by a brick wall. Sea views are had only from the upper windows. The exterior is an austere interpretation of Neo-Georgian, in a drab grey-purple brick said to have been specially made and imported from Italy. U-plan, originally open to gardens to the N but now closed with a later single-storey range. The main approach is from the E into the courtyard designed for visitors arriving by motorcar; the wings have half-columns on the ground floor between garages on the E

112. Barford Court (No. 157 Kingsway), 1934–7 by Robert Cromie, detail of staircase balustrade

side. In the centre of the N front, a chimney with stacks linked by an arch (a motif repeated elsewhere) and set between two almost semi-circular projecting towers linked by a first-floor balcony: one contains the staircase, the other has the understated front door set on the curve.

The garden front has a central projecting ground-floor bay forming a balcony above in front of an open loggia. A wheatear motif is used on external doors and perimeter gates. The interior is Art Deco and redolent of Cromie's cinema work, finished to a high standard with several pieces of built-in furniture. Reception rooms lined with flush panelling with inlaid detail. Contemporary light fittings, some set within diminishing ceiling recesses, and one extravagant tiered glass chandelier over the staircase, which also has a stepped balustrade with metal quadrants in diminishing layers of four. In the northern part of the garden a new building, sensitively designed in 1996 by *Peter Currie Architects* for the Royal Masonic Benevolent Institution who have run the site as a residential home since 1990.

Kingsway between St Aubyn's and Fourth Avenue was developed from the 1830s, e.g. Nos. 1–6 **Victoria Terrace**, an incomplete group of *c.* 1830 with quirky motifs, giant pilasters with capitals going Corinthian but enclosing single palmettes and shell-heads over windows that suggest the hand of *A.H. Wilds* (the equally peculiar oriel windows on cast-iron brackets must be later); **St Catherine's Terrace** (1852–3) with bold covered balconies canting forward around the bay windows; and **Courtenay Terrace** of the 1840s with S-facing bow fronts looking along individual private gardens towards the sea. Otherwise this part of Kingsway is characterized by Victorian hotels: the former St Aubyn's Hotel (now **Alibi** bar), of 1908 by *Arthur Packham* with a florid octagonal-domed corner; the **Sussex Hotel**, busy Italianate of 1855; **St Catherine's Lodge Hotel**, 1850s Jacobethan. Also mansion blocks and C20 blocks of flats: **St Aubyn's Mansions**, facing the sea, 1899 by *Lainson & Sons*, Free Renaissance style with mullioned windows, shaped gables and a corner turret; **Courtenay Gate**, a large four-square Neo-Georgian block of serviced apartments of 1934 by *Coleridge, Jennings & Soimenow*; **Flag Court**, 1958–9, by *T.P. Bennett & Son*, angled to maximize sea views and, unlike Courtenay Gate, with no attempt to soften its sheer bulk; and, on the corner of Medina Villas, **The Priory**, a block of flats by *Gotch & Partners*, 1961, brick, eight storeys, the top set back behind an open concrete frame. Crisply detailed balconies in tiers, painted white and made lighter by having glazed ends. The **King Alfred Centre** dominates the seafront W of St Aubyn's and is set to do so more dramatically if notorious proposals for a development including two tall buildings designed by *Frank Gehry* come to fruition. The existing buildings are dreadful: **Hove Marina** of 1937 by *Tom Humble*, Hove Borough Surveyor, and *Scott Brownrigg & Turner*'s ghastly **swimming pool** complex of 1980–2, designed apparently with no thought to context or sea views.

Suburban Developments

Cliftonville. The suburb was projected in 1851–2 by a syndicate of four local men. The seafront and streets N and S of Church Road came first, mostly called Villas and in their naming and style of housing displaying the fashion for the Italianate popularized by Osborne House on the Isle of Wight, e.g. **Osborne Villas** with pretty semi-detached stucco houses, just two storeys over basements, the canted bay windows with little tent roofs and fretted timber valances. Tudorbethan was also popular in Cliftonville, e.g. Nos. 40–3 **Medina Villas**, probably by *F.D. Bannister* who lived at No. 42. Bannister was the engineer to the London, Brighton & South Coast Railway and, according to Porter's *History of Hove* (1897), was the principal architect of Cliftonville. From the 1860s development spread N of Blatchington Road on former Stanford land sold for the building of the railway in 1840, stimulated by the opening of Cliftonville Station in 1865 (extended 1893 and renamed Hove Station from 1895 when the original Hove station situated off Holland Road closed).

The suburb's growth also led to the building of **Holy Trinity Church** at the N end of Ventnor Villas in 1863 by *James Woodman*. Tower added 1866, the N aisle in 1868. Polychromatic Gothic with plate tracery and an insubstantial battlemented S tower for which a spire was intended. On the chancel's S side a rarity, an external pulpit added in 1912. Ionic pilasters support a cavetto-moulded cornice. Evangelical tradition is evident also from the nave W extension which internally has a **gallery**, unusual for a church of the 1860s. Plastered interior, with the chancel roof trusses on foliate corbels and a plaster vault to the apse. The four-bay nave arcades have over-large carved capitals and the roof has arched trusses which intersect, like scissor braces, at the top. The aisle roofs have trusses of alternating design. **Font**, 1878, of Caen stone with columns of Sicilian marble. **Stained glass**, mostly by *Ward & Hughes*, 1869–76, with architectural canopies and stylized plant forms in the borders. One N aisle window, Easter garden scene, 1867, by *Hardman's*. One S aisle window, 1969, by *Marguerite Douglas-Thompson*, Jesus with Peter on the water, with swirling blue and white.

On the corner opposite, the **Central United Reformed Church**, built as a Congregational church in 1867 by *Horatio Goulty*. Ragstone, E.E. Gothic with tall two-light plate-traceried windows with stepped buttresses between. One composition with attached manse to the W: excessively tall dormers and paired lancet windows. In **Goldstone Villas** a former Primitive Methodist church of 1878 by *Thomas Wonnacott* (now **Europa House**), stuccoed and still in the classical style of the mid century. Redeveloped as offices for Olivetti in 1972 by *Edward Cullinan & Partners* who removed the rear wall and inserted a glazed, steel staircase. In **Denmark Villas**, spacious development of after 1865 but at the top the **Ralli Memorial Hall** of 1913 by *Read & Macdonald*, architects for much of the Cadogan and Grosvenor estates in London; both had trained in the offices of George & Peto. Restrained Renaissance style in red brick with stone-mullioned and transomed windows. Hexagonal porch entrance with balcony above.

Stanford's West Brighton Estate. The West Brighton Estate Co. leased fifty-seven acres of the Stanfords' West Brighton estate towards the seafront in 1871. *Sir James Knowles* drew up proposals for Grand Avenue and the streets to either side named, American-style, First, Second, Third and Fourth Avenues [110]. Only the two eastern seafront-facing blocks were built to Knowles's design and just one remains, on the corner of **Grand Avenue**, built in 1872–4 (later the Prince's Hotel, now Council Offices). Five storeys, a pediment in the centre and taller three-bay end pavilions of unequal height, that to the corner of Grand Avenue having an extra storey and a pyramid roof. The bald Italianate architecture set the mould for the initial development of the estate. Tactful extension to the N of 1978–81 by *Fitzroy Robinson Miller Bourne & Partners*. Yellow brick enveloped in a steel corset of balconies.

Development of **Grand Avenue** was surprisingly slow and in 1900 the company admitted, 'Grand Avenue has not proved a business success owing to the absence of demand for high-class residences.' The scale is generous, with the buildings set back behind strips of grass and side roads, effectively forming another sea-facing square. In the middle looking out to sea, a bronze **statue** of Queen Victoria in full regalia, by *Thomas Brock* (commissioned 1897, erected 1901). Portland stone plinth with inset bronze panels of allegorical reliefs. Corresponding at the avenue's N end is the Hove **war memorial**, 1921 by *Lutyens*, a granite Tuscan column topped by a bronze figure of St George, after Donatello.

113. No. 11 Grand Avenue, by Amos Faulkner, 1900–3

Some 1880s gault brick villas survive on the E side and a mansion block at the NW corner, but Grand Avenue today is dominated by eleven-storey blocks of flats of the 1930s and 1950s, mostly nondescript, except No. 4 (E side), of 1935–8, by *Murrell & Piggott* of London. *Moderne* style, in brown brick with Crittall windows. The façade is articulated with projections to either side with central recessed balconies and curved balconies set in the re-entrant angles. A high-level balcony links the two projections. Stuccoed ground floor with central entrance and a relief panel of Neptune above. At the NE corner, Nos. 8–11 of 1900–3 by *Amos Faulkner* for Willett. Faulkner had worked with Ernest Newton on the Willetts' development of the Camden Park estate at Chislehurst and here takes up Newton's Olde English style. Red brick with extensive tile-hanging and steep hipped tiled roofs. No. 9 has a broad two-storey bow window and an early C18-style porch canopy with pendants, whilst No. 11 [113] has prominent diamond-plan chimneys.

First Avenue. Developed in the 1870s–80s mostly with terraces rather than the detached and semi-detached villas that predominate elsewhere on the West Brighton estate. At the N end on either side **mews** running parallel to Church Road and on the w side the **Hove Place** pub, Tudor-style, set back, and squeezed in between the mews and a terrace but built in 1879 by *J. T. Chappell*. No. 37 is the last house in the terrace. The entrance and staircase halls have finely detailed early C18-style panelling of 1896 by *A. N. Prentice*. In **Second Avenue** several houses by *E. W. Hudson*, including No. 21 of 1878–9 with Gothic arches to the first floor, lugged corners to the upper-floor windows and a decorative canopied cast-iron balcony bridging between the two projecting bays. **Third Avenue**'s grandest house is No. 4 of 1878 by *W. Galsworthy Davie*, a pupil of Butterfield. Buff terracotta panels relieve the pale estate brick, with Aesthetic Movement-inspired decorative friezes and sunflowers. Especially attractive the entrance porch with sgraffito panels to the reveals, one with figures and inscription 'Come unto these yellow sands'. No. 5 is part of the same group of immensely tall detached houses at Nos. 1–4 **King's Gardens** of 1889 by *J. T. Chappell* (now flats). Queen Anne style of the urban mansion block by the seaside variety – with shaped gables, turrets and slab chimneystacks, of red brick (now mostly rendered over) and terracotta bands. Symmetrical as a group but individually asymmetrical. Inside, staircases with trelliswork panels to balustrade and as decorative panels beneath the string. Lifts were provided from the beginning.

Fourth Avenue has **The Hove Club** of 1897 by *Samuel Denman* in very free Jacobean style with a series of distinctive chimneys which rise from shaped gables, their flues framing the windows below. These have mullions and transoms with arched openings in the upper tier. Heavy timber and plaster detailing inside. Open-well staircase with iron balusters with sun motif. Facing, a good series of semi-detached houses of the 1890s, probably by *G.M. Jay*, several of whose designs were illustrated in the *Building News* in those years.

Church Road. The gault brick estate-style architecture predominates between Norton Road and Salisbury Road, but here treated as symmetrical terraces, more urban in scale and with ground-floor shops. Nos. 96–108 on the s side w of Fourth Avenue is typical whilst Nos. 105–119, opposite, effects a transition between the Cliftonville Italianate and the later Stanford Estate style. Nos. 91–103 (N side) has a Portland stone projection to the corner of Tisbury Road of 1927 for the **National Provincial Bank** by *F.C.R. Palmer*. Nos. 20–52 (s side) is on a larger scale. Here the main part has canted bays above the shopfronts and rises to four storeys, with the end pavilions rising higher, with a full extra storey at the western end, addressing the greater scale of Grand Avenue. The pavilion at the eastern end has big Gothic windows on the first floor and turns the corner into Second Avenue.

The Drive continues the spacious N–S axis set by Grand Avenue (originally the entire length from the seafront was named The Drive), crossed by Church Road and Eaton Road where stands Pearson's All Saints' Church (*see* p. 55). N of Church Road are immediately the characteristic, generously proportioned gault brick villas in the estate style, all relatively consistent, though varied in detail and intermingled with later buildings. No. 16 (w side) by *A. Cresswell*, 1882, marks a change to steeply pitched roofs and gables with decorative bargeboards and to a more elaborate porch. No. 22, called **Arundel House** (1898) is a red brick and terracotta mansion block in a Free Jacobean style. Asymmetrical with a pinnacled tower combining with a skyline of turrets and decorative chimneys. The tower has oriel windows supported on half-columns which mushroom out to form the corbelled supports. Castellated entrance with decorative frieze and finely detailed joggle-jointed lintel. N of Eaton Road are good exemplars of Willett's later activities at Nos. 69–79 (w side), designed by *H.B. Measures*, 1888–90. Red brick and terracotta in a Flemish–Queen Anne Revival style, asymmetrical and each one different. Brick and terracotta boundary walls with pretty little octagonal piers with ogee caps. No. 75 has a terracotta porch with mullioned windows and a semicircular oriel, its roof colliding with a gabled roof dormer. No. 73 has deliciously fanciful crouching creatures about to launch themselves from the shaped gable [114]. On the corner of Cromwell Road and The Drive, **Eaton Manor**, 1963, by *Hubbard Ford & Partners*, a heavy L-plan block of flats, purple brick and exposed concrete frame and ribbed concrete panels below windows. Symmetrical elevations, picking up the square and canted bays of Victorian Hove. The block is set over a basement car park with bridges from the pavement to the otherwise understated entrances.

The gault brick style of the early Stanford estate development by Willett's firm is still much in evidence on the nearby streets in spite of postwar rebuilding (e.g. houses in Cromwell Road, Eaton Gardens, Tisbury Road, together with the stables in Wilbury Grove (1878), Eaton Grove (1880) and Cambridge Grove (1882)). There is an undoubted attraction in the homogeneity and good proportions of this housing and those with an eye for detail will delight in the variety of cut and moulded brick, occasional use of terracotta and details of joinery and ironwork. However, the *Building News* in 1877 was not effusive, commenting, 'It is a pity . . . that the vulgar and bizarre kind of ornament we see is not condemned.'

Wilbury Road has a good mix, spread out. **Wilbury Lawn** (No. 44, N end) of 1905 by *J.H. Ball*, in a mixed Neo-Georgian style, the steeply pitched tiled roof looking early C18 but oddly asymmetrical and otherwise more Late Georgian in inspiration. Cement-rendered, with large un-Georgian dormers and a flat, rusticated surround to the front door. Jalousies to many of the windows. Large blocks of luxury interwar flats intrude further s: **Wilbury Grange** of 1937 by *Joseph Hill*, steel-framed and brick-faced with tiers of white-rendered balconies, with accommodation for servants provided at the top; and **Harewood Court**, larger, two parallel ranges linked at the N end by a lower pavilion, originally housing communal lounges and a smoking room. Designed in 1947 but not built until 1956, by *Denman & Son* for the Royal Masonic Benevolent Institution. The street range is divided into two seven-storey monoliths, stepped in at the corners and with five-storey shallow bows rising from the first floor.

114. No. 73 The Drive, by H.B. Measures, 1888–90, detail of the gable

Preston Manor and Preston Park

The manor of Preston was separate from Brighton but incorporated much of Hove (*see* p. 194) and Norden's survey of 1617 shows a substantial double-pile manor house facing Preston Road, 'well built with stone'. As the first village N of Brighton on the London road, Preston was a popular excursion from the town. The Preston Tea Gardens (located in a clump of elms at the junction of Preston Road and Preston Drove) were in existence by 1769, superseded in the 1830s by the Strawberry Gardens (just N of the village), which were grandly renamed the Tivoli Gardens *c.* 1852. From the mid C19 Brighton's suburbs encroached on the parish and by 1914 the village was wholly engulfed.

Preston Manor was rebuilt in 1738 by Thomas Western (of the earlier house the only evidence is moulded stone door surrounds in the basement) with its entrance facing N. This house forms the centre of the present building; E and W wings were added *c.* 1750, all clearly visible with separate roofs. In 1794 the Manor was sold to William Stanford, for whose family numerous changes were made, including a medievalizing tower placed in the middle of the garden front in the 1880s; this was reduced to a single storey in 1905 as part of major alterations by *C. Stanley Peach*, a family friend. He added a W wing, the enclosed veranda to the right of the entrance (the matching one on the left dates from 1910) and recast the interior, equipping the house for lavish entertaining. The Manor was bequeathed to Brighton Corporation by Sir Charles and Lady Thomas-Stanford, and opened to the public in 1933. Its real interest is the **interior**, displayed to show the life of an Edwardian gentry family and their servants. Architecturally it is a mix of *c.* 1738 (fine open-string **staircase**) with a heavy overlay by Peach of Neo-Georgian opulence (Ionic columns in the **entrance hall** and several chimney-pieces). The heavy pedimented doorcases in the **drawing room** date from 1924 by *C.H. Fox* of Brighton. The house's setting was changed radically with the widening of Preston Road in 1936 (demolishing lodge and stables) and again in 1972. SW of the house the **walled garden** was laid out as an 'old-fashioned' formal garden *c.* 1905; the walls themselves, though much rebuilt, date from the C17.

SE of the house is **St Peter's Church** (now in the care of The Churches Conservation Trust). Of flint. E.E. Nave and chancel and a thin W tower with pyramid roof and just simple single-lancet bell-openings, larger lancets otherwise, mostly renewed. The simple plan and the form and proportions of the tower suggest an earlier, C11, date but the details are all C13. Church and churchyard of entirely village character. C19 proposals for enlargement were set aside in favour of building an entirely new church to the N (St John & St Peter, 1902, by *Sir A. Blomfield & Sons*). The interior offers two delights: medieval wall paintings uncovered in 1830 and Victorian chancel. Substantial remains of an early C13 scheme of **wall painting** on the nave E and N walls. On the N wall a Nativity scene, badly damaged by fire in 1906 and, to the left of the chancel arch, the Martyrdom of Thomas Becket, and to the right, St Michael weighing souls. Excellent chancel restoration, 1877–8, by *Ewan Christian*, with a scheme of stencil decoration to walls and roof, restored sedilia and carved stalls. The **altar** is a reused chest tomb to Edward Elrington (d.1515) carved with the coats of arms of families associated with the Elringtons. Good armorial **stained glass**, also a charming vignette (N), 1957, by *Barton, Kinder & Alderson*. Nave windows of 1907 by *Lavers & Westlake*.

s of the house and church is **Preston Park**, Brighton's largest and first public park. 67 acres of meadowland were purchased from the Stanfords in 1883 – 'public parks are the best competitors for public houses' opined the *Brighton Herald* – and formally opened in November 1884, laid out along conventional lines with walks, plantations and perimeter carriage drives. Boundary walls and railings, by *Philip Lockwood*, Borough Surveyor, were swept away in the 1930s as part of the policy of 'opening up' the parks (*see* p. 84), especially when viewed from the motor car. On the E side, a pompous **clock tower**, in an odd mix of classical and Gothic styles, of 1891–2 by *Francis May*, Borough Surveyor. Brick, terracotta and stone, alternately square and octagonal in plan. NW of the clock tower the fake half-timbered **chalet** erected in 1887 as a tea room, with a veranda around, with the park police housed in the upper storey. Grand plans for modernization in the 1920s, including a six-acre lake, were drawn up by *Bertie MacLaren*, superintendent of the Brighton Parks Department, but implemented to a reduced scheme from 1929. It follows Thomas Mawson's 'geometric' idiom of strong axes interplaying with circular motifs, exemplified at the park's awkward triangular-shaped s end by a paved entrance with balustrades, a circular pool, rose garden and tea pavilion. The **pool**, in both its form and use of clean-cut concrete slabs, betrays Modern Movement influence, while the circular tea pavilion (**café**), especially admired by Goodhart-Rendel, has a stepped roof and pergola that allows the garden to flow into the building.

MacLaren also laid out **The Rookery**, opened in 1936 on the w side of Preston Road, against the railway embankment. This has dramatic natural stone rockwork with steep winding paths, a rustic bridge, thatched summerhouse and a waterfall or rocky cascade descending to a pond crossed by stepping stones, and planted with Alpine plants. Both The Rookery and the improvements to the park were achieved using unemployed labour, part of a Government-funded scheme to alleviate distress during the Depression.

115. Preston Park, clock tower, by Francis May, 1891–2

Stanmer and the University of Sussex

The village of **Stanmer**, 3m. NE of Brighton, is a relatively unspoilt one-street hamlet of the Sussex Downland kind. To its SW, standing in a traditional estate relationship across a large lawn, are Stanmer House and church.

Stanmer House was designed by *Nicholas Dubois* and built *c.* 1722–7 for Henry Pelham (d.1725), whose family bought the estate from the Gott family in 1712. It was completed for Thomas Pelham. The Pelhams were nationally one of the great Whig families and dominated Sussex politics. Why Dubois was chosen is unknown. He had been the translator of Palladio for Giacomo Leoni's edition of 1715–20 but the house is remarkably reticent, an exercise in a plain and gentlemanly classicism that is barely Neo-Palladian. The only clue is that Dubois was appointed Master Mason in the Office of Works in 1719 and may therefore have been attractive as a less expensive colleague of Vanbrugh, the chosen architect of Henry Pelham's cousin, the 1st Duke of Newcastle.

A very full statement of account among the Pelham papers reveals the names of all those involved in building, carrying and providing materials, as well as the total cost: £14,203 1s. 5½d., of which Dubois, as Surveyor, received £795 17s. 6d.

The **exterior** is of fine ashlar blocks of Wealden sandstone. Eight-bay E front, treated as seven symmetrical bays with a pedimented three-bay central projection and with one bay added in 1860, set back on the right with an end bay window. Long, rather asymmetrical nine-bay garden front to the S with an ungainly off-centre five-bay attic addition, possibly of the early 1770s. To this house was added *c.* 1812 an attic balustrade, closed-in porch, a tent-roofed veranda and balcony on the N side and an extraordinary four-bay giant Ionic colonnade closing the courtyard behind the house where it would only have been seen obliquely from the pleasure grounds. Only the porch survives. These features, and some internal alterations, were made for Thomas Pelham, the 2nd Earl of Chichester, to designs by *Joseph Kay*, with whom Pelham was later involved in developments at Hastings (they may have met during discussions on the new General Post Office in London). The colonnade was removed at the same time as the rear wing following 1945.

The interior is more rewarding than the exterior. Plain but not unimpressive **entrance hall** with plaster panelling, dado and niches with garland decoration, carried out by *William Wilton* of London, plasterer.

116. Stanmer House, entrance front, *c*. 1722–7

Impressive projecting full-height fire-surround in stone, abstract if rather Baroque in its classicism. **Staircase** beyond the hall, not obviously Palladian with two turned balusters to each tread and wreathed tread ends and a fully panelled upper landing with Ionic pilasters. Made by *Richard Boston* of Lewes, joyner, who provided much of the embellished work elsewhere in the house (*Henry Bean*, carpenter, also of Lewes, was paid for other work including doorcases). To the right of the hall the former **library** with bookcases in heavy Neo-Palladian style with much egg-and-dart decoration and one of a pair of mid-Victorian chimney-pieces in timber and marble with the Pelham buckle (the other is in the dining room).

The main rooms are s of the hall. First, a plainly panelled room, then the former **drawing room** with a good Adamish ceiling and door surrounds of the later C18 (perhaps of the early 1770s). The final room is the best: the **dining room** with a screen of Corinthian columns at its w end. Two pairs of fluted Corinthian columns and very fine plasterwork broadly English Rococo in style, i.e. largely and freely based on variants of wreathed and flowing foliage. There is reference to the introduction of two columns to the dining room in 1771–2 but there are four here and undated copies of manuscript notes (in the Brighton Local Studies Library), suggest that *Thomas Clarke, plaisterer*, received £68 on 23 April 1766 'being in full of a bill due to me ending January 1st 1762' for some Pelham work. Clarke, a plasterer of the highest skill, was commonly used by William Chambers, but the plasterwork here does not refer to Chambers's recently published *A Treatise on the Decorative Part of Civil Architecture* of 1759. Two pier glasses remain, without their narrow console tables, but the fire-surround has been replaced by a mid-Victorian near twin to that in the library. Flush to the wall, with an inset marble surround, it has none of the presence needed for such a lavish room.

Behind the house stands an early C18 **horse gin**, in a tall timber-framed building presumably built to house it. The engine, with a capacity to raise three tons of water an hour from a well 230 ft deep, was provided in the 1720s by *John Fowkes* of London, engine-maker, and cost £210. A second, smaller engine had a well-house built by *James Dawes*, bricklayer and rough-mason, who worked on the offices.

N, above the house, the **stable block** of 1778, later altered. Central arched entrance with pyramidal roof into a yard with stables on three sides. The original flint and brick ranges were raised during the C19 in red brick, presumably to increase the storage for hay above. It has not improved the building. To the NW the large former **kitchen garden** complex. The **grounds** have suffered over the years; the works that Dubois is known to have carried out – walls, pedestals, gates and a canal – were altered when the park was naturalized in the later C18 and the Pleasure Grounds to the w of the house were reworked. Other later works, including 'Sabrina's Tomb', have gone but the **Frankland Monument** of

117. Stanmer Church, 1838, interior looking E

1775 by *Richard Hayward* in *Coade* stone and resting on three tortoises, stands on the hillside to the s of the house.

In front of the house, to the e, is the **church**. It dates from 1838, the architect either *Joseph Butler* of Chichester (who signed drawings) or the otherwise unknown *Ralph Joanes* of Lewes (perhaps the *Ralph Jones* who designed the Greek Revival Town Hall at Worthing?). One would like to know more. Flint with stone dressings, with transepts, a thin w tower with recessed spire, and lancet windows. The mouldings and capitals inside are remarkably correct and the composition very graceful, even if the tower, as one might expect at this date, is a little weak. Inside, **w gallery** on two slender columns carrying the **organ** in its Gothick case. Arches to chancel and transepts, with continuous mouldings and capitals.

Interesting timber **furnishings**. The **lectern**, **altar** and w **doors** are by *Francis Jude Jones* (d.1937). His father, *Jude Jones* (1844–1919), was the estate carpenter and may have contributed the **commandment boards**, the **pulpit** and **bench ends**, which are considered earlier. **Stained glass**. e window: the Ascension by *Mayer & Co.*, given in 1887 in memory of the 3rd Earl of Chichester. **Monument**. Sir John Pelham, d.1580, with wife and son, d.1584. Small kneeling figures, brought from the church of Holy Trinity, Minories, London.

Sussex University lies ¾ m. se, in a very shallow valley on the edge of Stanmer Park. The campus can be reached by trains to Falmer station.

This was the second new university in postwar England (after Keele). Brighton Council, anxious to have a university, offered the site, which provided a leafy parkland setting similar to those of the nine other new universities (York, East Anglia, Essex, Lancaster, Warwick, Kent, Stirling, and Coleraine in Northern Ireland) founded after relaxation of controls on new foundations in 1958.

Sir Basil Spence (*Sir Basil Spence, Bonnington & Collins*) designed the **masterplan** in 1959, the university gained its Royal Charter in 1961 and the main buildings which form the core of the modern campus were built between 1961 and 1972 with some advice on landscaping from *Dame Sylvia Crowe*. Spence planned for only 800 students but by 1965 this was increased to 3,000 after ten years. It was from the first based around schools in the humanities and cross-curriculum courses, though this was limited in the sciences. Residential accommodation was at first omitted from the masterplan (it was assumed that students would live in off-season boarding houses) but added as the university expanded from the mid 1960s with new buildings further up the valley to the n and teaching buildings creeping up the slope to the e. More of the same followed from the 1970s onwards. Although Spence made no provision in his plan for the buildings required in this expansion, the character of his original group was so strong that it informs much of this later development, though there are one or two recent buildings, such as the Medical School up and behind Sussex House, which are not in character.

Money for building was not as tight at Sussex as at other universities of this generation, which is apparent in the quality of the **building materials**, especially. The buildings are remarkably homogeneous, their leitmotifs being heavy, chunky slabs of *in situ* concrete, often used as bands, and flat-arched pre-cast concrete vaults, both contrasted against the red brick walls, faced with stretchers only.

Spence's work here is thus emphatically different from his **style** before 1955, i.e. of Coventry Cathedral, where as Pevsner noted only the s porch, a late alteration in the original design, pointed the way to the University. What propelled Spence's work into this new direction is complex. Like Sheppard Robson & Partners at Churchill College, Cambridge (begun 1959), the most obvious sources are Le Corbusier's Maisons Jaoul (1954) and the Law Courts at Chandigarh (1953–5), particularly for the concrete arches, plain red brickwork and buttress-fins (features Spence also used at St Aidan's College, Durham (1962) and Glasgow Airport (1962–6)). His recent experience of large-scale master-planning at Edinburgh University (from 1954) must have been important too but there are distant memories of Lutyens's 'high game' here (he was in Lutyens's office briefly in 1929–30), and Spence himself referred to classical antiquity as an inspiration for both Falmer House and Pevensey I. This interest may be due to his time in Rome where he was designing the British Embassy in 1960, and Roman indeed seems the epic monumentality of the Sussex buildings with their rhythmic arches and grand exterior staircases, even if that formality is softened by the materials and the asymmetrical layout.

All of Spence's buildings address the open space of Fulton Court at the centre of the campus: Falmer House to the s, Arts to the n, Sciences to the e and the Library to the w. Although the grid plan remains strongly marked with its predisposition for grand views, the impact is distributed asymmetrically both in the grouping of buildings and in the buildings themselves. The main visual axis of the University from the Lewes road appears to run s to n on the pedestrian way through the middle of Falmer House to the pylon-like entrance of the Arts building, but it shifts e in Fulton Court onto a secondary s–n axis which runs alongside the science buildings (Pevensey, Chichester and Engineering) and then under Arts Road and past Bramber House (the former Refectory). The Library stands up the slope w of Fulton Court, and the later eastern extensions of Pevensey, Chichester and Engineering climb the sides of the slope to the e, bridging over another s–n axis, the prosaically named North-South Road where most of the post-1980 educational development is concentrated. Two buildings based on circles don't really fit the grid, the Meeting House just to the ne of Falmer House, and the Gardner Arts Centre to the sw [119].

A **tour** of the original buildings must begin with **Falmer House** (1960–2), which forms a sort of gatehouse and formal approach to the

118. Falmer House by Sir Basil Spence, 1960–2, e elevation to Fulton Court

open space of Fulton Court. The first building to be completed, it was designed as the main social centre, considered of major importance for the non-residential campus and soon outgrown. Its form is a traditional square quad, with the former refectory (Mandela Hall) projecting from the w range to the outside as well as into the courtyard, around which runs an almost continuous moat. Spence referred to the Colosseum as a spiritual source and indeed it possesses something of the awe-inspiring fragmentariness of the ancient ruin, due to the bold and wholly successful way in which on all floors the walls of two ranges (E and s) are left largely open. Spence suggested these spaces could later become rooms but he must surely have always intended this effect (and thought it might be hard to persuade the funders to pay for a building with a third of its space unused). Here it is especially the alternation of solid and void which seems at first quite arbitrary but turns out to follow rhythms one can react to, rhythms of brick and concrete, volume and space, cubic and arcuated. The skyline is horizontal except for the raised shallow tunnel vault of the refectory and the horns over the staircase, again Corbusian in spirit. Only the sheer outside wall of its staircase has another facing: knapped flint (inside as well) in deference to its downland location.

The main N–S axis passes through Falmer House into **Fulton Court**. To the E is **Pevensey I** (originally Physics; 1960–3), very much brick but with a continuous canopy in arched concrete. Three storeys and eleven bays, with plain brick columns up to the canopy and a second range of arches to a deep overhanging undercroft at ground level. Here Spence alluded to the Stoa of Attalus at Athens which had been restored in the mid 1950s. Plain sides with slit windows set apparently randomly. Central courtyard with steps up to garden and former entrance, now unused. **Chichester I** (Chemistry; 1962–5), immediately to the N, has a ten-bay front onto Fulton Court. Pronounced buttresses dividing the fenestration bays and arched openings only at lowest level. Entrance with stairs and ramp in the fifth bay from the left but with the main entrance up steps into the re-entrant court on s side, adjacent to the massively plain brick drum of the **Lecture Theatre**. This seems circular but isn't because Spence slightly shifted the two halves of the circle against each other. **Engineering I** (1964–6) to N, again more brick with laboratory/seminar block to s and big workshop block, now converted for teaching, to the N.

Arts A (1962–70 with **B** and **C** to its N) stands on axis with Falmer House, fronted by a lecture-theatre block which skilfully runs up the hill, widening and with the roof stepping as it does so. Tall concrete pylons mark the main entrance as emphatically as the stairs do the Library adjacent. Between Arts A and Arts B is a **courtyard** surrounded by a brick-arched cloister, the courtyard stepped up to both N and w, with a pool down at almost the lowest level to the E. Further still on this axis, and crossing Arts Road, are the later **Arts C** and **EDB**. They are in the manner of Arts B and create something like street architecture.

Arts C to E continue to the N, including, in **Arts D**, a seven-storey cruciform tower (with the unfortunate addition of a glazed fire-stair at its NE corner), something of a departure from the low-rise character of the rest of the campus.

The **Library** (1962–70) is a rather brooding presence overlooking Fulton Court to the W, with the main entrance at the top of a long and very formal flight of concrete stairs up the bank on which the Library sits. Paired slit windows in large panels of brickwork, which are divided by pairs of projecting buttress-fins; arched concrete panels at high level again, like Pevensey. The main entrance is set back behind spurs of wall which act as a gateway in front of the entrance. The Library was planned in three stages, complete in 1970, with the fourth stage by *Fielden & Mawson*, 1996–7. Within the first stage, close to the entrance, is the main staircase with a single flight running back over the entrance and emerging into a well-lit reading area.

s of the Library is the **Gardner Arts Centre** (1966–9), a multi-purpose space including an auditorium planned with assistance from *Sean Kenny*, architect and stage production designer. Consisting of blind red brick drums, it is based on two rings: an inner containing the main auditorium and an outer reduced by bites taken out of it to three sections, a single large one to the N and two smaller symmetrical ones to the S. A third ring is obfuscated by several towers of varying heights, the three largest close to the entrance.

The **Meeting House** (1965–7), a non-denominational worship space NE of Falmer House, is also circular. Here a drum of overlapping concrete blocks (now painted) is carried on brick fins surrounding an inset ground floor again with a moat; the conical roof is slightly asymmetrical. Internally, the 'hit and miss' arrangement of the blocks creates apertures for large panes of glass running round the walls and through the spectrum so the space is bathed in coloured light [120]. All the fittings, including what amount to chancel furnishings, were designed by Spence.

Sussex House (for the University administration), E of Falmer House, was the last of the specifically Spence buildings (1972) but lacks the dramatic presence of the rest, a more understated two-storey building in brick.

119. University of Sussex, Gardner Arts Centre, 1966–9

The additions to Spence's original plan adopt its character both to the N of Boiler House Hill (including Arts C and D and EDB) and to the E of the North-South Road (Pevensey II and III, Chichester II and III, Arundel Building and Engineering II). The four original **Residential Blocks** (Lancaster, York, Norwich and Essex Houses), all by *H. Hubbard Ford*, (1963–5), follow the same idiom, as do the Boiler House (1962, extended 1972) by *Spence*, and Bramber House (the new refectory), 1967, (later extended) by *Fitzroy Robinson & Partners* with Spence. Later student housing moves away from the predominant brick and concrete character of the s parts of the campus. **Park Village** (*Hughes, Lomax & Adutt*, 1969) is a successful development of staggered three-storey attached houses in red brick with some timber cladding but **East Slope Housing** is a disappointing development of split-level painted brick housing (*Maguire & Murray*, 1974–5, with Social Centre by *Phippen, Randall & Parkes*, 1979). Finally, a well-turned piece of Modernism, though ignoring its context in its zinc cladding, has recently been added as the entrance to Essex House by *John Pardy Architects* (2004).

Further Reading

There is a huge literature on Brighton and Hove and it extends into wider areas such as the history of the Regency period, for instance, and the expanding historiography of resorts and leisure towns. General works on spas and resorts include P. Hembry, *The English Spa 1560–1815; A Social History*, 1990 and P. Borsay, 'Health and Leisure Resorts 1700–1840' in P. Clark (ed.), *Cambridge Urban History of Britain*, Vol II, 1540–1840, 2000; with F. Gray, *Designing the Seaside: Architecture, Society and Nature*, 2006, and A. Brodie and G. Winter, *England's Seaside Resorts*, 2007, concentrating on their architectural expression.

Histories of the city start with **guidebooks** of which the first was Dr A. Relhan, *A Short History of Brighthelmston, with Remarks on its Air, and an Analysis of its Waters*, 1761. This was followed by the anonymous *The New Brighthelmstone Directory; or, Sketches in Miniature of the British Shore*, 1770; John Awsiter, *Thoughts on Brighthelmston*, 1788; Attree's *Topography of Brighton*, 1809 and C. Wright's *The Brighton Ambulator*, 1818. R. Sicklemore was a productive writer on Brighton including *The Epitome of Brighton* (1815), *The History of Brighton from the Earliest Period to the Present Time*, 1823, and *Descriptive Views of Brighton*, 1824. Later guides are J.A. Erredge, *History of Brighthelmstone*, 1862; H.C. Porter, *The History of Hove* (1897), J.G. Bishop, *A Peep into the Past: Brighton in the Olden Time*, 1880; Frederick Moorecroft, *Brighton Guide*, 1866; W.E. Nash, *Guide to Brighton*, 1886, with detailed walking tours of the town; and H.P. Clunn, *The Capital by the Sea*, 1953. J.D. Parry's *An Historical and Descriptive Account of the Coast of Sussex*, 1833, is another important source.

Timothy Carder's *The Encyclopaedia of Brighton*, 1990, a mine of information about the history and make-up of the town, isn't really a guidebook, nor is it a general history. Judy Middleton's similar *Encyclopaedia of Hove* (several volumes in Hove Library) is a main source for the history of Hove as is her earlier *A History of Hove*, 1979. J. and J. Ford's *Images of Brighton*, 1991, very usefully gathers together almost all the early views of the town and its buildings. The beginnings of the scholarly study of Brighton and Hove's **history** is a later C19 phenomenon, starting with H. Martin, *History of Brighton*, 1871; Lewis

121. Jaipur Gate, Hove, by Colonel Samuel Swinton Jacob and Surgeon Major Thomas Holbein Hendley

Melville, *Brighton: Its History, its Follies and its Fashions*, 1909; Osbert Sitwell and Margaret Barton, *Brighton*, 1935; E.W. Gilbert, *Brighton: Old Ocean's Bauble*, 1954, strong on the urban development of Brighton, and Clifford Musgrave, *Life in Brighton*, 1970, still the most complete history of the town. Sue Berry's *Georgian Brighton*, 2005, supersedes much of the previous discussion of the pre-1820 town as does her article, 'Myth and Reality in the Presentation of Resorts: Brighton and the emergence of the Prince and the fishing village myth, circa 1710–1824', *Sussex Archaeological Collections*, 140, 2002. Antony Dale's *Fashionable Brighton*, 1967, and *Brighton Town and Brighton People*, 1976, contain much of interest on both the architecture and history of the town.

Brighton has also attracted **squibs**, particularly early on, due to its celebrity culture. These included Peregrine Phillips, *A Diary kept in an excursion to Littlehampton near Arundel, and Brighthelmston in Sussex (Bew's Diary)*, 1780; *The New Brighton Guide*, 1796, by 'that amusing though somewhat acidulated' and 'jaundiced and venomous commentator' Anthony Pasquin (John Williams). Rather gentler are the journalist George Augustus Sala's *Things I have seen and People I have known*, 1894, and *Brighton as I knew it*, 1898. And they still come; a recent one is A. Seldon, *Brave New City: Brighton and Hove – Past, Present, Future*, 2002. **Early medical books** should also be mentioned: Dr Richard Russell, *Dessertatis de Tabe Clandulari et de Usu Aquae Marinae in Morbis Glandalarum*, 1750, translated as A *Dissertation on the Use of Sea Water in the Diseases of the Glands*, translated from the Latin by an Eminent Physician, 1752; this was followed by Dr A. Relhan's *A Short History of Brighthelmston, with Remarks on its Air, and an Analysis of its Waters*, 1761; Dr Kentish, Physician of Brighton, *An Essay on Seabathing and internal uses of Seawater*, 1788; J. Anderson, *A Practical Essay on the Good and Bad Effects of Sea-water and Sea-bathing*, 1795; Sake Deen Mahomed, *Shampooing: or, Benefits resulting from the Use of the Indian Medicated Vapour Bath*, 1822. The latest account of Dr Richard Russell is J.H. Farrant, 'Dr Richard Russell', *Dictionary of National Biography*, 2004; for Sake Deen Mahomed *see* J. Roles, 'Sake Deen Mahomed's Silver Cup', *Royal Pavilion & Museums Review*, 3, 1990.

Hove and particularly Brighton have long been **literary** subjects and many writers have lived, stayed and written in the city, including Dr Johnson and Fanny Burney, Charles Dickens, Lewis Carroll, Rudyard Kipling (in Rottingdean), Arnold Bennett, Terence Rattigan, Peter O'Donnell and Keith Waterhouse. Jane Austen describes the military encampments on Belle Vue Field (now Regency Square) in *Pride and Prejudice*, 1813; Harrison Ainsworth, living in Arundel Terrace, Kemp Town, set several novels in Brighton and around, including *Ovingdean Grange, a tale of the South Downs*, 1860, and *Old Court*, 1866, which describes the Old Ship Hotel, which also appears in William Makepeace Thackeray's *Vanity Fair*, 1869. Others include Edward Bradley (Cuthbert Bede), *Mattins and Muttons*, 1866; Georgette Heyer,

Regency Buck, 1935; Graham Greene, *Brighton Rock*, 1938, the film (1947, director, John Boulting) being shot on location in Brighton; Patrick Hamilton, *West Pier,* 1952 and Keith Waterhouse, *Palace Pier*, 2003. **Artists' impressions** of the town are illustrated in David Beevers, *Brighton Revealed, through artists' eyes, circa 1760–circa 1960*, exhibition catalogue, 1995; and John Roles and David Beevers, *A Pictorial History of Brighton*, 1993, is the best and most informative of the many collections of old photographs of the city.

Antony Dale to large part created the study of the Regency architecture of Brighton and Hove (and was for many years a committee member of the Brighton and Hove Regency Society). So for **architectural accounts**, apart from those mentioned above, study begins with his books including *The History and Architecture of Brighton*, 1972; *History of the Theatre Royal*, 1980; and *Brighton's Churches*, 1989. A very useful little primer on the buildings of the city and wider, *Guide to the Buildings of Brighton*, 1987, was produced by students of the School of Architecture and Interior Design at Brighton Polytechnic to mark the XVI World Congress of the International Union of Architects in Brighton that year. Howard Colvin's *A Biographical Dictionary of British Architects, 1600–1840*, 3rd edn, 1995, of course outlines the lives of individual architects. The RIBA Drawings Collection acquired a large collection of drawings by Busby in 1986 and these are discussed by Neil Bingham in *C.A. Busby, The Regency Architect of Brighton & Hove*, RIBA Heinz Gallery, 1991. Terraced housing, so important in the development of the city, is covered in Stefan Muthesius's *The English Terraced House*, 1982, and the ammonite capital in Michael Kerney, 'Ammonites in Architecture', *Country Life*, 27 January, 1983. H.S. Goodhart Rendel's characteristically perceptive article on 'The Churches of Brighton and Hove' appeared in *The Architectural Review*, 44, 1918, to be followed by H. Hamilton Maughan's *Some Brighton Churches*, 1922. Robert Elleray has dug out valuable information particularly on lost buildings in *The Victorian Churches of Sussex*, 1981, and *A refuge from reality; the cinemas of Brighton and Hove*, 1989.

L.F. Pearson, *Piers and other Seaside Architecture*, 2002, is a useful introduction to the history of piers and F. Gray, *Walking On Water: The West Pier Story*, 1998, is a reminder of its splendid history.

The **Royal Pavilion and the Dome** have a considerable literature of their own, including Humphry Repton, *Designs for the Pavilion at Brighton*, 1808; John Nash, *Views of the Royal Pavilion*, 1826 (published 1827), republished with introductory essay and commentary by Gervase Jackson-Stops, 1991; Henry D. Roberts, *A History of the Royal Pavilion*, 1931; Clifford Musgrave, *Royal Pavilion: an episode in the Romantic*, 1959; Patrick Conner, *Oriental Architecture in the West*, 1979; John Dinkel, *The Royal Pavilion, Brighton*, 1983, still the best introduction to the building; John Morley, *The Making of the Royal Pavilion*, 1984, really a very long, detailed and well-illustrated essay on the development of the internal decoration of the Pavilion; Megan Aldrich (ed.), *The Crace's,*

Royal Decorators 1768–1899, 1990; Virginia Hinze, 'The Re-creation of John Nash's Regency Garden at the Royal Pavilion, Brighton' in *Garden History*, 24(1) 1996; and Jessica Rutherford, *A Prince's Passion: The Life of the Royal Pavilion*, 2003, which discusses how the building was used. The wider work of John Nash is covered in John Summerson's *The Life and Work of John Nash, Architect*, 1980.

There are a number of recent detailed studies on individual buildings and sites, including C. Miele, 'The First Architect in the World' in *Brighton: Robert Adam, Marlborough House and Mrs Fitzherbert*, Sussex Archaeological Collections, 136, 1998 and David Beevers, *Guide to Preston Manor*, 1999. Sue Berry, 'Stanmer House and the Pelham Family, circa 1710–1810', *Sussex Archaeological Collections*, 142, 2004, and J. Goodfield and P. Robinson, *Stanmer and the Pelham Family*, 2007, give the latest position on that house. Ornamental gardens are examined in Sue Berry, 'Pleasure Gardens in Georgian and Regency Seaside Resorts: Brighton 1756–1840', in *Garden History* 28(2), 2000, and Virginia Hinze, *Brighton Parks Department – An exploration of its early history and of its formative Superintendent, Captain Bertie Hubbard MacLaren*, Architectural Association thesis, 1994. Embassy Court is described in *The Architectural Review* 78, 1935, and Janet Gooch describes *A History of Brighton General Hospital*, 1980.

Other aspects of the architectural history of the city are covered, inter alia, in the following publications: Sue Farrant, *Changes in Brighton and Hove's Suburbs: Patcham and Preston 1841–1871*, 1984; Sue Berry and others, *Preston: Downland Village to Brighton Suburb*, Preston Village Millennium Project, 2004; Sue Berry, 'Hotels, smells and water supplies; change in Brighton during the 1860s', *Sussex Past and Present*, 1994; H.T. Dawes, 'The Windmills and Millers of Brighton', *Journal of the Sussex Industrial Archaeological Society*, 1988; W.F. Pickering, 'The West Brighton Estate: Hove, a study in Victorian Urban Development', *Sussex Industrial History*, 5, Winter 1972–3; David Prout, 'Willett Built', *Victorian Society Annual*, 1989; and Jill Seddon, 'The Visual Arts in Regency Brighton and Hove', *The Georgian Group Journal*, 2003.

Finally, monographs on key individuals include Anthony Wagner and Antony Dale, *The Wagners of Brighton*, 1983, which gives biographies of the Rev. Henry Michell Wagner and his son Father Arthur Wagner and a lot of information about the churches, some now superseded. J. Pulling, *Volk's Railway, Brighton, 1883–1983*, 1983, and A.A. Jackson, *Volk's Railways, Brighton: An Illustrated History*, 1993, cover that Brighton institution. J.H. Turner, *The London, Brighton and South Coast Railway*, 3 vols, 1977–9, gives a full account of the history of that attractive railway company.

Finally, whilst information on the **internet** can be unreliable, a useful site for C19 stained glass has been Robert Eberhard's www.stainedglassrecords.org.

122. The Dome, staircase in the Art Gallery, detail of tiles

Glossary

Acanthus: *see* [2D].

Achievement: a complete display of armorial bearings.

Aedicule: architectural surround, usually a *pediment* on two columns or *pilasters*.

Aisle: subsidiary space alongside the body of a building, separated from it by columns, *piers*, or posts.

Almemmar: synagogue reading desk also known as bimah.

Ambulatory: aisle around the *sanctuary* of a church.

Ammonite: type of capital similar to the Ionic order, with volutes resembling whorled chambered fossilized shells.

Antae: simplified *pilasters*, usually applied to the ends of the enclosing walls of a *portico* (called *in antis*).

Antefixae: ornaments projecting at regular intervals above a Greek cornice, originally to conceal the ends of roof tiles.

Anthemion: classical ornament like a honeysuckle flower, *see* [2D].

Apse: semicircular or polygonal end, especially in a church.

Arabesque: non-figurative surface decoration consisting of flowing lines, foliage scrolls etc., based on geometrical patterns.

Arcade: series of arches supported by *piers* or columns.

Arch: for types *see* [4].

Architrave: *see* [2A]. Also moulded surround to a window or door.

Ark: chest or cupboard housing the tables of Jewish law in a synagogue.

Art Deco: a self-consciously up-to-date interwar style of bold simplified patterns, often derived from non-European art.

Ashlar: large rectangular masonry blocks wrought to even faces.

Astylar: with no columns or vertical features.

Attic: small top storey within a roof. Also the storey above the main *entablature* of a classical façade.

Baldacchino: solid canopy, usually free-standing and over an altar.

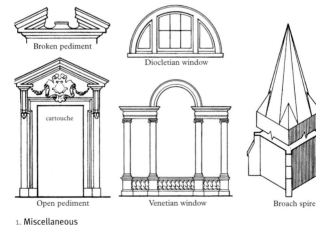

Broken pediment

Diocletian window

cartouche

Open pediment

Venetian window

Broach spire

1. Miscellaneous

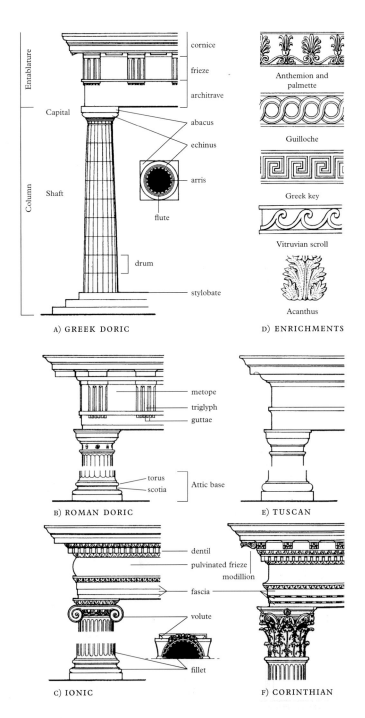

A) GREEK DORIC

Entablature
- cornice
- frieze
- architrave

Capital
- abacus
- echinus

Column
- Shaft
- arris
- flute
- drum
- stylobate

D) ENRICHMENTS

Anthemion and palmette

Guilloche

Greek key

Vitruvian scroll

Acanthus

B) ROMAN DORIC
- metope
- triglyph
- guttae
- torus
- scotia
- Attic base

C) IONIC
- dentil
- pulvinated frieze
- modillion
- fascia
- volute
- fillet

E) TUSCAN

F) CORINTHIAN

2. Classical orders and enrichments

Baluster: pillar or pedestal of bellied form; used together in a balustrade.

Bargeboards: boards, often carved or pierced (called fretted), fixed beneath the eaves of a gable to cover and protect the rafters.

Baroque: style originating in Rome *c.* 1600 and current in England *c.* 1620–1720, characterized by dramatic massing and silhouette and the use of the giant order.

Barrel vault: one with a simple arched profile.

Batter: intentional inward inclination of a wall face.

Bay: division of an elevation by regular vertical features such as columns, windows, etc.

Bay window: one projecting from the face of a building. *Canted*: with a straight front and angled sides. *Bow window*: curved.

Bellcote: small gabled or roofed housing for a bell or bells.

Billet: Norman ornament of small half-cylindrical or rectangular blocks.

Blocked: columns, etc. interrupted by regular projecting blocks (blocking).

Bolection moulding: bold convex and concave moulding, used especially in the late C17 and early C18.

Bow window: *see* Bay window

Brise-soleil (French): a sunscreen of projecting fins or slats.

Broach spire: *see* [1].

Brutalist: used for later 1950s–70s Modernist architecture displaying rough or unfinished concrete, massive forms and abrupt juxtapositions.

Cable moulding: like twisted strands of a rope; also called rope moulding.

Capital: head feature of a column or *pilaster*; for classical types *see* [2].

Cartouche: *see* [1].

Cast iron: hard and brittle iron, cast in a mould to the required shape.

Cavetto: classical concave moulding of quarter-round section.

Chancel: the E part or end of a church, where the altar is placed.

Ciborium: a fixed canopy over an altar, usually vaulted and supported on four columns; also called a baldacchino.

Clerestory: uppermost storey of an interior, pierced by windows.

Coade stone: ceramic artificial stone made in Lambeth 1769–*c.*1840 by Eleanor Coade (d.1821) and her associates.

Concrete: composition of cement (calcined lime and clay), aggregate (small stones and rock chippings), sand and water.

Console: bracket of double-curved profile.

Corbel: projecting block supporting something above.

Corinthian; cornice: *see* [2F; 2A].

Cottage orné: artfully rustic small house.

Cupola: a small dome used as a crowning feature.

Curtain wall: a non-load-bearing external wall applied to a framed structure, in architecture of the C20 onwards.

Dado: finishing of the lower part of an internal wall.

Decorated (Dec): English Gothic architecture, late C13 to late C14.

Dentil: *see* [2C].

Distyle: with two columns.

Doric: *see* [2A, 2B].

Dressings: the stone or brickwork worked to a finished face about an angle, opening, or other feature.

Early English (E.E.): English Gothic architecture, late C12 to late C13.

Entablature: *see* [2A].

dormer

Hipped roof

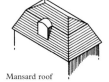

Mansard roof

Flemish or Dutch gable

3. Roofs and gables

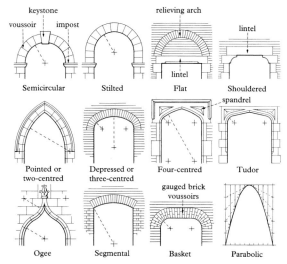

4. Arches

Entasis: very slight convex deviation from a straight line, used to prevent an optical illusion of concavity.

Fasces: bundle of straight rods bound together.

Fenestration: the arrangement of windows in a façade.

Fluting: series of concave grooves (flutes).

Foil: (lit. leaf): lobe formed by the cusping of a circular or other shape in tracery. Trefoil (three), quatrefoil (four), cinquefoil (five), and multifoil express the number of lobes in a shape.

Foliate: decorated with leaves.

Gambrel roof: a hipped roof which turns to a gablet at the ridge.

Giant order: a classical *order* that is two or more storeys high.

Gibbs surround: C18 treatment of an opening with blocked architraves, seen particularly in the work of James Gibbs (1682–1754).

Gothic: the style of the later Middle Ages, characterized by the pointed arch and *rib-vault*.

Groin vault: one composed of intesecting *barrel vaults*.

Guilloche: *see* [2D].

Herm: (lit. the god Hermes): male head or bust on a pedestal.

Hindoo: Indian style of exotic orientalizing architecture.

Hipped roof: *see* [3].

Hoodmould: projecting moulding above arch or *lintel* to throw off water.

Hydraulic power: use of water under high pressure to work machinery.

Impost: horizontal moulding at the springing of an arch.

In antis: of columns, set in an opening (properly between simplified *pilasters* called *antae*).

Ionic: *see* [2C].

Jetty: a projecting upper storey on a timber-framed building.

Joggle: the joining of two stones to prevent them slipping, by a notch in one and a projection in the other.

Lancet: slender, single-light pointed-arched window; *see* [6].

Lantern: a windowed turret crowning a roof, tower or dome.

Light: compartment of a window.

Lintel: horizontal beam or stone bridging an opening.

Loggia: open gallery with arches or columns.

Lunette: semicircular window or panel.

Machicolation: openings between *corbels* that support a projecting *parapet*.

Mathematical tiles: facing tiles with the appearance of brick.

Metope: see [2B].

Modillion: see [2F].

Mouchette: a curved dagger-shaped motif in tracery.

Mullion: vertical member between window *lights*.

Narthex: enclosed vestibule or porch at the main entrance to a church.

Nave: the body of a church w of the crossing or chancel, often flanked by aisles.

Newel: central or corner post of a staircase.

Nogging: brick infilling of a timber frame.

Ogee: of an arch, dome, etc., with double-curved pointed profile.

Order: one of a series of recessed arches and jambs forming a splayed medieval opening, e.g. a doorway or arcade arch. Also, an upright structural member used in series, especially in classical architecture.

Orders (classical): for types *see* [2].

Oriel: window projecting above ground level.

Palmette: see [2D].

Pantile: roof tile of curved **S**-shaped section.

Pargetting: (lit. plastering): exterior plaster decoration, either moulded in relief or incised.

Parapet: wall for protection of a sudden drop, e.g. on a bridge, or to conceal a roof.

Pavilion: ornamental building for occasional use; or a projecting subdivision of a larger building (hence *pavilion roof*).

Pediment: a formalized gable, derived from that of a classical temple; also used over doors, windows, etc. For types *see* [1].

Perpendicular (Perp): English Gothic architecture from the late C14 to early C16.

Pier: a large masonry or brick support, often for an arch.

Pilaster: flat representation of a classical column in shallow relief.

Pilotis: French C20-century term for pillars or stilts that support a building above an open ground.

Polychromy: the use of contrasting coloured materials such as bricks as decoration, particularly associated with mid-C19 Gothic styles.

Porte cochère: (French, lit. gate for coaches); porch large enough to admit wheeled vehicles.

Portico: porch with roof and (frequently) *pediment* supported by a row of columns.

Purlin: horizontal longitudinal timber in a roof structure.

Quoins: dressed or otherwise emphasized stones at the angles of a building.

Rafter: horizontal longitudinal timber in a roof structure.

Reeded: decorated with small parallel convex mouldings.

Render: a uniform covering for external walls as a weather protection, either of lime and sand or cement and sand. When worked to a fine surface called *stucco*.

Reredos: painted and/or sculpted screen behind and above an altar.

Retable: painted or carved panel standing on or at the back of an altar, usually attached to it.

Rib-vault: masonry framework of intersecting arches (ribs) supporting vault cells.

Rococo: style current *c.* 1720 and *c.* 1760, characterized by a serpentine line and playful, scrolled decoration.

Roll moulding: medieval moulding of part-circular section.

Rood: crucifix flanked by the Virgin and St John, usually over the entry into the chancel, set on a beam (rood beam) or painted on the wall.

Rustication: exaggerated treatment of masonry to give the effect of strength.

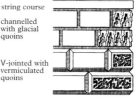

string course

channelled with glacial quoins

V-jointed with vermiculated quoins

5. Rustication

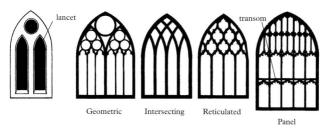

6. Tracery

lancet · Geometric · Intersecting · Reticulated · transom · Panel

Sanctuary: in a church, the area around the main altar.

Scagliola: composition imitating marble.

Sedilia: seats for the priests in the *chancel* wall of a church or chapel.

Sgraffito: decoration scratched, often in plaster, to reveal a pattern in another colour beneath.

Shiplap: see weather-boarding

Soffit: underside of an *arch*, *lintel*, etc.

Stall: fixed seat in the choir of *chancel* of a church for the clergy or choir.

Stiff-leaf: carved decoration in the form of thick uncurling foliage; originally late c12–early c13.

String course: horizontal course projecting from a wall surface.

Stucco: durable lime plaster, shaped into ornamental features or used externally as a protective coating.

Swag: ornament in the form of drapery suspended from both ends.

Tabernacle: canopied structure in a church or chapel to contain the reserved sacrament or a relic.

Tester: (lit. head); flat canopy over a tomb or pulpit, where it is also called a sounding-board.

Tracery: openwork pattern of masonry or timber in the upper part of an opening, *see* [6].

Transept: transverse portion of a church.

Transom: horizontal member between window lights; *see* [6].

Tread: horizontal part of a step. The tread end may be carved on a staircase.

Triforium: middle storey of a church interior treated as an arcaded wall passage or blind *arcade*.

Truss: braced framework, spanning between supports.

Tuscan: *see* [2E].

Tympanum: the area enclosed by an arch or *pediment*.

Vault: an arched stone roof, sometimes imitated in timber, plaster etc.

Venetian window: *see* [1].

Vitruvian scroll: wave-like classical ornament.

Voussoirs: wedge-shaped stones forming an arch.

Waggon roof: with the appearance of the inside of a wagon tilt; often ceiled.

Waterleaf: a broad tapering leaf shape that turns over at the top, used especially on late c12 capitals (hence waterleaf capital) and some classical mouldings.

Weather-boarding: wall cladding of overlapping horizontal feather-edge boards. Known as shiplap if of rectangular section with a rebate cut on each edge.

Wrought iron: ductile iron that is strong in tension, forged into decorative patterns or forged and rolled into e.g. bars, joists, boiler plates.

Index
of Artists, Architects and Other Persons Mentioned

The names of architects and artists working in Brighton and Hove are given in *italic*, with entries for partnerships and group practices listed after entries for a single name. Page references in italic include relevant illustrations.

Index
of Localities, Streets and Buildings

Principal references are in **bold** type; page references including relevant illustrations are in *italic*. 'dem.' = 'demolished'

Illustration Acknowledgements

Every effort has been made to contact or trace all copyright holders. The publishers will be glad to make good any errors or omissions brought to our attention in future editions.

We are grateful to the following for permission to reproduce illustrative material:

A special debt of gratitude is owed to English Heritage and its photographer, James O. Davies, who took the photographs for this volume.

Especial thanks to Mrs Antony Dale and to P. J. and S. P. Berry for help with period illustrations. Thanks are also due to The Royal Pavilion & Museums for permission to photograph the Pavilion.

Building News: 75, 86
English Heritage (NMR): 42
English Heritage (James O. Davies): 2, 3, 4, 6, 8, 9, 10, 11, 12, 13, 15, 16, 17, 20, 22, 24, 27, 28, 29, 30, 31, 32, 34, 35, 36, 40, 41, 43, 44, 47, 48, 49, 50, 51, 52, 54, 55, 56, 58, 59, 61, 62, 64, 65, 66, 67, 68, 72, 73, 74, 76, 77, 80, 81, 82, 83, 85, 87, 88, 89, 90, 93, 94, 96, 98, 99, 101, 102, 103, 104, 105, 107, 111, 112, 113, 114, 115, 116, 117, 118, 119, 120
Alan Fagan: 21
Illustrated London News: 70
Oxford Designers & Illustrators: 1, 37, 46, 53, 60, 69, 78, 84, 91, 97, 106, 109
RIBA: 63
The Royal Pavilion & Museums (Brighton and Hove): 14, 38, 39, 71, 100, 110
TATE: 95